THE EUROPEAN UNION SE

D1553770

General Editors: Neill Nugent, William E. Paterson,

The European Union series is designed to provide an authoritative library on the European Union, ranging from general introductory texts to definitive assessments of key institutions and actors, policies and policy processes, and the role of member states.

Books in the series are written by leading scholars in their fields and reflect the most up-to-date research and debate. Particular attention is paid to accessibility and clear presentation for a wide audience of students, practitioners and interested general readers. The series consists of four major strands:

- General textbooks
- The major institutions and actors
- The main areas of policy
- The member states and the Union

The series editors are **Neill Nugent**, Professor of Politics and Jean Monnet Professor of European Integration, Manchester Metropolitan University, and **William E. Paterson**, Director of the Institute of German Studies, University of Birmingham.

Their co-editor until his death in July 1999, **Vincent Wright**, was a Fellow of Nuffield College, Oxford University. He played an immensely valuable role in the founding and development of *The European Union Series* and is greatly missed.

Feedback on the series and book proposals are always welcome and should be sent to Steven Kennedy, Palgrave, Houndmills, Basingstoke, Hampshire RG21 6XS, UK, or by e-mail to *s.kennedy@palgrave.com*

General textbooks

Published

Desmond Dinan **Ever Closer Union: An Introduction to European Integration (2nd edn)**
[Rights: World excluding North and South America, Philippines & Japan]
Desmond Dinan **Encyclopedia of the European Union**
[Rights: Europe only]
Simon Hix **The Political System of the European Union**
John McCormick **Understanding the European Union: A Concise Introduction**
Neill Nugent **The Government and Politics of the European Union (4th edn)**
[Rights: World excluding USA and dependencies and Canada]
John Peterson and Elizabeth Bomberg **Decision-making in the European Union**

Ben Rosamond **Theories of European Integration**

Forthcoming

Simon Bulmer and Andrew Scott **European Union: Economics, Policy and Politics**
Andrew Scott **The Political Economy of the European Union**
Richard Sinnott **Understanding European Integration**

Also planned

The History of the European Union
The European Union Source Book
The European Union Reader

The major institutions and actors

Published

Renaud Dehousse **The European Court of Justice**
Justin Greenwood **Representing Interests in the European Union**

(continued overleaf)

**Series Standing Order (*outside North
America only*)**

ISBN 0–333–71695–7 hardcover
ISBN 0–333–69352–3 paperback

Full details from www.palgrave.com

The European Union and the Third World

Martin Holland

palgrave

First published 2002 by
PALGRAVE
Houndmills, Basingstoke, Hampshire RG21 6XS and
175 Fifth Avenue, New York, N.Y. 10010
Companies and representatives throughout the world

PALGRAVE is the new global academic imprint of
St. Martin's Press LLC Scholarly and Reference Division and
Palgrave Publishers Ltd (formerly Macmillan Press Ltd).

ISBN 0–333–65904-X hardback
ISBN 0–333–65905-8 paperback

This book is printed on paper suitable for recycling and
made from fully managed and sustained forest sources.

A catalogue record for this book is available
from the British Library.

Library of Congress Cataloging-in-Publication Data

Holland, Martin, 1954–
        The European Union and the Third World / Martin Holland.
            p.   cm. – (The European Union series)
        Includes bibliographical references and index.
        ISBN 0-333-65904-X – ISBN 0-333-65905-8 (pbk.)
            1. European Union countries–Foreign economic relations–Developing
        countries.   2. Developing countries–Foreign economic relations–
        European Union countries.   I. Title   II. European Union series
        (Palgrave (Firm))

        HF1531.Z4   D445   2002
        337.40172′4–dc21

10   9   8   7   6   5   4   3   2   1
11   10   09   08   07   06   05   04   03   02

Printed in China

Contents

List of Tables, Figures and Boxes

Tables

Figures and Boxes

List of Abbreviations

ACP	African, Caribbean and Pacific countries
ALA	Asia–Latin American (Committee)
APEC	Asia–Pacific Economic Cooperation
ASEAN	Association of South East Asian Nations
ASEM	Asia–Europe Meeting
CAP	Common Agricultural Policy
CEEC	Central and Eastern European Countries
CFSP	Common Foreign and Security Policy
CIS	Confederation of Independent States
COREPER	Committee of Permanent Representatives
DAC	Development Assistance Committee (of the OECD)
DGI	Directorate General for External Economic Relations
DGVIII	Directorate General for Development
EAMA	Associated African States and Madagascar
EBA	Everything but Arms
EC	European Community
ECHO	European Community Humanitarian Office
EDF	European Development Fund
EEC	European Economic Community
EIB	European Investment Bank
EMU	Economic and Monetary Union
ESAF	Enhanced Structural Adjustment Facility
EU	European Union
EUA	European Units of Account
Eurodad	European Network on Debt and Development
FDI	Foreign Direct Investment
FIC	Forum Island Countries
FRY	Former Republic of Yugoslavia
FTA	Free Trade Areas
FTAA	Free Trade Area of the Americas
GATT	General Agreement on Tariffs and Trade
GDP	Gross Domestic Product
GNP	Gross National Product
GSP	Generalized System of Preferences

G7	Group of Seven
HDI	Human Development Index
HIC	High-Income Country
HIPC	Highly Indebted Poor Countries
IGC	Inter-Governmental Conference
IMF	International Monetary Fund
LDC	Least Developed Country
LIC	Low-Income Country
LMIC	Lower Middle-Income Country
Maghreb	Countries of Algeria, Morocco and Touisia
Mashrek	Countries of Egypt, Jordan, Lebanon and Syria
MERCOSUR	Mercado Común del Sur
MFA	Multi-fibre Agreement
MFN	Most Favoured Nation
NAFTA	North American Free Trade Agreement
NGO	Non-Governmental Organization
NICs	Newly Industrialized Countries
NIS	Newly Independent States (of the former USSR)
OCT	French Overseas Collectivities and Territories
ODA	Official Development Assistance
OECD	Organization for Economic Cooperation and Development
QMV	Qualified Majority Voting
SADC	Southern African Development Community
SAP	Structural Adjustment Programme
SCR	Service Commun Relex ('Joint Service for the Management of Community Aid to Non-Member Countries')
SEM	Single European Market
STABEX	Stabilization of Export Earnings Scheme
SYSMIN	Stabilization Scheme for Mineral Products
TEU	Treaty on European Union
UK	United Kingdom
UMIC	Upper Middle-Income Country
UN	United Nations
UNDP	United Nations Development Programme
WTO	World Trade Organization
ZANU-PF	Zimbabwe African National Union–Patriotic Front

Preface

This has been without any doubt a difficult book to write. Not only is the topic vast and complex, the parameters within which the EU has operated its policy with the Developing or Third World have undergone radical and seemingly continual reform in recent years. This text incorporates all these significant changes, including a full analysis of the Cotonou Partnership Agreement of June 2000 and the 'Everything but Arms' initiative of March 2001. Hopefully, the analysis will remain both provocative and relevant for years to come even if the policy details continue to change in the future. The analysis poses a number of simple but related questions. First, can the EU demonstrate a distinct development policy separate and superior to that of the Member States? Second, how far have traditional development policy assumptions been replaced by a global liberalized agenda based on free trade? Third, how successfully has the EU linked development policy with its foreign policy activities under CFSP? And lastly, what is the impact of external relations – particularly development policy – on the integration process *per se*?

The conceptualization as well as writing of this book has spanned several years and locations. My gratitude and appreciation go to Heribert Weiland and other colleagues at the Arnold Bergstraesser Institut, University of Freiburg, Germany, and to the Alexander von Humboldt Foundation for their continuing fellowship support; to Apirat Petchsiri and the graduate students of the European Union Studies Programme at Chulalongkorn University, Bangkok, Thailand; and to my colleagues at the Centre for Research on Europe at the University of Canterbury, New Zealand. Special thanks goes to the Rockefeller Foundation for the award of a Bellagio residency fellowship which enabled me to complete the first draft of this manuscript while at the indescribably wonderful Villa Serbelloni on Lake Como Italy in the summer of 2000. Lastly, I hope this book goes some way to repay the debt I owe to my wife, Ann Marie: the completion of this manuscript would not have been possible without her love, support, understanding and patience.

Villa Serbelloni   MARTIN HOLLAND

Author's note

Throughout this book, it can safely be assumed that one Euro equals one Ecu and/or EUA.

For

Ann Marie
who makes me complete

Introduction:
Setting the Context

Europe's formal relations with the developing world are as old as the European Community (EC) itself. However, the shape and the content of those relations have altered significantly since the signing of the Treaty of Rome in 1957. Successive enlargements, differential rates of global development, the collapse of communist ideology in Central and Eastern Europe and the reorganization of international trade under the auspices of the World Trade Organization (WTO) have all contributed to redefining the European Union's (EU) external relations with the Third World. These changes were nowhere more dramatically portrayed than in the Lomé Convention (1975–2000). The Convention – linking the EU with the African, Caribbean and Pacific (ACP) developing countries – was considered the hallmark of the EU's policy with the Third World, yet it failed to meet the needs and expectations of the new millennium and underwent a comprehensive and critical review from 1997 onwards. The new century also witnessed parallel revisions undertaken in Europe's relations with Latin America, Asia and elsewhere. This text examines these changes and identifies common themes as well as contrasting examples. Most significantly, the argument presents development policy within the wider context of Europe's integration process and suggests that theories of integration are the appropriate tools for understanding not just Europe's internal politics, but its external relations as well.

In order to contextualize development policy, the EU's engagement with the Third World is best described as a policy patchwork. In addition to the ACP states, it incorporates Latin America, China, India, most of Asia and arguably North Africa. Europe has negotiated framework cooperation agreements with some 15 Asian and Latin American countries; has similar agreements with three regional groupings (the Association of South

1

East Asian Nations (ASEAN), Andean Pact and Central America); began the Asia–Europe Meeting (ASEM) process; operates cooperation or association agreements with the Maghreb and Mashrek states as well as with four other Mediterranean countries; and, lastly, also has special relationships with a multitude of member state overseas departments and territories. However, by far the most structured and important historical relationship has been the Lomé Convention, which in June 2000 was superseded by the Cotonou Agreement and now embraces almost all the developing countries of the Caribbean, Pacific and sub-Saharan Africa.

Consequently, Europe's traditional view of development has been specific but comparatively limited. The developing world was defined as principally those former member state colonies in Africa, the Caribbean and the Pacific and dealt with under the Lomé framework; only this relationship was historical, institutionalized, comprehensive and based on the principle of non-reciprocity. In contrast, relations with the Indian sub-continent, Asia and Latin America have been comparatively new, *ad hoc*, fragmented and generally more limited in scope. Such a dichotomy (based on past practice rather than development criteria) was always difficult to sustain, and has become increasingly indefensible. The collapse of communism in Central and Eastern Europe further complicated what was already an untenable position: throughout the 1990s development aid was increasingly shifted in favour of these emerging democratic European states. Clearly, Europe's old definitions of development needs were proving to be hopelessly inadequate, raising more issues than they solved.

A more inclusive definition of the developing world was needed for the EU that recognized regional disparities and sought a common approach to common problems. Geography and history were no longer an acceptable or sufficient rationale. Consequently, from 1997 onwards the EU fundamentally reviewed its network of relations with regions of its traditional partners in the developing world (ACP, Asia, Latin America) in an attempt to produce a new policy paradigm that was consistent, comprehensive and common in origin, approach and criteria. Formally, and if somewhat belatedly, this motivation was founded in the treaty obligations agreed to at Maastricht. Article 130u of the Treaty on European Union states:

Community policy in the sphere of development co-operation, which shall be complementary to the policies pursued by the Member States, shall foster:
- the sustainable economic and social development of the developing countries, and more particularly the most disadvantaged among them;
- the smooth and gradual integration of the developing countries into the world economy;
- the campaign against poverty in the developing countries.

Thus the trinity of coordination, coherence and complementarity governing the EU's external policies was extended to development. Europe's relations with the developing world came under greater scrutiny and past practice was challenged both externally and internally. It has become increasingly unfashionable for states and other international actors to follow traditional development strategies because of their modest successes over the past half century. More immediately, priority has been given to the transitional economies of the states of Central and Eastern Europe at the expense of the non-European developing world. For the European Union, charity has increasingly appeared to begin closer to home.

Where is the developing world?

From the EU's perspective, determining what constitutes the Third World has been complicated rather than simplified by its past reliance on the Lomé Convention as the principal line of demarcation. But the Lomé framework, whilst extensive, never provided a comprehensive approach towards the developing world and one of its greatest weaknesses was its somewhat idiosyncratic and incremental nature. For example, consider the following comparison of two countries at the end of the 1990s. Both share a European colonial legacy; they have comparably poor per capita GDPs (Gross Domestic Product); display similar low literacy and life expectancy levels; and the external trade patterns for both are based on a limited range of primary products. Both, clearly, are developing countries, arguably amongst the least developed. In this example, however, only one, Angola, was a member of the Lomé Convention, the

EU's then preferred framework for relations with the developing world. The other, Cambodia, remained outside. Similar
parallels can be made between Nigeria (a comparatively afflu-
ent Lomé state) and India, a developing country outside the
Convention, or between Dominica and Vietnam. Out of the 48
least developed countries in the world as listed by the United
Nations, 9 were excluded from the fourth Lomé Convention
that only expired in 2000.

These illustrations symbolize a central problem – the patchwork nature of the EU's development policy. A consistent and
comprehensive approach has been absent: incrementalism and
adhocery spiced with pragmatism and post-colonial *Angst* has
resulted in Europe's fragmented and increasing complexity of
relations with the countries of Africa, Asia, the Caribbean, Latin
America and the Pacific Island states. More vociferous critics
argue that such a status quo is indefensible. The question is
whether this geographical diversity requires policy pluralism, or
is a simple coherent global approach more appropriate and ultimately more effective in realizing development goals?

Defining the 'Third World' has always been problematic.
Even the term itself raises political sensitivities. What criteria
should be applied: ideology; poverty; geography; economic
performance; aid; or exclusion from the global economy?
Obviously, reliance on just a single criterion is inadequate. However, each, at some time, has been utilized as the demarcation
between the 'First' and 'Third' World. Analysis as recent as 1990
defined the Third World as 'non-European, non-communist and
poor' (O'Neill and Vincent, 1990, p. ix). The tumultuous international events of the 1990s overturned not just communism,
but also the simplicity of ideology as a definitional development
criterion. The former stability of global political geography
has dissipated to such an extent that the traditional usage of
the term 'developing country' is no longer a clearly delineated
concept. The variety of nomenclature is revealing: the 'Third
World', 'Developing World', 'the South', 'under-developed',
'non-industrialized' or even 'Other World' have all been applied
to the same general category of countries, albeit each with specific inclusions and exclusions. To further complicate matters,
just after the birth of the European Community in the late 1950s
there were just 83 member countries in the United Nations. By
1989 this had risen to 156 members and by 1996 to 185. Faced

with more than one hundred 'new' nations, old designations have seemed increasingly redundant.

At one level it is argued that the Third World can be defined most simply by identifying geographically what constitutes the First and Second/transitional Worlds – definition by exclusion of the 'other'. If we accept this proposition the Third World is composed of all states other than those of Western, Central and Eastern Europe, Russia and the Confederation of Independent States (CIS), Japan, Australasia and North America, mirroring a broad North–South divide (the antipodes excepted). Such simplicity sits uneasily with the reality of crudely defining the economies of Brazil, Singapore, Venezuela, United Arab Emirates, Kuwait or even South Africa as simply developing.

An alternative strategy is to work from the bottom up. The OECD-defined 48 Least Developed Countries (LDCs) obviously fit the rubric; so too do all the 77 ACP (African, Caribbean and Pacific) full member states of the 2000 Cotonou Partnership Agreement, the successor to the previous Lomé Conventions. Once the arithmetic approaches three figures, choices become open to interpretation. What of the states on Europe's southern border? Do, perhaps, the 'economies in transition' of Eastern Europe, or those developing countries on the Mediterranean rim qualify? Further afield, is it valid to classify Latin America, China, India and the vast majority of Asia as an undifferentiated Third World category?

What criteria, then, can Europe use to distinguish between the complex and differentiated categories of the developed and developing world? Certainly a crude dichotomy is unsatisfactory. Perhaps statistics provide a reliable guide to this definitional problem? If so, whose statistics should be used: the OECD, the World Bank, the European Community or the third countries themselves?

The World Bank's *World Development Report 1997* uses 1995 GNP per capita statistics as the main criterion to establish four basic categories of development (covering 210 'countries'). These are (note strange gap between US$3020 and US$3036!):

- Low-income (US$765 or less)
- Lower-middle-income (US$766–3020)
- Upper-middle-income (US$3036–9385)
- High-income (US$ 9386 and above).

The analysis identified 63 low-income economies, 65 lower-middle-income, 30 upper-middle-income and the remaining 52 as high-income economies. The *Report* goes on to state that low- and middle-income economies 'are sometimes referred to as developing economies'; but whilst the 'use of the term is convenient . . . Classification by income does not necessarily reflect development status'(!) (pp. 264–5). Defining the Third World from these World Bank categories is also complicated by geography. For example, 16 lower-middle-income and 7 low-income countries are from Central and Eastern Europe and Russia – economies in transition certainly, but not normally seen as part of the Third World.

In the OECD 1996 Development Assistance Committee's report *Development Cooperation* a different but related methodology is adopted. Focusing on just those developing countries that were ODA (Official Development Aid) recipients, five categories were identified, again using the criterion of per capita GNP (although based on 1992 data):

- Least Developed Countries (LDCs)
- Low-Income Countries (LICs) (less than $675)
- Lower Middle-Income Countries (LMICs) ($676–$2695)
- Upper Middle-Income Countries (UMICs) ($2696–$8355)
- High-Income Countries (HICs) (greater than $8355).

Forty-eight LDCs, 16 LICs, 65 LMICs, 32 UMICs and 6 HICs (see OECD, p. A101) were identified. Two additional categories were used to distinguish between aid to 14 countries and territories in transition (CEECs: Central and Eastern European Countries and NICs: Newly Independent States of the Former Soviet Union) and 6 states designated 'more advanced developing countries' (such as Kuwait, Singapore or the United Arab Emirates). However, nine CEEC/NIS states were still defined as either LIC or LMIC states – traditional Third World categories – blurring the usefulness of the index for defining development status.

The Human Development Index (HDI) offers yet another perspective. This United Nations Development Programme (UNDP) approach supplements indices that focus crudely on GNP bases. It employs indicators based on the criteria of longevity (life expectancy), educational level and income per head: whilst still imperfect, many argue that it gives a better assessment of 'development' as opposed to poverty. The 1999 HDI Report rank-ordered 174 countries and produced some surprising results. For example, the ACP country of Barbados ranked number 30 above EU candidate countries Malta (32), Slovenia (33), Czech Republic (36) and Poland (44)! In fact, five Caribbean ACP States were ranked in the top 50 places. Less surprisingly, every country ranked below 150 was an ACP member (http://www.undp.org/hdro/HDI.html).

Faced with this ambiguity, in this study a precise GNP per capita definition of the Third World is avoided in favour of an essentially geographically based interpretation that reflects the reality and actual practice of the EU's development relations. Marginal countries that are excluded from this study are those that fall into either the World Bank 'higher income' bracket or the OECD 'more advanced developing countries' classification. Most significantly, none of the CEEC/NIS states are included here. This is despite the fact that a number meet the GNP per capita criterion and, as is argued elsewhere in this text, during the 1990s these new states took the lion's share of aid. Indeed, the priority given to their reconstruction highlighted the problems within the EU's fragmented approach to global development *per se*.

Context

It has become commonplace to draw attention to the complications introduced by the pillared approach to post-Maastricht EU policy-making. The Treaty on European Union's (TEU) intergovernmental compromise, which introduced the idea of policy pillars that distinguish between competences and decision-making methods according to policy sector, has undoubtedly exacerbated rather than reduced the ability for the EU to act as a single actor. The cordoning and sanitization of 'foreign policy' as a pillar II intergovernmental competence under the Common Foreign and Security Policy (CFSP) has excessively narrowed the domain for EU foreign policy action. Almost in every instance, pillar I *communautaire* competences are required to implement CFSP in practice. This consequence is nowhere more clearly evident than in relations with the developing world,

TABLE I.1   *Distribution of CFSP Joint Actions and Common Positions adopted, 1997–99*

Focus of CFSP action	Total number of Common Positions/ Joint Actions
Eastern Europe Ukraine, Russia, Belarus, Afghanistan, Albania, ex-Yugoslavia/Balkans	64 (43 of which were directed at the Balkans/FRY)
ACP countries Ethiopia, Rwanda/Great Lakes, Africa, Congo, Sierra Leone, Angola, Nigeria	29
Non-ACP developing countries Libya, Indonesia, East Timor, Middle East, North Korea, Iraq, Cuba, Myanmar	14
Thematic issues Nuclear non-proliferation, anti- personnel mines, weapons of dual purpose, biological weapons	22

Source: *European Foreign Affairs Review* (1998, 1999, 2000).

which illustrate both the impracticality of this segmentation, as well as the policy contradictions that can result. Of course, this policy *apartheid* was necessary for reasons related to intra-European debates on integration and the price in terms of a diluted EU external presence was one a majority of member states were willing to pay. For third countries the notion that Europe's relations with the South (particular through Lomé) constitute something other than foreign policy is absurd. But it is an absurdity that the EU insists on preserving.

The CFSP – particularly joint actions and common positions – inevitably contaminates the purity of the TEU's policy pillars. But both the intergovernmental as well as pillar I trade relations between the EU and the developing world remain distinct from CFSP. The accompanying Table highlights how permeable the policy boundaries established under the TEU are. The range of CFSP joint actions, common positions and decisions with developing countries is high and has become the EU's major foreign policy focus outside the Balkans and Eastern Europe. In 1998, for example, Africa accounted for 6 of the 22 common positions taken by the EU, and Asia a further 5: three of the EU's 20 joint actions related to Africa (Allen and Smith, 1999, p. 89). But it is only these joint actions and common positions that are dealt with as foreign policy under pillar II procedures. The problems of coordination between CFSP objectives and those conducted by the EU under pillar I are dealt with elsewhere in this volume. Suffice it to say at this stage that the existence of the CFSP both complements and complicates EU development policy.

The collapse of the Berlin Wall (intriguingly exactly on the 101st anniversary of the birth of Jean Monnet) has done more to redefine the context of the EU's development policy than any other contemporary single event. The East, not the South, became the principal focus of EU development assistance throughout the 1990s. This new geopolitical context has also cast a shadow that extends significantly into the future in the form of enlargement. Arguably, by 2010 at the latest, the EU may have expanded to include perhaps as many as ten new members – the majority if not all of which will be comparatively poor by current EU standards despite the development assistance of the 1990s. Under these circumstances, the willingness or ability of the EU to continue with traditional development support has been questioned. Consequently, whilst at one level the negotiations for enlarging the EU appear to be a strictly intra-EU issue, the implications do set the context within which existing and future relations with the developing world are determined. Arguably, part of the explanation behind the EU's determination to redefine the basis of the Lomé Convention is suggested by the context of enlargement.

Similarly, Agenda 2000 and the related Inter-Governmental Conference (IGC) issues relating to institutional reform also impact upon the EU's development policy – albeit in an indirect way. The need to move beyond the constraints of consensus towards majority voting has implications for all external relations. In particular, the new emphasis on enhanced cooperation as a decision-making style could see the EU adopting differentiated layers of relationships with the developing world. No longer may it be necessary for the fifteen to find a consensus to formulate policy: an inner core group of states may prefer to extend their joint activity to introduce a more extensive collective European policy. Of course, no such policy can contradict the existing *acquis* but undoubtedly this flexibility can be regarded as a potential policy vanguard and as such it can implicitly set the future policy direction of the EU as a whole. Potentially, enhanced cooperation can create path-dependency by creating a new level of collective policy for the core group of states that can ultimately lead to a new collective future policy status quo for all member states. This tendency can be applied – at least in theory – to initiatives in development policy. As past enlargements have already shown, northern and southern EU states have different development policy perspectives and it seems quite possible that a Nordic dimension could use enhanced cooperation to advance collective development policy for a smaller number of states. This possibility at least does influence the context of EU decision-making. The former use of consensus as a policy brake, if not redundant as a threat, is no longer an absolute veto.

Turning from the internal European contexts that help to shape development perspectives, there are two important external arenas that constrain EU policy: the WTO and global debt-reduction initiatives. The failed 1999 Seattle WTO meeting illustrated both the inter-related nature of the EU and WTO agendas and the importance of incorporating development concerns as a central feature of global liberalization. Simply, whatever independent initiatives the EU may wish to make in development policy, these need to be both compatible with WTO rules and consistent with developing country aspirations. As the banana saga of the late 1990s illustrated, the global context of WTO institutions is a clear and legitimate constraint of EU policy formation. Similarly, the G7 initiative of 1998/9 on global debt reduction for categories of developing countries helped to shape the emergence of a common EU stance on the issue. Thus institutional frameworks outside those of the EU have had – and will continue to have – an impact of the direction and application of specifically EU development policy.

Other examples could be added to this list of external and internal agents – the global consensus on poverty, the environment and women's development in particular. However, the important point at least from the perspective of this text is that clearly context does matter. Despite being the world's largest trader and having experienced some 50 years of collective action the EU cannot act in a fully autonomous manner but is, like all international actors, constrained by a multiple series of contexts, both intra-European and global.

In summary, context matters. Europe's development policy does not operate in a vacuum – whether theoretical or empirical. Policy choices are constrained by the varied contexts (internal, external and global) within which the EU operates. This general conclusion has significant policy implications and this section has outlined a number of particular contexts that have influenced the EU's relationship with the developing world (such as CFSP, enlargement, Agenda 2000, the WTO and global debt initiatives).

Objectives and challenges: the focus of the study

The task of this text is to explore this mosaic of relations – historically, institutionally and in terms of contemporary policies – and to provide a comprehensive overview that both respects the uniqueness of each policy sector and demonstrates, where applicable, the commonalities of the EU's global relations with the developing world. This tension has been the hallmark of EU–Third World relations to date and recent reforms were in part designed to address the issue of differentiation.

An aspect of integration?

The primary focus is on the EU policy-making process. In particular, the link between internal EU integration and external relations is emphasized. The debates pertaining to a deeper Union and the integration process are not confined purely to Europe's own Single Market and Monetary Union programmes; they influence and direct the policies adopted towards the external world. At a simplistic theoretical level, this analysis suggests that there is a simple 'spillover' from the level of political and economic integration within the EU into the area of development policy. Collective external action is dependent on the political will of the EU's elite; without their agreement policy reformulation is impossible given its intergovernmental character. The purpose of this book is not to provide a detailed description of each EU–developing country bilateral relationship, or even to provide an exhaustive account of the various treaties and

agreements. Rather, it provides a thematic analysis and overview that locates development policy in the wider integration
debate. (See Chapter 9 for a fuller discussion of this theoretical
application.) Where specific examples and cases are discussed
in various chapters, these are by way of illustration of more
general issues.

A case for subsidiarity?

A fundamental question posed in this analysis is to what extent
should there be an EU development policy? What can the EU
do better – in terms of development – than the member states?
Can a more effective development policy be conducted bilaterally between member states and third countries directly than
can be achieved 'collectively' at the EU level? Simply, but pro-
vocatively, is development policy a case for subsidiarity? The
concept of subsidiarity introduced in the Maastricht Treaty has
traditionally (and legally) been regarded as confined to discussions of intra-EU policy competences. Subsidiarity is interpreted
legally as a requirement that EU policy only be implemented
where there is a clear advantage over the bilateral implementation of that policy by individual member states. Brussels has to
demonstrate that things can be done better collectively than by
the individual governments acting separately. Within the EU's
internal policies this concept has been problematic enough: in
external relations, both intergovernmental and *communautaire*,
the difficulties are magnified.

However, the principle (at least in a general if not precise legal
sense) is relevant to the current external relations debate. The
onus is on the EU to demonstrate that the EU is better in conducting and delivering development policy to the Third World
than are the member states. If this cannot be demonstrated a re-
nationalization of development policy could emerge, a tendency
consistent with the general intergovernmental interpretation of
subsidiarity. The challenge, then, is to what extent can the EU
demonstrate both a *distinct* development role for itself as well
as a *superior* one to that of the member states? Whilst development policy will continue to be an area of mixed competences
and commitments between the member states and the EU, the
recent trend has been towards increasing the role of the Union.

And yet to avoid duplication the EU needs to establish a distinct role in development policy separate from that already conducted by the member states. As one senior Commission official has suggested, there seems little point in Europe running a sixteenth programme for the sake of it. Member states can choose whether to commit their resources bilaterally or through the EU system: what clear advantages can the Community route offer? Historically, what has been lacking is any coherent and accepted yardstick that can determine what aspects of development cooperation are best done bilaterally by member states, and what are better done collectively at the Community level.

In some respects the EU makes a unique contribution to development aid. First, through the Lomé Convention the EU attempted to introduce a greater degree of equality into the development relationship than traditional bilateral arrangements. Second, largely thanks to pressure from the European Parliament, Europe initiated policy and debate on a number of development issues, such as women and development, reproductive healthcare, AIDS, the environment and development, and refugees. Third, a bottom-up philosophy tends to emphasize cooperation with NGOs as the appropriate deliverer of development assistance. Overall, it can be argued that collective EU development policy adds value if only by virtue of its scale of assistance, particularly in areas such as emergency food aid and through Lomé funds. However, in general in the past there has been a deafening silence in answer to the questions of Europe's distinctive development role and what policy elements are best coordinated at the EU level. Only in 2000 did the Commission finally begin to address this fundamental concern.

Whilst Treaty Article 130 lists distinctive features of EU development policy, currently these are not exclusive domains: however, it might provide a guide to the EU–member state division for future policy sectors. Many proposals to define and specify a distinct EU role have been tabled. For example, the EU could focus primarily on poverty alleviation (as required by the TEU). This radical approach would see EU assistance focus on the least developed countries, leaving bilateral member-state relations to cover the other developing countries. Such a division runs counter to the past twenty-five years of Lomé relations that have grouped all types of developing country together under a single convention. Any dismantling of the ACP framework would require significant member-state cooperation and goodwill in order to plug the resultant gaps. Obviously this touches on the central issue of the role of the Council. Intergovernmental agendas suggest that neither the extension of EU policy competences nor a redistribution of competences between the Union and its member states will be easily achieved. Others have called for the EU to act as the 'wholesaler' of development assistance (supporting the structure of development) with member states acting as 'retailers' in the local markets (actually implementing specific programmes on the ground). Another proposal emphasizes conditionality concerning 'democracy and the rule of law . . . human rights and fundamental freedoms' as a distinctive competence of EU policy. Thus whatever bilateral relations might exist would be governed by EU-level definitions of human rights and democratic conditionality. The operation of the European Community Humanitarian Office (ECHO) adds credence to Europe's civilian humanitarian identity. However, the current consensus is for parallel organizations to exist rather than to create an exclusive EU role. Rationalization rather than duplication may be to the greater benefit of developing countries in the post-Lomé world. These and other themes are explored in greater detail in the following chapters.

Optional or fundamental?

Confronting this fundamental question – does the EU need a development policy – is essential. Is any such policy merely an optional extension of the process of integration, like social or regional policy, or is it a core function, even perhaps a democratic obligation? We cannot take as given the necessity of a development policy beyond the technical framework established by the Common Commercial Policy. However, there are a number of altruistic as well as self-interested reasons that suggest that a development policy is not optional, but fundamental to the process of European integration and the EU's global role.

Included among these motivations based on self-interest is the desire to avoid destabilization caused by increased immigration and refugee crises. Whilst a Europe just for Europeans is not the policy of the EU, improving the living standards of the Third World may reduce the economic attraction of migration (both legal and illegal) to Western Europe. The maintenance of resource supplies remains a factor, although one that has diminished since the collapse of the Soviet Union. With the opening up of markets and resources in the former Soviet sphere of influence, the EU is no longer exclusively dependent on the developing countries for certain products and raw materials. A further motivation can be found in the EU's support for the exploitation of export markets and the general promotion of global free trade. As is discussed elsewhere in this book the EU is committed to integrating the Third World into the global trading system, but preferably on the basis of free trade despite the developing world's scepticism. Lastly, the EU has long held a desire to emerge as a global actor – both economic as well as political. The development agenda allows it to play such a political role through its economic power as the world's largest trader.

More altruistically, the EU's development policy expresses its belief in democracy. The pervasive application of conditionality concerning human rights, good governance and democracy should not be misinterpreted as the imposition of European values on reluctant developing states. Typically, developing countries welcome this conditionality as it can help them safeguard and extend democratic practices domestically. Similarly, EU policy encourages and supports regional integration in the developing world. Even under the past Lomé umbrella there were provisions for the promotion of regional integration projects, such as the Southern African Development Community (SADC) for example. Obviously, as the world's most advanced form of regional cooperation, the EU has a philosophical commitment to integration; however, it would be somewhat churlish to regard this as a selfish motivation. The rationale is primarily altruistic. Finally, there is the assumption (already touched on) that Europe's internal integration cannot be treated in splendid isolation but is inextricably linked with its external relations. What happens within the EU integration process has fundamental repercussions for the developing world – economically, socially and environmentally. The consequences of a failed Single Market, or Monetary Union would not be confined to Europe: they would impact directly on the fragile economies of the developing world. The development of the Third World is, therefore, inextricably linked to the internal success of European integration.

Of course, some argue that development policy is not a 'core' European policy in the sense that the Common Agricultural Policy (CAP) or the Single Market are. Whilst not advocating the re-nationalization of development policy (in line with a strict interpretation of subsidiarity) it would become an EU policy sector to which the concept of enhanced cooperation might be appropriately applied. This has been conceived as a method to enable those states that are willing and able to do so to press ahead towards fuller European integration more quickly than others. Thus the pace of integration is no longer determined by the slowest member state, and importantly, such flexibility would enable closer forms of cooperation, that could otherwise take place only outside the Treaty framework, to be kept under the Treaty umbrella. For example, the Nordic countries have traditionally placed a greater emphasis on the development agenda than other EU states. In a post-Lomé context either that saw the member states fundamentally divided over policy options or where a decision was adopted that reduced the content of development policy, the Nordic states and others may wish to promote (or 'enhance') development policy through the mechanism of flexibility. A number of states, therefore, would extend European policy whilst operating under the treaty framework (within the obligatory rider that any such activity was consistent with the *acquis communautaire* and existing EC policies). Whilst the content of any such 'enhanced cooperation' as well as the number of participating countries are unknown, theoretically development policy may in future become an unexpected candidate for the use of enhanced cooperation – a case of conceptual and empirical spillover perhaps?

By necessity this text provides an empirical account of the historical development of the EU's Third World policy; however, it offers more than a repetitive, descriptive and statistical recital of information easily found elsewhere (see Lister 1997a; Grilli, 1993). The text presents thematic and theoretical arguments that provide the context for analysing EU policy. Obviously, the reform of the Lomé Convention is a significant theme, but as already argued above, the EU's policy towards developing countries reaches far beyond this treaty-based agreement with the ACP states. Both the strengths and the weaknesses of EU policy (in content and scope) are the focus of this analysis.

Change, reform and differentiation

There is no ideal time to write about the EU: it is constantly evolving and susceptible to the vagaries of electoral change in the member states. The same is true for Europe's policy with the Third World. The last decade of the twentieth century witnessed monumental global change: ideological, economic and strategic. These changes directly impacted on our perceptions and expectations about the developing world. From the mid-1990s Europe's development policy has been in a state of flux and it will continue to evolve into the new millennium. Consequently, this text presents the debates that have shaped the new policy options and offers broad parameters within which future changes can be located and interpreted. Why did the EU undertake such a complete re-evaluation of its development framework at the end of the twentieth century? The rationale for reform was initiated by a growing dissatisfaction with the Lomé structures. The motivations were diverse, but cumulatively compelling, at least from a European perspective.

First, there was the record of European assistance to date. Few, if any, of the Lomé countries had seen a radical transformation in their economic well-being: dependency continued to define their relationship with Europe. Second, as noted earlier, the preferences and resources given to Central and Eastern Europe had largely been at the expense of the ACP states: the cake had not sufficiently increased to cope with both these development demands. Third, the WTO began to cast a critical eye in general over preferential agreements, and specifically with respect to the existing Lomé preferences (which had an interim WTO waiver), arguing that these were inconsistent with the trend towards open markets. In response, the Commission of the EU was active in promoting a global free trade philosophy. Fourth, and perhaps paradoxically, trade figures suggested that the 'privileged' position of Lomé countries and the value of their preferential treatment had been significantly eroded since 1989. The Lomé states were no longer at the apex of the 'pyramid of privilege'. Further, many of the states in Asia had substantially out-performed those of the ACP despite receiving no concessionary privileges.

Last, the calls for reform reflected a growing recognition of the diversity within the so-called developing world and the obvious inconsistencies in the EU's geographical ambit. It became increasingly difficult to explain what common interests bound the Lomé states together or distinguished them from the majority of non-Lomé developing countries. The ACP was an acronym, but it also became increasingly anachronistic. The ACP secretariat argued that the rationale for the grouping is more than post-colonial history and clearly the large size of the ACP group does provide certain negotiating advantages (for both the ACP and the EU). However, the existence of regional provisions within the existing Lomé framework worked to emphasize the diversity of needs rather than enhance the 'coherence' of the ACP community. Increasingly 'differentiation' became the clarion call for the new development policy agenda.

Future challenges

This text raises many of the future challenges that face the EU's policy towards the Third World beyond 2000. The first is the question of development funding. To what extent can financial assistance and trade preferences be redistributed away from the countries of Central and Eastern Europe and back to the 'traditional' definition of Third World developing states? An overall increase in support is not an option. Second, the lessons from past enlargements suggest that the next wave of membership will impact on the EU's development policy: the status quo is not viable. Third, within the changing context some member states will strive to maintain and protect their special historical ties with particular countries or developing regions. Balancing this with more general reform issues may prove contentious, particularly for the French and the British. Fourth, global trends will influence the EU's policy options. The WTO provides a new constraint upon EU policy as any new trading relationship with the developing world has to be consistent with WTO regulations. The 1990s dispute over Lomé banana preferences is just one small indication of the new environment in which EU policy must now operate. Fifth, and related, is the move towards global regionalism that provoked a restructuring of the EU's development relations. Perhaps the greatest challenge lies in the EU differentiating between levels, or types, of developing country, discriminating between countries that up to the year 2000 had largely been treated on an equal footing despite their apparent different levels of development. Sixth, the framework for relations will be problematic. Should the principle of non-reciprocity be retained (albeit for a reduced category of states) or should the philosophy of Free Trade Areas (FTA) be applied uniformly irrespective of the level of development? And last, as set out in both the Maastricht and Amsterdam Treaties, the reduction of poverty is the development policy goal. However, has the EU provided itself with adequate and appropriate instruments and policies for such an ambitious task? Simply, is such a humanitarian policy goal achievable?

As is typically the case in most EU policy areas, development and relations with the Third World combine a number of otherwise discrete policy sectors and institutional actors. For example, it involves external trade relations in general as well as Lomé relations specifically: the role of the European Community Humanitarian Office has increased significantly whereas the CFSP has been used spasmodically to achieve development policy goals. Consequently, both *communautaire* pillar I European Community competences are utilized in conjunction with pillar II *intergovernmental* procedures. The actors include the member states in the Council, the European Parliament and the Commission (which itself divides competence for development policy between at least five Directorates General). As is explored in the following chapters, whilst such policy diversification has both strengths and weaknesses, the problems of coordination and complementarity are undoubtedly exacerbated by this diffusion.

The relationship between the CFSP and development policy is a clear illustration of this problem. The Maastricht Treaty demands a linkage despite the pillared structure that separates development policy from intergovernmental CFSP. Article C of the Common Provisions is explicit:

> The Union shall in particular ensure the consistency of its external activities as a whole in the context of its external relations, security, economic and development policies. The Council and Commission shall be responsible for ensuring such consistency. They shall ensure the implementation of these policies, each in accordance with its respective powers.

The challenge is to balance Europe's array of external objectives and responsibilities. Development policy, in its broadest sense, is part of the EU's CFSP personality and one of its instruments. Joint actions, for example, can have development implications: the 1993–5 joint action on South Africa provides a good illustration of this relationship. As a global actor the EU requires a comprehensive network of external policies that combine trade, environment, development as well as the more traditionally recognizable foreign policy issues together. Achieving coordination, coherence and complementarity between and across these sectors within the Union is a mammoth task (and one that has been compounded by the Maastricht 'reforms'). But it is also an essential task and one, as already suggested, unavoidably linked to the integration debate *per se*. In such a scenario development policy cannot be an optional extra, but constitutes a core component of Europe's external relations and CFSP.

The chapters

The remainder of this introduction provides a synopsis of the individual chapters. Whilst each chapter focuses on a specific area of European development policy, the themes and ideas raised in this introduction permeate the discussion throughout. The EU has set itself the task of fundamental reform of its relations with the Third World. As such it is legitimate and necessary to question whether the reforms are based on a coherent philosophy or represent a series of disjointed political compromises that do little to reconceptualize development policy. Why should there be an EU policy? What should be its content? How is it to be executed? Who are the actors? And, crucially, how is it to be funded? These are all central issues that require analysis.

Chapters 1 and 2 provide an historical and a geographical overview of EU–Third World relations. Here the dichotomy between relations with the ACP states and non-ACP countries (in Asia and Latin America) is the organizing principle, with a separate chapter devoted to each of these two groups. Chapter 1 considers the origins, motivations and content of Europe's development policy towards the ACP and contrasts the earliest period of relations (the Yaoundé Convention) with the successive Lomé Conventions. Chapter 2 explores the comparatively rudimentary relations with Latin America (particularly with MERCOSUR) and those with Asia (through both ASEAN and the ASEM process). The framework for relations, trade and aid are all considered, highlighting the contrasts as well as the similarities with EU–ACP relations.

Chapter 3 draws on some of the arguments suggested in the earlier chapters. It examines the institutional relations that structure the EU–Third World dialogue as well as the decision-making processes within the EU that shape development policy. The internal reforms of the Prodi Commission are contrasted with the Santer Commission structure of 1995–99. The management of the Commission's external assistance programme as well as the rationale behind the reorganization of Directorate Generals is reviewed. The chapter concludes with a discussion of ECHO and the role of humanitarian aid. The main argument of this chapter is that poor administrative and implementation structures have hampered the delivery of development policy and structural reform is a necessary precondition for a more effective EU development policy in future. Chapter 4 debates the merits, effects and consequences of two specific EU concerns: complementarity and conditionality. Complementarity has become a guiding principle for the organization of all EU policy sectors. The realization of this goal in development policy is, however, complex and problematic. Political conditionality (in the form of good governance, democracy, the rule of law and Human Rights) has become a pervasive element of EU external relations, and yet its application remains disputed. Economic conditionality (structural adjustment, liberalization and debt) is similarly contentious, but also remains a core element of European policy. The chapter examines two contemporary cases (Zimbabwe and Fiji) that address some of the issues of implementing conditionality.

Chapter 5 explores a number of trade policy regimes used by the EU – from Generalized System of Preferences (GSP) to Lomé, reciprocity and WTO obligations. Europe's promotion of global regional integration is also considered. The EU's trade policy debates – which contrast preferential regimes with liberalized free trade areas – provide the theoretical context for examining the trade data. The chapter provides a summary of the patterns of trade between the EU and the developing world (distinguishing between the ACP, MERCOSUR and ASEAN/ ASEM frameworks) The conclusion of the analysis is that trade mechanisms are not simply a technical question: their choice is inherently political. Chapter 6 provides a background to the reform processes of the late 1990s that have seen the Lomé Convention fundamentally challenged and the basis of EU– Third World relations radically altered. Four phases of change are identified: the 1996/7 Green Paper exercise; the resultant Commission guidelines; the Council negotiating mandate; and the eventual negotiating process. The chapter sets out the institutional and policy framework options that were effectively to shape EU–Third World for the next two decades. It concludes with an assessment of the implications of the reforms for policy coordination, coherence and complementarity – the official mantra governing external relations and development policy.

Chapter 7 is devoted to a critical account of the new Cotonou Partnership Agreement of 2000. Key differences from the previous Lomé regime are highlighted, as are any similarities with new agreements being signed with other parts of the developing world in Asia and Latin America. The chapter argues that the Cotonou Agreement, if successful, could become the blueprint for the global application of the EU's development programme. The objectives and institutional structure are outlined, the nature of the political dialogue and conditionalities discussed, and innovations identified. The differentiation within the ACP according to development status (separating out the Least Developed Countries) yet retaining the ACP umbrella for the purposes of constructing regional free trade agreements between the EU and six ACP groupings is critically reviewed.

Chapter 8 looks towards the future challenges faced by the EU. First the problems associated with actually implementing the Cotonou provisions are reviewed. Second, the 'Everything but Arms' initiative is discussed together with the significant policy developments of early 2001 in which the EU adopted a new trade framework for the world's 48 LDCs. The chapter draws some general conclusions about Europe's development policy and suggests topics for further analysis as development policy evolves. This new approach brings together for the first time both ACP and non-ACP countries under one regime. Lastly, Chapter 9 discusses the appropriate conceptual framework for analysing EU development policy. It argues that integration theory normally used to explain internal EU policies and processes can also be used to successfully conceptualize development policy and external relations.

Conclusion

To conclude, the focus of this analysis of development policy with the Third World has consciously chosen to adopt a region-to-region approach. Thus the chapters are concerned with EU relations with the four principal blocs that describe the developing world – the ACP, MERCOSUR, ASEAN and ASEM. This approach is obviously open to the criticism that bilateral relations between the EU and individual developing countries are not given sufficient recognition. For example, relations with India or Pakistan are not included here, nor are the countries of Central America. However, this individual level of analysis is the necessary and unavoidable price to be paid for providing a broader perspective of EU development policy. The text – mirroring the EU itself – utilizes economies of scale by looking at region-to-region relations. Indeed, the very fact that the EU seeks such regional dialogues and agreements underlines that this approach is the appropriate perspective.

Writing about development policy as the process evolves is as precarious as it is ambitious. This text seeks to identify the content of the policy debate and to theorize about the relationship between EU development policy and the integration process. As such, the ideas adopted are innovative and hypothetical. However, a core theoretical lacuna has been suggested that necessitates an answer: *does the EU play a distinct role in development policy?* Subsidiarity could yet provide the answer, albeit one that is critical of the EU's claim to distinctiveness. Conversely, enhanced cooperation could suggest that development policy was no longer a core policy within the Union, but one where a variable geometry approach is most appropriate. However, any such reformulation of the EU's role has to recognize and accommodate the objective of consistency in external relations and development policy as expressly articulated in the Maastricht Treaty.

For much of the developing world the reality of the new millennium started on 29 February 2000, the date the Lomé IV

Convention expired. Traditionally, the EU has been the developing world's most significant democratic partner. However, the Commission's 1996 *Green Paper on Relations between the European Union and the ACP countries* that considered reforming the Lomé Convention launched a process that many believe has fundamentally altered this relationship. Development policy currently faces a crossroads and many of the assumptions and certainties of the past four decades are under scrutiny.

Development policy reform is a continual process, the outcome of which remains undecided and susceptible to sudden change. Forging a consensus within the EU member states is always hard and the European Parliament will certainly be active – and its approval is required for any new treaty-based agreement. Despite the clear free trade policy tendencies of Europe, the history of the EU suggests that ambitious proposals that challenge the status quo more often lead to incremental and pragmatic change than to wholesale reform. However, the response of the Third World is crucial. Collectively they may be able to shape the debate to their mutual advantage; however, if no consensus emerges on their shared interests the EU may again be able to dictate the terms of the dialogue. Whatever the outcome, clearly there will be winners and losers. The 1975–2000 status quo could not be maintained.

Whether the late-1990s reform process was just another manifestation of *fin de siècle* euphoria, or a more sober re-evaluation of the EU's global role and limitations, the new millennium has signified a watershed in development policy.

Chapter 1

Four Decades of African, Caribbean and Pacific Relations

This chapter begins by addressing two basic questions: what were the origins of the EU's development policy; and, what were the motivations? These simple questions need to be examined in some detail in order to convey the context within which development policy has evolved since 1957. Many of the current debates concerning the restructuring of relations with the Third World can only be understood through such an historical perspective.

The 1957 Treaty of Rome establishing the then EEC was a document that challenged the pre-existing assumptions about state sovereignty. These assumptions were not exclusively internal in their implications but extended to a state's external affairs as well. The internal integration of the European market had direct and serious consequences for third countries and the position of the developing world was addressed, albeit imperfectly, in the founding Treaty. Of course, bilateral relations have persisted and act to complement the European relationship with the developing world; significantly, however, the scope and scale of these bilateral ties have been progressively modified. Whilst the Treaty was myopic in its largely francophone definition of the Third World this framework represents the origin of Europe's fragmented and differentiated approach.

The original signatories to the Treaty of Rome all sought special arrangements for those matters that were of particular importance to them: agricultural, political and colonial. For France, the protection of the relationship with its colonial dependencies was one such priority. Significantly, throughout the discussions that led to the Spaak Report, which set the framework for the original European Community, no mention was made of colonial relations, and only as late as May 1956 did France table the issue. The other member states were reluctant to involve the EC in what was to most a French external

25

affair, with the Dutch and the Germans the most critical. However, as expressed by one commentator, 'France's move was shrewdly timed: by making a satisfactory agreement on provisions for its dependencies a sine qua non for its signature of the Treaty, French bargaining power was maximized' (Ravenhill, 1985, p. 48). Consequently, on French insistence, provisions for 'association' for all dependencies were included in Part IV of the Treaty: a contractual treaty-based relationship was created that established both the basis and rationale for subsequent arrangements such as the Yaoundé and Lomé Conventions.

Associated status was given to specific overseas collectivities and territories (OCTs) that had 'special relations' with a member state. Initially this only involved relations between 31 OCTs and four member states (France, Belgium, Italy and the Netherlands) but was expanded with the first enlargement in 1973. French colonial ties predominated and incorporated the states of French West Africa, French Equatorial Africa as well as island dependencies in the Pacific and elsewhere. Article 131 sets out the parameters of these original provisions:

> The purpose of association shall be to promote the economic and social development of the countries and territories and to establish close economic relations between them and the Community as a whole.
> . . . association shall serve primarily to further the interests and prosperity of the inhabitants . . . in order to lead them to the economic, social and cultural development to which they aspire.

In essence, both member states and colonial dependencies were to be treated similarly with respect to trade access, investment and the reduction and eventual abolition of customs duties (with the exception of certain 'sensitive' products). A consequence of this was that other third country developing states were discriminated against. The contractual nature of the relationship was important as a legal obligation was established on member states 'to contribute to the investments required for the progressive development of these countries and territories' (Article 132.3). The exclusive mechanism chosen for the task of providing aid was the European Development Fund (EDF). The role of the EDF has grown significantly (both in the scale and scope of funding) and it still remains one of the key instruments of Europe's policy with the developing world. Despite this assistance and the market preferences given to their exports, the associated states generally failed to improve their economic profiles over this period.

Not surprisingly, Articles 131–6 have subsequently been criticized for perpetuating the existing colonial dependency. Whilst with hindsight this certainly seems the case, two ancillary factors are pertinent. First, in the context of the time, these Articles were more significant for underlining at the very beginning of European integration that an external developmental relationship could not be ignored. Clearly, Europe's global role and responsibility was to be valued and part of the wider notion of integration: the then Community was much more ambitious than is perhaps commonly acknowledged. As Monnet argued, the Community was 'not a coal and steel producers' association: it is the beginning of Europe' – with all that phrase implies internally and externally (1978, p. 392). But second, the selectivity of the countries included foreshadowed what was to become the central problem in Europe's relationship with the developing world – historical ties rather than need has been the driving rationale behind preferential treatment. It has taken more than four decades to begin to unravel this selectivity in Europe's definition of the developing world.

The Yaoundé Conventions

Whilst these provisions still apply to a small number of territories today, in the early 1960s the majority of OCTs gained their independence and new arrangements were appropriate and necessary. Consequently, by the mid-1960s the vast majority of African states found their relations with the EC structured through a completely new and separate treaty: the first Yaoundé Convention. The foundation of the Convention was the recognition of the national sovereignty of the participating countries. It established preferential trading arrangements between the Six and 18, principally francophone, countries. These were known as the Associated African States and Madagascar (EAMA in its original French acronym) and were composed of: Burundi, Cameroon, Central African Republic, Chad, Congo, Dahomey,

Gabon, Ivory Coast, Madagascar, Mali, Mauritania, Niger, Rwanda, Senegal, Somalia, Togo, Upper Volta and Zaire.

There were three distinct and original features to the Convention: a) its comprehensive character; b) the multilateral framework; and c) its joint institutions. First, uniquely for the time, the Convention linked a range of separate development policies under a single integrated approach. Financial aid, technical assistance and training, trade preferences and investment and capital movements were all covered. Second, the Convention was the first example of a common contractual basis for relations between the industrialized and the developing world. This multilateral framework made it easier to adopt a regional approach to issues and promoted regional cooperation amongst the EAMA group. Third, the three joint institutions of the Association were created (the Council, the Parliamentary Conference and the Court of Arbitration). The Council contained one representative from each of the EAMA and Community member states, met annually and could issue binding decisions based on joint agreement. The Parliamentary Conference had only advisory status, whereas the Court was the final arbiter where informal procedures in the Council were unable to resolve disputes arising under the Convention. It was never called upon to do so, however.

The first Yaoundé Convention expired in 1969 – although its provisions were renewed for a further five-year period ending in 1975. During the lifetime of this second Convention the first enlargement of the Community took place. UK membership and the question of Commonwealth relations necessitated a major review of external relations. However, this first decade of treaty-based relations between Europe and the developing world provided the context within which the subsequent Lomé Conventions were debated and designed. Community support for the EAMA was directed principally through the EDF and the European Investment Bank (EIB). Under Yaoundé I a total of 666 million EUA (European Units of Account) was provided in EDF aid and a further 64 million in the form of EIB loans. Under Yaoundé II, EDF aid rose to 843 million with a further 90 million provided by EIB loans (Commission, 1986, p. 15). During this period the Community provided approximately 20 per cent of the total official aid received by the 18 signatory states. Three times this amount was provided by continued bilateral assistance from individual member states (mainly France, Belgium and increasingly Germany). The combination of Community-level aid and bilateral aid is the hallmark of Europe's past and present relationship with the developing world. Whilst the balance may have changed from Convention to Convention, this essential element has never been challenged. Community-level aid supplements and supports bilateral action: it has never been designed to replace it entirely.

Two serious problems underlay the seeming largesse of the EDF: disbursement of funds and narrow sectoral support. First, typically, from 1957 to 1975 only a third of EDF funds were successfully disbursed during the lifetime of the respective agreements. Second, the greatest proportion of EDF aid was given to infrastructural projects virtually excluding development of the industrial sector. As such, the EDF mirrored the bilateral practices of former colonial donor states.

The basic principles of the Convention followed those found in the Community's own Treaty of Rome and partly foreshadowed the core elements of the Cotonou Agreement that was to be signed in the year 2000. Over time it was hoped to establish the abolition of customs barriers; reciprocal duty-free access; abolition on quantitative quotas on exports; and the extension of most-favoured-nation status to EC member states. The trade content of the Conventions provided for EAMA imports into the Community free from customs duties and quotas for all agricultural and industrial products – except those that were in direct competition with European producers. Whilst the exceptions were criticized, under Yaoundé II EAMA producers in these categories were given limited but preferential access over other third countries. More importantly, the trade preferences enjoyed by the EAMA were progressively eroded due to the EC lowering or abolishing duties on a range of tropical products – such as coffee, cocoa, tea, pineapples and nutmeg. In addition, products such as copper, iron ore, cotton, rubber and oil seed, which were the main EAMA exports, were never subject to EC tariffs in general. Consequently, the Convention could not provide them with any preferential access to the European market. Overall, the economic benefits provided by the Convention appeared marginal and were openly criticized by the 18 signatories and two member states, Germany and the Netherlands. The impression was given that the Yaoundé states were

TABLE 1.1   *EC imports from and exports to the developing world, 1958–67*

	1958 % imports	1967 % imports	1958 % exports	1967 % exports
Yaoundé States	5.6	4.2	4.4	2.9
Latin America	10.2	8.9	10.1	6.5
Africa (non-EAMA)	9.4	10.3	12.3	6.5
Middle-East	11.2	9.5	4.4	4.1
SE Asia/Oceania	4.8	3.7	6.5	4.9

Source: Commission (1969), Annexe I.

just 'suppliers of the residual market that the Community producers could not fill and at best provided them with a slight
advantage over third countries' (Ravenhill, 1985, p. 56). To
compound the trading problem, Yaoundé was based upon the
principle of reciprocity.

The Yaoundé Convention only linked Europe to a small
segment of the developing world and in it the seeds of Europe's
future piecemeal approach to First–Third World relations can
be traced. Obviously, the 18 Yaoundé countries' share in total
external trade was relatively small. Importantly, however, the
pattern of trade over the 1958–67 period declined (see Table
1.1). In 1958, 5.6 per cent of Community imports came from
the Yaoundé States, this figure falling to 4.2 per cent by 1967.
Community exports to the EAMA stood at 4.4 per cent in 1958,
but only represented 2.9 per cent a decade later and the resultant Community trade deficit with the Yaoundé States rose from
US$22 million to US$378 million over the period. There was a
typical asymmetry in the goods traded: 72 per cent of Yaoundé
exports to Europe were primary products whereas 85 per cent
of the Community's exports were industrial in origin (Commission, 1969, p. 10).

Whilst the first ten years of the Community saw a general
increase in the EC's share of world trade (which by 1967 saw the
Community the leading global importer [18 per cent] and
exporter [20 per cent], as shown above the developing world's
share of this trade declined. Overall, trade with the developing
world – like that with the Yaoundé States – declined during the
Community's first decade. In 1958 the developing countries sup-

plied 42 per cent of the EC's imports and took 39 per cent of Europe's exports. By 1967 these figures had fallen to 38 per cent and 27 per cent respectively. During the same period the EC reduced its import of raw materials from 30 per cent to 22 per cent. Consequently the Community's trade deficit with the developing world rose from US$700 million in 1958 to $3225 million in 1967. What is perhaps most surprising is that if these figures are broken down regionally, Latin America, non-EAMA Africa and the Middle East were all more important markets for the EC. Only trade with SE Asia approached the modest levels of the Yaoundé States (see Table 1.1). And yet at this stage Europe's relationship with the wider developing world lacked the formalized relationship of the Yaoundé Convention. No special privileges existed that gave concessions to these Third World nations.

This broader trend continued to be reflected for the duration of Yaoundé II. Whereas the EAMA states provided 13.4 per cent of the developing world's exports to the EC in 1958, this declined to a 7.4 per cent share by 1974. Similarly, the EAMA states received 11.6 per cent of the EC's exports to the developing world in 1958, falling to 8.4 per cent in 1974 (Ravenhill, 1985, p. 61).

What, then, was so special about the Yaoundé states and what were Europe's motivations? Were they purely economic and arguably neo-colonial, or more developmental in origin? Certainly, Europe's global competitors, especially the USA, may have viewed the association as prejudicial and incompatible with the framework of the General Agreement on Tariffs and Trade (GATT). The difficulties that were to become endemic within the economies of the developing world were already apparent by the time the Yaoundé Convention was signed. Its provisions lacked the necessary drive to alter the historical relationship. Whilst the free trade principle was seen as assisting development, in practice the limited concessions tended to maintain, even strengthen, the dependency relationship. Without the principle of non-reciprocity, the charge of economic neo-colonialism was hard to refute. The majority of the associated states were part of the French franc currency zone and the provisions of the Convention tended to distort normal economic patterns of development.

More critically, many interpreted the Yaoundé Convention as a poorly disguised extension of French foreign and colonial policy. As one analysis pointed out, the undeniable dependency of francophone Africa on France for aid and trade 'existed independently of the EEC and was in no way consequential to it' with the majority of original member states 'extremely loath to become involved with former African colonies'(Cosgrove-Twitchett, 1978, p. 122). There was no political dimension to the Convention whatsoever: the notion of good governance conditionality had yet to be conceived. The relationship was essentially one that was a consequence of historical ties that were increasingly difficult to organize as the Community began to expand from its clear francophone base to incorporate the English-speaking developing world.

In summary, many of the issues pertinent to Europe–Third World relations under subsequent Lomé Conventions, as well as to the future, can be traced to the earlier Yaoundé agreements. As discussed here, they include ineffectual trading concessions; the disbursement of EDF funds; the colonial basis for preferences and country selectivity; an emphasis on infrastructure aid; the question of reciprocity; and last, but far from least, the dominance of the development agenda by France.

The Lomé Conventions: I and II (1976–85)

More than any other factor, the enlargement of the European Community from the original Six to the Nine in 1973 foreshadowed a restructuring of external relations. Whilst Denmark and Ireland did not have any colonial legacies, one of the key areas of concern raised by British membership was protecting and maintaining relations with Commonwealth developing countries. Geographically this demanded extending the African focus of Yaoundé to include both Caribbean and Pacific states – although the Indian sub-continent was to remain excluded. There was a profound distinction between the Commonwealth ethos based upon an open trading relationship and respect for sovereignty, and the paternalism of France and latterly the Community that 'suggested the Community had little respect for the newly won sovereignty of the Associates' (Ravenhill, 1985, p. 72). Conceptually, it became necessary to mesh the narrowly defined EAMA interests with the more diverse needs of Commonwealth countries. A simple extension of the Yaoundé pro-

visions was contemplated and explored, but ultimately a specifically tailored and integrated Convention was produced that
sought to protect French sensitivities yet meet British demands.
The views of the developing countries, whilst sought, appeared
of secondary importance to the process.

A secondary motivation behind this first definition of the
Community's development policy was the widely felt disappointment about the impact of Yaoundé. As already noted, the
trading preferences were progressively eroded and the introduction of the Generalized System of Preferences (GSP) scheme
in 1971 was indicative of a broadening of Europe's external relations. The development objectives of the Convention remained
unfulfilled and the exclusivity of membership (largely francophone) encouraged charges of neo-colonialism. Some member
states viewed the prospect of future British membership as an
opportunity to open a wider development debate, an idea that
was vigorously supported by the Commission who wished to
see its bureaucratic authority strengthened in this area.

As a transitional arrangement, Protocol 22 (annexed to
Britain's Treaty of Accession) provided 20 Commonwealth
states with the opportunity to negotiate a long-term agreement with the Community. Three options presented themselves:
simply to enlarge Yaoundé; to sign individual bilateral agreements; or, to collectively agree on a preferential trade agreement.
In its 1972 policy Memorandum to the Council of Ministers,
the Commission effectively defined the parameters for the policy
debate, largely allayed the fears of both the EAMA and Commonwealth states, and addressed both French and British concerns. A formidable achievement by any standards! In it the
notion of membership eligibility was widened beyond former
colonial dependencies, development assistance was extended
and reformed; non-reciprocity became a core principle; and,
paternalism was replaced by the concept of partnership (Commission, 1973). However, the Commission's clarity did not
necessarily reflect unanimity at the member state level and the
negotiations were contentious and hard-fought between the
Nine. Conversely, despite their regional diversity and linguistic
division, the developing countries emphasized their shared
mutual interests. A consensus was forged and throughout the
negotiations this new African, Pacific and Caribbean (ACP)
grouping acted through a single spokesperson.

Formal negotiations between the Community and the respective developing countries began in mid-July 1973, some 18 months prior to the expiry of Yaoundé II. It was not until July 1974, however, that the Nine could agree on the outline for the new agreement. Eventually, French opposition to a non-reciprocal arrangement was dropped, an agricultural compromise was fashioned, and on German insistence, an aid ceiling was established. Only the question of sugar remained problematic – how to balance Britain's Commonwealth sugar preferences within a CAP that already produced a significant surplus in sugar beet. Sugar came to symbolize the level of support the UK was prepared to commit to its Commonwealth partners and the ACP made signing of any overall agreement conditional on this issue alone. A compromise on this final issue was only reached at the eleventh hour, on 1 February 1975. Commonwealth producers were granted an annual access of 1.4 million tons at a guaranteed price, and domestic production was allowed to expand within the already over-supplied European market.

The resulting Lomé Convention replaced one acronym and political and economic entity (EAMA) on the world stage with a new configuration: the African, Caribbean and Pacific states – the ACP. Lomé I was signed on 28 February 1975 and came into force on 1 April 1976 linking the then 9 European Community states with 46 developing countries. This new ACP grouping comprised the original 18 Yaoundé states and Mauritius; 6 other African states; and 21 less-developed Commonwealth countries. Of these Commonwealth states 12 were African, 6 from the Caribbean and 3 the Pacific. However, during the five-year duration of Lomé I the number of signatories quickly rose to 53 – signalling a consistent pattern of growth in Lomé membership that lasted until the end of the twentieth century.

The most distinctive feature of the Lomé Convention was a commitment to an equal partnership between Europe and the ACP. The preamble committed the signatory states 'to establish, on the basis of complete equality between partners, close and continuing cooperation in a spirit of international solidarity' and to 'seek a more just and more balanced economic order'. In part, this change in approach was a response to the perception that the Yaoundé arrangements had perpetuated dependency rather than promoted development. In part, too, it was a reflection of the Commonwealth philosophy that stood in stark contrast to the francophone style of colonial relationship. At one level the idea of partnership was formally reflected in the trade relationship, its legal base and in the structure of the institutional framework. At another level, a simple commitment to the principle of partnership can be criticized as ineffectual because such a dialogue could never be between equal partners. As is examined in the chapters that follow, a European agenda has clearly prevailed. This mismatch between ambition and actual practice notwithstanding, the goals of the Convention were innovative and established a first–third world relationship that was progressive and unparalleled for its time.

The institutional framework combined the Yaoundé structures with the commitment to partnership. Three principal institutions were established: the ACP–EC Council of Ministers; the Committee of Ambassadors; and, the Joint Consultative Assembly. Like its predecessor, the Council was composed of the ACP and European member states and a Commission representative. Normally, it was convened annually and was mandated to oversee the general scope of the Convention's work and to implement and review policies to attain its objectives. The Committee of Ambassadors assisted the Council in these tasks and met with greater frequency. The joint consultative assembly was the largest institution and was composed of an equal number of ACP parliamentarians and representatives from the European Parliament. As the name implied, its powers were consultative not binding. However, the assembly has proved to be an energetic body and active in proposing recommendations and resolutions to the Council for consideration. In particular, its criticisms of cumbersome procedures and delays in disbursement of funds have been vigorous and helped to promote reforms. The only major departure from the previous institutional structure was the absence of a judicial arbitration procedure. The Court of Arbitration was never convened under Yaoundé; the Lomé philosophy sought political rather than legal solutions to disputes. The tasks of all these institutions evolved during the lifetime of the Convention and innovations (such as the Article 108 Committee in 1980) were introduced. However, the basic structures set out in Lomé I persisted until the end of Lomé IV a quarter-century later.

The major policy objectives of the Convention were as commendable as they were ambitious: the promotion of EC–ACP trade; agricultural and industrial development; special aid for the least developed states; and, support for regional cooperation. At the policy level, Lomé I was much more than just an extension of the preceding Convention. The shortcomings of Yaoundé had been rightly criticized and Lomé sought to address these in two specific ways: first, by dropping reciprocity; and second by the introduction of an export stabilization scheme. (These, and other unique aspects of European policy are examined in greater detail in Chapters 6 and 7.) The decision to relinquish reverse preferences and embrace non-reciprocity was of greater psychological than economic importance. The ACP states were now required simply to treat EC exports at least as favourably as exports from other developed nations. The effect on the EC's pattern of external trade was, however, marginal.

STABEX – the system for the stabilization of export earnings from agricultural commodities – was the major innovation of Lomé I. Its objective was to provide funds to ACP countries to cover production shortfalls or price fluctuations for specific agriculture products exported to Europe. Whilst the actual trigger mechanisms and operation of STABEX were complex, the system was in principle extremely simple. The system was important because many ACP states were dependent on a limited number of products making them especially susceptible to variations in world market prices. STABEX can be equated with an insurance policy for the ACP: the EC guaranteed a minimum earnings threshold for these specified exports and compensated for any loss of revenue caused by lower prices or loss of production. Twenty-nine products were covered under the first Convention, rising to 44 in Lomé II.

Obviously, the benefits were not equally distributed among the ACP. Under Lomé I more than one third of available support went to groundnut production (139.4 million ecus) and just three states (Senegal, Sudan and Mauritania) accounted for 38.1 per cent of the available funds. This uneven spread continued under Lomé II, albeit with some product and country variation. Three products (coffee, cocoa and groundnuts) took four-fifths of the budget with three states (Senegal, Ghana and Ivory Coast) accounting for 38.5 per cent between them. Payments for groundnuts saw Senegal alone benefit by 155.7 million ecus

TABLE 1.2   *STABEX transfers by product category, Lomé I and II*

Product	Lomé I Ecu m.	% total transfers	Lomé II Ecu m.	% total transfers
Coffee	14.5	3.8	246.6	37.4
Cocoa	1.5	0.4	148.8	22.6
Cotton	43.4	11.5	36.5	5.5
Copra/coconut	10.6	2.8	31.6	4.8
Groundnuts	139.4	36.9	133.3	20.2
Iron ore	61.8	16.4	*	*
Oilcake	17.6	4.7	14.0	2.1
Raw sisal	20.6	5.5	9.1	1.4
Wood	40.0	10.6	0.4	0.1
All other	28.1	7.4	39.2	5.9
Totals	**377.5**	**100.0**	**659.5**	**100.0**

between 1976 and 1985 (see Tables 1.2 and 1.3) and the top six beneficiaries under each Convention took around 60 per cent of funds. The underlying philosophy of STABEX proved to be its Achilles heel during these initial years. Global recession and a fall in commodity prices saw requests for STABEX compensation exceed the allocated budget. By 1980, the start of the second Convention, the budget could only match roughly half of all funding requests and a year later there was a funding deficit of 341 million ecus. Whilst the budget was in balance by the end of Lomé II, the scheme was clearly a victim of its own success and inevitably an inadequate response to fluctuations in the global economy. Despite these initial problems Lomé's popularity increased; 7 newly independent former British dependencies joined the Convention making a total of 60 signatories, with a further 3 joining during the five years of the agreement. Only one of these (Zimbabwe) was from Africa, the remainder being Pacific or Caribbean island states, signalling a changing geopolitical balance within the ACP grouping. Lomé II varied little from the Lomé I framework institutionally and in basic approach: two developments were, however, introduced – a greater emphasis on the least developed countries and the introduction of SYSMIN. At the beginning of Lomé I, 24 of the 46 states were classified as Least Developed Countries (LDCs).

TABLE 1.3   *STABEX transfers by country, Lomé I and II*

Country	Lomé I	
	Ecu m.	% total transfers
Senegal	65.1	17.2
Sudan	41.8	11.1
Mauritania	37.0	9.8
Niger	22.7	6.0
Tanzania	20.7	5.5
Uganda	20.6	5.5
Benin	20.4	5.4
Others	149.2	39.5
Totals	377.5	100.0

Country	Lomé II	
	Ecu m.	% total transfers
Senegal	90.6	13.7
Ghana	85.4	12.9
Ivory Coast	78.4	11.9
Papua New Guinea	50.7	7.7
Kenya	44.9	6.8
Sudan	40.7	6.2
Others	268.8	40.8
Totals	659.5	100.0

Note: * Less than 1% of total transfers.
Source: Commission (1986), pp. 24–5.

Over the next decade this rose to 35 and Lomé II placed a renewed emphasis on LDCs and landlocked states. Consequently, programme aid and EIB loans disproportionately went to these states. SYSMIN was arguably a more immediately significant extension. This 'special financing facility' for mineral exports was based on similar principles to those of STABEX. This provided those ACP states heavily dependent on mining exports to the EC a degree of protection from loss of production or price collapses. Lomé II provided 282 million ecus for this and covered copper and cobalt, phosphates, manganese, bauxite and aluminium, tin and iron ore.

Any assessment of the impact of the first decade of the Lomé Convention has to begin by acknowledging its foresight in its commitment to partnership and desire to help integrate the economies of the developing countries into the global market. Second, Lomé eschewed any form of neo-colonial ties: the ACP states were not required to offer the EC special preferences, nor were they prohibited from trading with other developed countries. Third, no political conditionality was imposed: the domestic politics of signatory states were largely ignored. And, as indicated in the above analysis, a range of development assistance programmes as well as trade preferences was introduced. However, any evaluation also has to acknowledge the gap between the Convention's intentions and its actual effect on relations. Perhaps most critically, the impact on the balance of trade has been marginal. Whilst the ACP enjoyed a trade surplus with the EC, this was also the position prior to Lomé. In terms of product, the Convention had the perverse effect of promoting ACP dependency on raw materials as an export base in exchange for importing primarily industrial goods from Europe. During the negotiations for Lomé II the European Parliament issued a particularly critical Report:

> The structure of ACP–EEC trade reveals an acute imbalance, both among products exported and among the ACP exporting countries . . . this structure has changed very little and largely retains the features of the colonial period. . . . The rule of free trade is meaningless for countries which, at the present stage, because of their production structures, have practically nothing to export to the Community. (Focke Report, 1980, p. 14)

The often-quoted figure of 99.5 per cent customs-free access for ACP exports was misleading. Not only were specific agricultural exports excluded, the figure referred to only existing products, not to potential exports. Finished products in the industrial, agricultural and commercial sectors were excluded and something like 70 per cent of ACP exports could enter Europe duty-free under GSP arrangements anyhow. Even the well-intentioned STABEX and SYSMIN schemes have been criticized for rewarding failure rather than success. They could act

as a disincentive as neither encouraged better production or efficiency. Those countries that actually increased their production
capacity and exports gained nothing under the schemes. Lastly,
even the more inclusive scope of Lomé covered only a small
percentage of the EC's trade with the Third World and, consequently, was a modest contribution to a meaningful North–
South dialogue.

On balance, Lomé was clearly superior to its predecessor, the
Yaoundé Convention and it symbolized a watershed in post-
colonial relations with the developing world. Lomé not only
removed reciprocity, it expanded the scope of relations beyond
the historical aspects of trade. Equality and stability replaced
dependency as the defining characteristics. Obviously, not every
ACP or European demand could be met – indeed, both sides
were guilty of creating future problems by seeing only their
interpretation of the agreement. The first Lomé decade has been
characterized as one of falling hopes, even if the culprit was the
successive oil crises and global recession rather than the Convention. But Lomé was historically important for creating a new
actor in international affairs – the ACP – and it was this framework that dominated Europe's perspective on Third World relations for the remainder of the twentieth century. Whether
the motivations were selfish or altruistic, however, probably
remains largely a matter of interpretation.

Lomé III and IV

The external global context has always been influential in determining the parameters for Europe–Third World relations. The
oil shocks and resultant recession of the 1970s fundamentally
changed the context within which Europe conducted its development policy. It became increasingly apparent that the economic decline in Africa (and to a lesser extent the Pacific and
Caribbean states) was not a temporary phenomenon; if development were to be achieved, Lomé III would have to do more
than continue the existing framework. For example, between
1980 and 1987 African per capita GDP declined by an annual
average of 2.6 per cent, investment fell whilst simultaneously
the debt burden rose inexorably. In contrast, the 1980s
witnessed a period of phenomenal economic growth in the

developing economies of South East Asia. Increasingly, international financial institutions such as the World Bank and the International Monetary Fund (IMF) became instrumental to the management of development and brought with them the new disciplines and doctrines of structural adjustment programmes (SAPs). By 1989, 30 such programmes were in place in Africa alone (*The Courier*, 1990, p. 27). Consequently, the focus of Europe's policy began to change to address these broader adjustment issues and to look for an international consensus on macroeconomic assistance.

It was in this context that Lomé III was negotiated. Greece had joined the Community in 1981 and Spain and Portugal were set to do so in 1986. It was the then Twelve and 66 ACP states that were party to Lomé III. Whilst still imperfect in its geographical spread, these 66 states represented roughly half of the total global number of developing states and contained 15 per cent of the developing world's population. Africa continued to dominate (45 states); 29 ACP states were also Commonwealth members with a further 21 members of the Franco-African summit. Despite ten years of interaction the ACP only clearly expressed its identity in relation to Europe: individual ACP states took on a variety of group identities depending on the chosen fora. Europe's relations with the Third World remained at best idiosyncratic and incomplete. But Lomé continued to symbolize Europe's imperfect definition of development cooperation.

The third Convention sought to 'promote and expedite the economic, cultural and social development of the ACP states and consolidate and diversify relations in a spirit of solidarity and mutual trust' (Article 1). In concrete terms, however, there were comparatively few innovations to the Lomé framework and as such it failed to address adequately the development crisis that engulfed the Third World during the 1980s. The euphoria and hyperbole that greeted the signing of the first Convention in 1975 was markedly absent. Lomé no longer appeared to be the best model for development given the deterioration of most developing country economies. Indeed, there is a strong case that rather than heralding a new interdependence, after fifteen years Lomé had merely re-established North–South dependency (Grilli, 1993, p. 36). The new emphasis on thematic issues (climate, environment, health) as well as commitments to

social and cultural cooperation lacked substance. The more significant change was the application of conditionality, something
that the ACP had previously resisted. Agreements on EC private
investment safeguards and conditional funding for adjustment
programmes heralded a watershed in the relationship and provided a glimpse of a new agenda that was to dominate the
1990s. Any economic bargaining power the ACP had previously
enjoyed began to dissipate and the leverage provided by moral
arguments appeared increasingly ineffective.

Unlike previous Conventions, Lomé IV was a ten-year agreement (with a mid-term financial review) expiring in the year
2000. Once again, changes in the international environment
were to dictate the content and direction of policy. Compounding the plight of the Lomé countries, the collapse of communism heralded a new and more immediate development priority
for the EC – that of Eastern and Central Europe. Throughout
the 1990s Europe's funding priorities clearly shifted from the
traditional Lomé states to those closer to home (see Introduction). In addition, the '1992' Single European Market (SEM)
project, the GATT Uruguay Round and the establishment of the
WTO all posed potentially new trade challenges to an already
embattled Third World. If not forgotten, the Lomé states
appeared to face increasing marginalization.

After fourteen months of negotiations the new Convention
between the Twelve and 68 ACP states was signed on 15 Decem-
ber 1989, once more in the Togolese capital of Lomé. Initially
Lomé IV covered more than 450 million people, rising to 570
million in some 70 states by the time of the mid-term review in
1995. However, it was only in the last months of 1989 that the
agreement was cobbled together under the then French presidency. In general, Europe dictated the agenda and ACP demands
– such as debt relief – went unheeded. The EDF budget was
increased to 12 billion ecus (a nominal increase of around 40
per cent from the Lomé III figure of 8.8 billion). In real terms,
however, the increase was marginal and significantly below that
called for by the ACP; the amount was raised to 14.6 billion
ecus at the 1995 mid-term review (see Table 1.4). Such outcomes
reflected both the hardening attitude of member states as well
as the poor bureaucratic resources of the ACP Secretariat. The
much-prized principle of partnership at the core of the Lomé
model appeared distinctly compromised.

TABLE 1.4 Financing of development cooperation, 1958–2000

Convention	Fund	Date	No. states	EIB** (Ecu m.)	EDF* (Ecu m.)	Total (Ecu m.)
Treaty of Rome	EDF 1	1.1.1958	31	–	581	581
Yaoundé I	EDF 2	1.7.1964	18	64	666	830
Yaoundé II	EDF 3	1.1.1971	19	90	843	933
Lomé I	EDF 4	1.4.1976	46	390	3 124	3 514
Lomé II	EDF 5	1.1.1981	57	685	4 754	5 439
Lomé III	EDF 6	1.5.1986	66	1100	7 754	8 854
Lomé IV	EDF 7	1.3.1990	69	1200	10 800	12 000
Lomé IV (review)	EDF 8	4.11.1995	70	1658	12 967	14 625

Notes: * Includes grants, special loans, STABEX, SYSMIN.
     ** Own resources, loans.

Source: *The Courier* (1990) no. 120, p. 26, and (1996) no. 155, p. 12.

A key element in Lomé IV was the renewed emphasis on conditionality – economic and political. For the first time, aid was explicitly earmarked for Structural Adjustment Support with financial resources coming from the existing EDF budget. Approximately 10 per cent of funds were designated for this purpose – 1150 million ecus in EDF7 rising to 1400 million in EDF8. Flexibility rather than a standard approach was emphasized in the new Convention. Article 244 guarantees that

> (a) the ACP States shall bear primary responsibility for the analysis of the problems to be solved and the preparation of reform programmes;
> (b) support programmes shall be adapted to the different situation in each ACP State and be sensitive to the social conditions, culture and environment of these States; . . .
> (e) the right of the ACP States to determine the direction of their development strategies and priorities shall be recognized and respected;
> . . .
> (i) support shall be given in the context of a joint assessment between the Community and the ACP State concerned on the reform measures being undertaken or contemplated either at a macro-economic or sectoral level.

Whilst ACP states were included in the policy debate on economic reform, clearly European approval was a funding prerequisite. Article 243 defined as appropriate the type of initiatives that promote GDP and employment, increase productivity and foster economic diversification whilst simultaneously improving 'the social and economic well-being' of the population and ensuring 'that adjustment is economically viable and socially and politically bearable'. These structural reform conditions were only modestly amended in 1995 by extending the process to the regional level. Broadly speaking, the EU mirrored the World Bank view on SAPs – despite any strong empirical evidence that such an approach was generally beneficial for development (Lister, 1997b, p. 116). The Convention's assertion that the ACP 'shall determine the development principles, strategies and models for their economies and societies in all sovereignty' (Article 3) sat uncomfortably with this recognition of *Realpolitik*. It was only during the 1997–8 Green Paper debate on Europe's post-Lomé relations with the Developing World that this established orthodoxy began to be challenged.

Only minor modifications were made to the trade preferences of Lomé IV – despite the erosion of the so-called pyramid of privilege for ACP states – although some relaxation in the 'rules of origin' for manufactured products were gained. The only significant EU concession was to extend the funding basis of STABEX and SYSMIN, although this fell far short of ACP expectations. Debt, rather than trade preferences, had become the more important problem by the end of the 1980s. Whilst Articles 239–42 introduced the issue of debt repayment on to the Community agenda, this 'major development issue' remained largely the primary domain of member states and international organizations. At this stage, Europe did not want to establish a new precedent in this area. Once again, the importance of consistency and complementarity between EU and member state policy was highlighted. The recognition of this issue was welcome, yet Europe's collective response remained cautious and respected the role of the member states. Given the EU's limited financial involvement (just 1.2 per cent of the ACP debt-servicing costs were with the EU) it was argued that it was inappropriate and ineffective for the EU to become the dominant forum for addressing debt relief. Whether this view was justified or not, ignoring the Community dimension on debt stood in stark contrast to the wider Lomé philosophy of partnership.

Conversely, the new Convention included a number of policy innovations: the environment; human rights; women; and cultural cooperation. The emphasis on human rights was arguably the most ambitious of these. The general principles and objectives of the Convention directly linked development with 'respect for and promotion of all human rights' and economic well-being. Such rights are:

> legitimate aspirations of individuals and peoples. The rights in question are all human rights, the various categories thereof being indivisible and inter-related, each having its own legitimacy: non-discriminatory treatment; fundamental human rights; civil and political rights; economic, social and cultural rights. (Article 5)

In particular, EU–ACP cooperation was required to accommodate 'the cultural dimension and social implications' of development and permit 'men and women to participate and benefit on equal terms' (Article 13). Articles 139–48 of the Convention expand on these cultural and social concepts and the topic of women and development was covered by Article 153. Here, the EU supported ACP efforts aimed at 'enhancing the status of women, improving their living conditions, expanding their economic and social role and promoting their full participation in the production and development process on equal terms with men'. Other social policies included health, education and training, population issues and the environment. Cumulatively these further extended the Convention's scope beyond its purely trade-related origins and confirmed that political and social conditionality was to constitute a new direction in European development policy. The differences, rather than the similarities, between the original Convention and Lomé IV were becoming increasingly pronounced. Whilst the status quo was retained in the overall trade relationship, new motivations heralded a psychological shift in EU–Third World relations.

By the time of the scheduled 1995 mid-term review, the global development context had significantly shifted from the parameters that had set the 1989 agreement – and the shift further disadvantaged the developing countries. A number of states faced increasing economic crises and donor fatigue was becoming endemic. The traditional ideological and geo-strategic balance had collapsed as former communist societies increasingly embraced democratization. Internally, the Maastricht Treaty of 1992 established new development cooperation objectives and obligations and through the 1995 enlargement different development perspectives were introduced by the new member states of Austria, Finland and Sweden (Vernier, 1996, p. 8). Only the mid-term renewal of the financial protocol of Lomé IV was mandatory; in all other respects it was anticipated that the Convention would run unaltered for a decade. However, largely on EU insistence, the review process was extended beyond funding issues in response to the changing global context, the effect of liberalization on the erosion of preferences, and problems associated with the actual implementation of the Lomé system.

By employing the provisions under Article 366, both the ACP and the member states were entitled to modify aspects of the agreement. Although all decisions were consensual, the modifications adopted principally reflected the EU's new agenda rather than ACP concerns. The review lasted 13 months with the revised agreement being signed by 70 ACP states in November 1995. Three broad areas were reviewed: institutional and political issues; trade and sectoral issues; and development financing. Consensus existed on amending a wide range of issues, notably reference to democratic principles, the fundamental importance of trade in the development process and the introduction of two-tranche programming. Conversely, differences existed over EDF funding, access to the SEM and the relaxation of the rules of origin for ACP products.

The main focus of the trade debates departed from the traditional Lomé preoccupation with preferential access to a more inclusive approach for creating a better trading environment. The arguments were as much political as they were economic and reflected the agenda of the then GATT negotiations. Two new Articles introduced the idea of trade development, and were aimed at 'developing, diversifying and increasing ACP States' trade and improving their competitiveness' domestically and internationally (Article 15a). Mirroring the commitment of the Maastricht Treaty, Article 6a called for the gradual integration of the ACP economies into the world economy and described the function of trade as 'energizing the development process'. Preferential access was not totally absent from the mid-term review, however, and debate proved contentious. A compromise position saw a modest expansion in product access and a relaxation in quantitative restrictions. The most acrimonious area, however, concerned rules of origin. Finally only modest changes were accepted that encouraged regional cooperation between member and non-member states. In contrast, the reform of STABEX was not controversial and funds for the system were raised by some 20 per cent to 1.8 billion ecus.

The final issue to be renegotiated was the new financial protocol – EDF8. This increased overall funding for Lomé by 22 per cent to 14.6 billion ecus, although in real terms the value remained static: one member state, the UK, even reduced its contribution! The difficulties in obtaining a financial agreement were further underlined by the ratification process. It was June 1998 before the EDF8 began distributing these new funds. Given that enlargement meant that there were now 15 rather than 12 donors, the overall funding level disappointed the ACP recipients. Again, this reflected the EU's new development priorities in Central and Eastern Europe and reflected a general worldwide downward trend affecting bilateral and multilateral aid. Programme aid remained at the heart of the EU's approach. Minor changes were made to the structural adjustment provisions and the application of EIB resources. The EU successfully resisted a request for the unilateral cancellation of ACP debts but did offer some financial relief (worth 135 million ecus in loans) and drafted a new declaration annexed to the Convention in which:

> The Community reaffirms its willingness to contribute constructively and actively to the alleviation of the debt burden of the ACP States.
>
> In this context, it agrees to transform into grants all the special loans of the previous Conventions, which have not yet been committed.
>
> The Community also confirms its determination to pursue the discussion of these questions in the appropriate fora, taking into account the specific difficulties of the ACP States. (Annex LXXXIV)

One innovation, however, introduced broad conditionality to the objectives of EU aid policy. The Convention was amended to read: 'In support of the development strategies of the ACP States, due account shall be taken of the objectives and priorities of the Community's cooperation policy, and the ACP States' development policies and priorities' (Article 4). The EU objectives and priorities were derived from the Maastricht Treaty (Article 133U) and mirrored commitments given elsewhere, namely: sustainable economic and social development; the reintegration of ACP economies into the world economy; alleviation of poverty; support for democratic and legitimate government; and the protection of human rights and liberties. Although a policy 'dialogue' was established, clearly ACP states were expected to embrace these principles within their own respective development approaches if Lomé assistance was to be granted. The most direct expression of this new expectation was in the move to a two-tranche system for indicative programmes. By withholding 30 per cent of funds until effective implementation of a programme is established, the EU can sanction those states that fail to meet the agreed 'dialogue' objectives.

Institution-building: from Lomé to Cotonou

Lomé was the most institutionalized of all the EU's group-to-group dialogues and its longevity was in part a consequence of the reliability and contractual permanence of this institutionalization. As seen above, the first Convention established three principal bodies – the Council of Ministers, the Committee of Ambassadors and the joint consultative assembly – and the powers and functions of each institution are specified in Articles 338–55 of Lomé IV. The principle of partnership defined, at least formally, their composition and function. As Article 338 states: 'The Council of Ministers shall act by agreement between the Community on the one hand and the ACP States on the other.'

The Council was composed of the ACP, European member states and a Commission representative. Normally, it was convened annually and is mandated to oversee the general scope of the Convention's work and to implement and review policies to attain its objectives. Where necessary, committees or *ad hoc* working parties were created to assist the Council (Article 342). The presidency of the Council alternated between an EU member state and an ACP state. Council decisions were binding. Under Article 345, the Council could, however, delegate its authority to the Committee of Ambassadors. More generally, the Committee of Ambassadors assisted the Council in executing its tasks and met with greater frequency and at least once every six months (Article 346.3).

The joint consultative assembly met biannually. Its membership was composed of an equal number of ACP parliamentarians (or designated representatives) and Members of the European Parliament. This democratic requirement was introduced in 1995: prior to this the ACP delegates were often ambassadors or civil servants, not elected representatives. In those cases where no ACP parliament existed, representatives were subject to the approval of the joint assembly (Article 32.1). As the name implied, the assembly's powers were consultative not binding and its limited powers defined in Article 350. It could consider the Council's annual report; adopt resolutions relating to the Convention; and 'submit to the Council of Ministers any conclusions and make any recommendations it considers appropriate'. As noted above, however, the assembly was often an energetic body. Conspicuous by its absence in the institutional structure was any judicial arbitration mechanism; the Lomé philosophy sought political rather than legal solutions to disputes.

Whilst the basic structures established in Lomé I had persisted for 25 years, the tasks of all these institutions evolved during the lifetime of the Convention. For example, at the mid-term review of Lomé IV, the political dialogue within the ACP–EC Council of Ministers framework was 'enlarged' in an attempt to make it more 'effective' and, where necessary, extended the dialogue outside the Lomé framework (Article 30.3). Good governance, democracy and human rights typically came to dominate the EU–ACP political dialogue: this was extended to cover 'issues and problems of foreign policy and security' (Preamble). Interestingly, provision was also made for regional dialogues, perhaps foreshadowing the possible regionalization of ACP relations after the year 2000.

The major policy reform saw the human rights provisions of Article 5 extended in a carrot and stick approach. Good governance was given additional emphasis and 'respect for human rights, democratic principles and the rule of law' defined as 'an *essential* element' of the Convention. To facilitate this, some 80 million ecus were reserved under the new financial protocol for institutional and administrative reforms 'aimed at democratisation, a strengthening of the rule of law and good governance'. As a measure of the EU's commitment to promoting democratic and human rights, any ACP state that failed to meet these Article 5 criteria faced, in the last resort, suspension from the Convention. Whilst there was consensus on the importance of institutionalizing democratic practices, the line between paternalism and partnership became harder to define.

In the context of change, the Lomé institutions could play a powerful role. As the history of the EU's own institutional development shows, once established, institutions become resilient and resistant to comprehensive change. Incrementalism rather than radical reform set the parameters. Consequently, whilst the Commission's Green Paper and Guidelines for negotiating beyond Lomé IV suggested fundamental institutional and policy reforms, the inertia applied by the existing institutional status quo was an important factor constraining change (see Chapter 6).

Conclusion

To summarize, this historical overview of EU–ACP relations forms the starting point for this analysis of Europe's relations with the Third World. The Lomé Convention was traditionally the major development framework: the rationale was largely historical rather than rational. What became increasingly clear during the last five years of Lomé IV was that the ACP countries could no longer rely upon either privileged access or continued financial aid from this special relationship. However, escaping the tyranny of acronyms proved difficult for the European Union and the ACP still retains a unique place within Europe's wider development policy.

Despite this resilience Lomé IV provoked concern about the longer-term viability of its preferential philosophy. The Uruguay Round of GATT drew attention to Lomé's inconsistencies with the broad principles of trade liberalization. Whilst a waiver was eventually granted under the GATT and the subsequent WTO regime, clearly existing practice was becoming increasingly indefensible. The evolution of EU development policy mirrored the internal development of European integration process itself. Initially geographically restricted and limited in ambition, both integration and development policy expanded in scope, content and ambition over the past four decades. By the year 2000 the incremental policy-making style of the Lomé Conventions was forced to address a globally more contemporary approach to relations with the developing world. In contrast to this long history of institutionalism and policy development, as the next chapter outlines, Europe's links with the non-Lomé developing states have been comparatively rudimentary and *ad hoc* in nature.

Chapter 2

Latin America and Asia

The most vociferous criticism of the Lomé regime was its unbalanced and exclusive nature. Some would even argue that the EU has never had a genuine Third World policy and that the motivations driving Europe's development policy have always been Afro-centric. All 48 sub-Saharan African states were party to Lomé IV, whereas the island states of the Pacific and the Caribbean were not uniformly covered. Overall, some 90 per cent of the ACP population are African. As one commentator has argued:

> Concentration on Africa means the relative neglect of other regions of 'more' interest to the EC, however 'interest' may be defined: if in terms of poverty, the exclusion of India and Bangladesh is hard to justify; if in terms of commercial importance, the absence of South America and South-East Asia is odd; and if in terms of international politics and military strategy then, again, Africa plus some islands in the Caribbean and the Pacific is not an obvious focus. (Stevens, 1983, p. 144)

As we have seen the Convention was originally designed to place the ACP at the top of the 'pyramid of privilege' by providing a more favourable trading regime than that offered to any other developing country. Whilst the ACP's position has declined, those directly disadvantaged have not been the ACP, but the developing countries of Asia and South America, all of which were excluded from the Convention.

Latin America

Despite the formalized relations with the Caribbean, Latin America has always been on the fringes and marginal to

Europe's mainstream development. This distant relationship is somewhat puzzling given the cultural, religious, historical and trading ties that exit. As was shown in Table 1.1 during the EC's first decade, Latin America was an equally important trading partner compared with Africa as a whole (and far more important than the Yaoundé states). Many of the products that Europe sourced from Africa were available from Latin America and supplies arguably more secure. Further, Latin America seemed to provide a wealthier potential market for European exports policy (Grilli, 1993, pp. 226–7). Why, then, the apparent neglect?

An explanation can be found in the historical context of the 1950s when the Community's policies and interests were defined – not in dispassionate economic analysis. Despite significant German and Italian migrant populations, the absence of a direct member state colonial heritage mitigated against creating a preferential-type framework. Consequently, largely on French insistence only, Africa received initial preferential treatment. EU external relations in these formative years reflected, if on a larger scale, individual bilateral interests. A separate collective European perspective had not been established and in foreign relations priority was given to francophone concerns. As Chapter 1 outlined, the metamorphosis to wider ACP interests was, again, principally the result of a new bilateral concern, this time British. Similarly, the accession of Spain and Portugal to the Community in 1985 provided a new bilateral pressure, finally, this time for a more inclusive and formalized approach to European–Latin American relations.

Given the modest concession originally given to the Yaoundé states the absence of a formalized cooperation agreement with Latin America should not be surprising. The first priority of fledgling European Community was to generate internal economic cohesion and growth; external relations were very much of secondary importance and only given prominence if advocated by a leading member state – such as France. Italian attempts to promote relations with Latin America did not carry the same weight. For all third countries, the combination of a common EC external tariff and specific preferences for African states posed a real trading challenge. It has only been with the expanding ambitions of the EU to play an international role that a comprehensive approach to external relations has become evident. The 'neglect' of relations with Latin America – as well as with other regional groupings – was very much a consequence of the internal dynamics of European integration.

Furthermore, Europe's commercial intervention within the region was always confronted with the geopolitical reality of the USA. Even where South American states have sought to reduce their trade dependency on the USA, this reorientation has met with countervailing pressure from Washington. Consequently, asymmetry has typically characterized EU–Latin American relations: economic links have been underdeveloped compared to the greater importance given to political aspects of the relationship. Consequently, during the 1980s Latin America was at the very bottom of the pyramid of privileges, outranked by the preferences offered to the ACP, the Mediterranean states, the Gulf and even ASEAN. In contrast, the 1980s process of democratization provided Europe with a platform on which to enhance a political relationship.

One reason why the EU was able to conduct a dialogue with the Yaoundé states was because they already had an institutional framework within which cooperation could be developed. In contrast, no such common institutional framework linked the various Latin American states together: a group-to-group dialogue did not exist. 'Latin America' as a term is not analytically that helpful, incorporating as it does, some 20 states (Argentina, Bolivia, Brazil, Chile, Colombia, Costa Rica, Cuba, Dominican Republic, El Salvador, Ecuador, Guatemala, Haiti, Honduras, Mexico, Nicaragua, Panama, Paraguay, Peru, Uruguay and Venezuela). As the following discussion shows, the pan-continental approach is too unwieldy with distinctions necessarily drawn between Central America, Southern America, the Rio Group and latterly MERCOSUR, which is discussed below. Whilst a number of initiatives have succeeded in establishing a framework for relations between the EU and regional sub-groupings over the past two decades, almost all have failed to transform the relationship significantly. The inability of the Latin American countries themselves to agree on the principle of an FTA until the late 1990s was also an important impediment to institutionalizing relations. The following brief history focuses on the key developments.

Early relations

Italy was instrumental in initiating the EC's dialogue with Latin America. In 1969 the Commission issued its first-ever report on the relationship; and the so-called 'Brussels dialogue' began soon after (establishing regular meetings between the Latin American Ambassadors and EU officials in Brussels). The introduction of GSP provisions in 1971 also opened up the prospect of a fairer trading regime with Europe. More generally, 'The GSPs also marked the beginning of a rebalancing of the positions of Latin America and Asia in the hierarchy of trade privileges granted by the Community to developing countries' (Grilli, 1993, p. 235). In contrast with this collective approach, bilateral relations with three Latin American countries – Argentina, Uruguay and Brazil – were also established in the early 1970s. The mid-1970s also witnessed the introduction of Community aid to the region (although historically this has mainly gone to Central American countries). However, these initiatives proved to be Pyrrhic victories in the face of the signing of the first Lomé Convention in 1975. Whether rightly or wrongly, Europe gave the clear impression that Latin America was not party to its development strategy and could not expect preferential concessions. The accession of the UK reinforced Africa's privileged status, and by extending this favouritism to Latin America's Caribbean neighbours, added insult to perceived injury.

A decade had elapsed before a dialogue was effectively re-established and sub-regional frameworks created. This signalled a renewed political interest in regional democratization as well as, obviously, the 1985 accession of Spain and Portugal. An initial cooperation agreement between the Community and the five Andean Pact countries (Bolivia, Colombia, Ecuador, Peru and Venezuela) was signed in 1983 and extend into a more focused Framework Agreement of Cooperation a decade later. Similarly, a Cooperation Agreement with partner countries of the General Central American Economic Integration Treaty was signed in 1985, and subsequently followed by a cooperation framework agreement with Costa Rica, El Salvador, Guatemala, Honduras, Nicaragua and Panama in 1993. Of greatest regional significance was the 1992 Inter-institutional Cooperation Agreement and the 1995 Inter-regional Framework Agreement signed with MERCOSUR (Mercado Común del Sur), both of which were designed to strengthen regional political cooperation and lead to the progressive liberalization of trade. Cumulatively, these developments symbolized Europe's 'rediscovery' of Latin America and underlined the region's efforts to liberalize, consolidate democratic institutions and embrace regional integration.

Regional integration was particularly marked during the 1990s. MERCOSUR brought together Argentina, Brazil, Paraguay and Uruguay (with Chile an associate member). The Andean Pact transformed in 1996 into the Andean Community. Free trade agreements link Colombia, Venezuela, Mexico and Chile and in 1998 the Andean Community and MERCOSUR completed a framework agreement with a view to creating a continental-wide free trade area. To supplement this, the EU concluded an FTA with Mexico in 2000. This consistent and progressive regional trend has helped to raise the profile and priority of Latin America from the EU's developing country perspective. However, MERCOSUR has increasingly become the EU's preferred framework for relations arguably at the expense of the other Latin American cooperation agreements signed with the EU. MERCOSUR now comprises roughly 50 per cent of total EU exports to Latin America. Indeed, the region's overall economic relationship at the end of the 1990s was comparatively fragile. Between 1990 and 1998, the percentage of Latin America's total exports going to the EU has fallen from 24 per cent to 14 per cent and the EU share of Latin America's total imports decreased from 21 per cent to 18 per cent. One consequence of this has been the reversal of a trade surplus (US$12.4 bn) favouring Latin America in 1990 to a large trade deficit (US$15.7 bn) with the EU by 1998 (Grisanti, 2000, p. 6).

MERCOSUR

The delayed nature of the relationship with Latin America has meant that the debate on non-reciprocity that characterized Lomé has been bypassed in favour of adopting free trade as the starting point for discussion. The idea of establishing an EU–MERCOSUR FTA was first floated in 1994. The resultant 1995 Framework Agreement paved the way, if cautiously and at a measured pace, for the debate on gradual and reciprocal trade liberalization with a view to creating an eventual free trade zone. This is envisaged as a relative long-term process with implementation commencing in perhaps 2005 at the earliest, with the prospect of 10–15 year transition periods for selected products (in line with WTO practice). This prolonged transition would also allow MERCOSUR to mature institutionally and for other frameworks for South American regional integration to emerge, as well as provide the EU with a further breathing-space before implementing the required CAP reforms (Dauster, 1998, p. 448). More generally, relations with MERCOSUR provide the EU with another venue through which it can begin to extend and define a coherent global external policy (Bessa-Rodrigues, 1999, p. 85). Relations with Latin America (as well as those with Asia) constitute the remaining missing elements in the EU's international actor profile.

The next significant impetus came at the joint Heads of Government meeting in June 1999. However, agreement on a timetable or the scope of tariff reductions proved impossible at this stage. This prevarication meant that before any such negotiations commenced, the post-Lomé discussions would be largely concluded and several years' experience of the prototype EU–South African FTA gained. The delay was largely due to French reticence stemming from the possible agricultural implications of any such free trade agreement for Europe's farmers. As the protracted discussions over a South African FTA had shown, the CAP constitutes a negotiating impediment that often makes the EU an inflexible negotiating partner.

Typically, agriculture already composes half of MERCO-SUR's exports to the EU. Intentionally, no timetable deadline has been set other than that implied by the parallel WTO discussions: a new WTO round of global liberalization is a precondition for the FTA proposal – and the so-called Millennium Round may take up to 2005 to conclude successfully. The Chirac–Jospin French Government seems likely to weigh any global concessions made in the WTO context against any further special concessions towards South American free trade. As conjectured in the Introduction and in Chapter 9, only an understanding of the multi-level complexity of EU policy-making provides the necessary theoretical context within which to understand this process.

The EU's prospective FTA partner states comprise the four MERCOSUR members plus, since 1996, two associate members – Bolivia and Chile. These six have a combined population of some 200 million. The economic arguments had been building throughout the previous decade during which time the EU had become MERCOSUR's largest trading partner and supplier of foreign direct investment supplanting the USA's economic dominance everywhere else in the Americas (except, of course, Cuba). For example, in 1997 MERCOSUR's largest export market was the EU (at 31 per cent, with the USA second on 19 per cent); similarly, the EU provided the highest proportion of imports (33 per cent compared with 27 per cent for the USA). Projections based on these figures suggest that such a proposed FTA would create a market of 575 million consumers (with existing trade worth US$140 bn). The EU's economic importance to Chile mirrors this MERCOSUR pattern. However, as noted above, the 1990s have also been a decade of deficits for South America. Whilst the EU has increased its exports to the region by 164 per cent, Latin America's exports to the EU have only grown by 29 per cent (*The Economist*, 26 June 1999, p. 69). However, whilst trade with Latin America has rapidly overtaken that of the ACP states, it still remains marginal for the EU, equivalent to roughly just 6 per cent of the EU's overall foreign trade. In contrast, Europe remains the region's largest foreign aid donor. (See Chapter 5 for additional economic commentary.)

For the EU, the proposed Latin American FTA does not signify any departure from the dominant economic philosophy of the 1990: free trade is consistent with its global approach and international rivalry with the United States for trading dominance. Indeed, the prospect of a USA-led Free Trade Area of the Americas (FTAA) composed of a 34-country group from north to south proposed for the year 2005 was an additional motivation for the Europeans. Such a grouping could result in trade with the EU declining significantly.

For the five Latin American states, arguably the FTA has a number of advantages. First, it provides a new economic option to the historical dependency on trade with the USA. Second, and consequentially, balance and diversity in the region's external relations may be enhanced. Third, such cooperation provides a further incentive towards the longer-term objective of South

American intra-regional integration. And fourth, the competing options of an EU–FTA or an American FTAA provides at least the possibility for MERCOSUR to extract a better preferential arrangement by playing Europe off against the USA as the negotiations develop. Such a strategic advantage is normally absent when third countries are confronted with EU proposals.

In summary, interregional cooperation between the EU and Latin America remains a long-term objective reflecting both a desire for liberalized market access and a degree of 'parity' with the USA regionally (Allen and Smith, 1999, p. 102). While there is now an established cycle of formal meetings (with the San José Group, the Rio Group and Andean countries for example), one cannot but be struck by the comparative limitations of the relationship rather than its substantive impact. In contrast with the architectural clarity of the EU–ACP relationship, the multiplicity of institutional frameworks also distracts from the coherence of EU–Latin American relations. This dilemma, however, is not unique to South America but is also reflected in Europe's relations with Asia – as discussed in the following section.

Asia: beginning a dialogue

In keeping with the EU's peculiar segmentation of the developing world, it is revealing that the Asia–Europe Meeting (ASEM), which established a regular forum for dialogue, was only established as late as 1996. In comparison with the ACP states and even Latin America, prior to this Asian development was not a policy priority and accorded little recognition. This peripheral relationship was all the more puzzling given that Asia in many ways has a shared colonial history with other parts of the developing world. France, Great Britain, Portugal and the Netherlands all had post-colonial links in the region, creating a triangle of interests that encompassed India, Indochina and Indonesia. In addition to the shared cultural aspects of language, much of Asia could also provide a similar range of agricultural and tropical goods that were originally supplied by the Yaoundé and latterly ACP states. Contrary to the evidence of hindsight, from the perspective of the 1950s, Asia seemed a less appealing partner than Africa or Latin America. It was geographically remote, generally poor, comparatively diverse, and regarded as a less reliable source of supplies for raw materials needed by Europe (if largely because of the Cold-War context of Soviet and Chinese regional influence). The original six members of the 1957 European Economic Community considered the influence of the UK in the region as a further disincentive. Commonwealth ties and a pervasive influence of the English language served to convey the impression that many parts of Asia remained essentially British domains. At the simplest level, it came down to a question of priorities. The fledgling Community had modest resources and limited external ambition. The importance of francophone Africa initially precluded all other options, including ties with Asia. By the time of UK membership, the Asian context had changed considerably and it was already becoming apparent that Asia had become an export competitor for Europe rather than a dependent partner in need of assistance. Thus despite the strong ties between the UK and the Indian sub-continent in particular, no Asian country was permitted to join the Lomé Convention. This missed opportunity essentially confined Asian–EU relations to the lowest of priorities for the next two decades.

During this period European policy became fragmented and lacked any clearly articulated overall Asian strategy other than a rationale based around a particular economic advantage. In a sense, this was an inevitable and appropriate response and reflected the increasingly disparate nature of Asia as an economic grouping. Europe's relations could be located along a continuum running from benevolent humanitarianism to competitive disinterest along which three distinct groups could be identified. To the one extreme, South Asia (including India, Pakistan and Bangladesh) remained economically underdeveloped and eligible for European humanitarian aid although not for preferential trade arrangements. Towards the middle of the continuum were those countries (largely the then ASEAN group of Indonesia, Malaysia, Thailand and the Philippines) that began to develop complementary economies to Europe and who shared a broad political (anti-communist) agenda. To the other extreme the Newly Industrialized Countries (NICs) of East Asia (such as Taiwan, Hong Kong, Singapore and South Korea) began to pose a real and increasingly competitive threat to key areas of European production. This economic growth made the NICs incompatible with the non-reciprocal philosophy that shaped Lomé in the early 1970s (Grilli, 1993, pp. 271–2). During the 1970s and 1980s this continuum became polarized as a larger number of countries progressed to the NIC camp. Consequently, these states were largely excluded by definition from Europe's development perspective and without any issues or strong advocates to promote their cause, Europe–Asian relations continued in the form of benign neglect.

Although pragmatism was a common link in European attitudes towards these three Asian groups, there were policy differences in Europe's relations with South Asia, ASEAN and the NICs. Grilli has characterized Europe's posture towards South Asia as 'mildly sympathetic . . . with minimal effective involvement in terms of economic assistance' (1993, p. 276). Under the 1971 GSP regime three South Asian states were categorized as least developed and gained the best market access – even if their export potential meant that they could take little advantage of the concessions. Other bilateral commercial cooperation agreements were subsequently signed during the 1970s with India, Sri Lanka, Pakistan and Bangladesh but only on the MFN basis giving no special preferences. Of course, direct aid was provided outside these agreements for rural development to promote both food supply and food security. The bulk of European aid to Asia was concentrated on South Asia within which India increasingly dominated. However, aid to South Asia only represented around 7 per cent of Europe's total aid budget, and in absolute and relative terms bilateral aid from member states was more important. As Grilli has noted, 'with more than two and a half times the population of sub-Saharan Africa and a substantially lower per capita income, South Asia received five times less financial aid from the Community during 1976–88' (p. 280). Given the concentration of the world's poor in South Asia it remains to be seen how the EU's new priority of poverty alleviation can be directed towards the region without diminishing efforts made elsewhere, especially in Africa. However, unless poverty eradication in Asia is prioritized, the EU will be unable to meet its self-imposed treaty obligations or persuade many that its policy framework is either appropriate or effective.

In 1980 relations with ASEAN became structured through a region-to-region agreement, the EC–ASEAN Economic and Commercial Cooperation Agreement. Launched in 1967, ASEAN has grown from its 5 original members now to include all 10 South East Asian countries (Cambodia was the last to join in 1999). The formalization of the Agreement disguised the fact that little substantive change was initially implemented and normal GSP levels remained the extent of preferential treatment (McMahon, 1998, p. 235). A number of ASEAN countries began to lose even this advantage for specific products and they were 'graduated' out of the system during the 1990s. Singapore, for example, no longer receives GSP from the EU. For most tropical agricultural products, however, ASEAN exports remained disadvantaged by pre-existing Lomé preferences. The signing of a series of bilateral trade and cooperation agreements between 1982 and 1987 with Indonesia, China, Thailand, Singapore, Malaysia, Korea and the Philippines, and with Vietnam in 1994, largely served to confirm the status quo (van Reisen, 1999, p. 138). However, the value of EU–ASEAN two-way trade has increased annually, from a low of 22.4 billion ecus in 1988 to almost three times this figure at 65.7 billion ecus by 1996. The EU has become ASEAN's second largest export market and third largest trading partner (after Japan and the USA). The late 1990s Asian financial crisis distorted the normal pattern of EU–ASEAN balance of trade and since 1998 Europe has experienced a significant trade deficit (see Chapter 5 for more detailed trade figures analysis). In terms of institutional structure, Joint Co-operation Committee meetings are held every 18 months and there is an annual political dialogue held at ministerial level. The major contemporary focus of the political dialogue is through the ASEAN Regional Forum that was established in 1994 to promote regional peace and stability. It remains Asia's only collective security arrangement and the EU participates as a full member. The accession of Myanmar to ASEAN has, however, affected the expansion of the political dialogue since 1997.

The attitude towards ASEAN countries will change, of course, as they continue to develop and mirror the NICs economies more closely. Unlike other parts of Asia, the NICs were best placed to gain advantage from the GSP regime. Beyond this formal trading arrangement, up until the 1990s protectionism and hostility rather than benign intent were more typical of European responses to the NICs. Across a wide range of manufactured and industrial products the NICs became a major threat to domestic European producers. Consequently, tariff and non-tariff barriers were applied and general agreements (such as the Multi-fibre Agreement – MFA) were promoted. The NICs have also attracted a particularly high number of anti-dumping actions by the Commission.

This history of European indifference ended with the 1994 Commission document *Towards a New Asia Strategy*. The motivation was both internal and external. Clearly, Asia represented a striking omission in the EU's profile as the world's leading trading power. There was also a 'credibility gap' in EU relations with Asia that the *Strategy* document sought to address. The economic opportunities that Asia presented, especially in the post-1989 context, were consistent with the EU's global economic agenda and newfound devotion to trade liberalization. A more coherent and regionally sophisticated European response to Asia was long overdue. The policy objectives were to increase the EU's economic presence in the region, develop and extend the political dialogue and to assist in reducing Asian poverty levels. In keeping with the tone of the mid-1990s, Europe's role in promoting democracy, good governance and the rule of law was given equal importance with economic gains (van Reisen, 1999, p. 139).

For the purposes of the Commission document Asia was recategorized into three regions (South Asia, East Asia and South-West Asia). Direct bilateral partnership agreements with individual countries were concluded where possible (with India and Bangladesh for example). However, the geography of Asian regional integration presented the EU with some initial institutional problems. The Asia–Europe Meeting (ASEM) involving 10 states became the chosen format for dialogue with South East Asia. This new grouping brought together Brunei, China, Indonesia, Japan, South Korea, Malaysia, Philippines, Singapore, Thailand and Vietnam. In terms of economic development the 10 were diverse (Singapore and Vietnam for example) and three of them (China, Japan and South Korea) were not members of the region's most established political and economic grouping – ASEAN. Further, both Myanmar and Laos were members of ASEAN but excluded from the ASEM process. In contrast to the newness of ASEM, formalized relations with ASEAN were comparatively developed: as noted already, as early as 1980 an ASEAN–EC cooperation agreement had been signed. EU–ASEAN relations were given a new stimulus by the

1997 so-called 'New Dynamic' initiative designed to consolidate and deepen economic relations. The durability of this accord was underlined in July 2000 when the EU agreed to extend the Agreement to both Laos and Cambodia (the latter having acceded to ASEAN in 1999). Of more importance perhaps was a strong emphasis on political dialogue and EU support for greater Asian regional integration and security issues. Efforts in the 1990s to deepen the political relationship were thwarted by conflicts over human rights conditionality (see Chapter 4). The accession of Myanmar to ASEAN in 1997 has further complicated this situation. Consequently, while the EU–ASEAN relationship has endured, it has failed to mature sufficiently and the economic and political aspirations remain largely unfulfilled. Whilst the prospect of an ASEAN free trade area by 2009 provided some incentive for the EU to persevere with the relationship, a new, wider framework for EU–Asian relations (ASEM) was simultaneously developed during the mid-1990s. The question is whether this new institutional framework can be more successful in reconciling political concerns and promoting economic relations (McMahon, 1998, pp. 236–41).

The trade dimension: ASEM I, II, III

The inaugural 1996 ASEM Heads of Government meeting in Bangkok, brought together the Fifteen plus the Commission and 10 regional states – Brunei, China, Indonesia, Japan, South Korea, Malaysia, the Philippines, Singapore, Thailand and Vietnam. Clearly, three of these (Brunei, Japan and Singapore) do not fit even the most generous definition of development and a further three states (Japan, China and South Korea) were not part of ASEAN. To an extent ASEM mirrors a European constructed reality (in the same way that the ACP only exist within an EU context). Thus although ASEM is an important part of the EU's overall development approach, it provides neither an exclusive nor comprehensive approach to Asian development issues. However, the EU's broader global economic interests beyond simply development policy may be better served by the ASEM process rather than by ASEAN, as it encompasses the Japanese economy as well as the potential benefits of access to China's market. Consequently, the parallel ASEM and ASEAN tracks can jointly provide a more balanced regional approach (with the exception of the countries of South Asia). ASEM appears more adept at addressing the 'big picture' issues (such as the Asian economic crisis) whilst relations through ASEAN provides for more detailed specific focus and a vehicle where political issue can be raised (albeit without dramatic effect) (Allen and Smith, 1999, p. 101).

Economically, EU–ASEM relations are of significance, particularly in comparison with the declining economic importance of the ACP states. Tables 2.1 and 2.2 provide import and export data for the 1995–99 period (Lee, 2000, pp. 4–6). During these five years the overall volume of EU–ASEM trade increased by around 30 per cent. All 10 ASEM countries saw the value of their exports to the EU increase annually: whilst Japan remained the single largest exporter, China provided the most significant increase during the period (from €26 366 m. to €49 169 m.). Conversely, EU exports to ASEM countries have stagnated, reflecting the reduced demand caused by the Asian economic crisis of the late 1990s. In only two ASEM markets (Japan and China) did EU exports marginally increase: elsewhere there was a general decline. Consequently, the balance of trade has increasing grown in favour of the ASEM partners (see Table 2.3): the EU has been a much more important export market for ASEM than East Asia is for the EU. Prior to the Asian financial crisis the balance of trade favouring ASEM was generally stable at around €30 billion, with this level tripling by the end of the 1990s. Correcting this imbalance will certainly be a priority if the ASEM process is to be maintained and developed.

The picture for Foreign Direct Investment (FDI) is somewhat different and in part compensates for the imbalance in trade flows. Globally, the EU is considered to be the world's largest investor – both for outward investment and as a FDI recipient. However, the developing countries of Asia rank well below the USA and Latin America in terms of their share of the EU's FDI (with intra-EU FDI by far the most important market). Despite this lower priority, the EU's share of FDI within the ASEM region has grown: by 1996 it represented 12.3 per cent of FDI and had overtaken the USA and was on a par with the FDI levels of Japan. Conversely, with the exception of Japan and South Korea, the ASEM countries have traditionally exhibited lower levels of FDI outside of Asia. This tendency was again

TABLE 2.1   *EU imports from ASEM, 1995–99 (€m.)*

	1995	1996	1997	1998	1999
South Korea	10922	11095	13068	15952	17889
Japan	54282	52326	59548	65663	69872
China	26366	29981	37366	41800	49269
ASEAN 7	34475	37677	44666	50459	51757
TOTAL	**126045**	**131079**	**154648**	**173874**	**188787**

TABLE 2.2   *EU exports to ASEM, 1995–99 (€m.)*

	1995	1996	1997	1998	1999
South Korea	12276	14029	13827	8735	11061
Japan	32604	34991	35040	30909	34511
China	14662	14487	16014	17139	19049
ASEAN 7	36753	40294	44462	29830	30104
TOTAL	**96295**	**103801**	**109343**	**86613**	**94725**

TABLE 2.3   *EU–ASEM balance of trade, 1995–99 (€m.)*

	1995	1996	1997	1998	1999
South Korea	1354	2934	759	−7217	−6827
Japan	−21678	−17334	−24507	−34754	−35361
China	−11674	−15495	−21351	−24661	−30221
ASEAN 7	2280	2618	−206	−20628	−21654
TOTAL	**−29718**	**−27277**	**−45305**	**−87260**	**−94063**

Source (all three Tables): *Eurostat*, External and Intra-European Union Trade, monthly statistics, 2000.4, cited in Lee (2000).

exacerbated by the Asian financial crisis (Chirathivat, 2000, pp. 2–4).

The initiative for an EU–Asia meeting came from Singapore and the ASEAN group in response to the 1994 Commission document. ASEM was originally conceived as a comprehensive platform for dialogue and cooperation reflecting the emergent role of Asian economic 'Tigers' and Europe's somewhat marginal involvement in the region. The 10 Asian members have a total population of 1834 million, almost five times that of the EU but with a combined GDP per capita figure of US$6232 compared with US$8174 for the EU. Several factors have been used to explain the motivations behind the ASEM process. First, economics played a mutually attractive role. From the EU perspective, clearly the trade imbalance had to be addressed; from the ASEM perspective the expansion of the EU Single Market and the lingering suspicions about 'fortress Europe' suggested the necessity for dialogue. Second, the global context of accelerated regionalization served further to underline the vacuous nature of EU–Asian relations and provided added incentive to create at least a dialogue, if not a set of institutions. ASEM, in many ways, appeared to provide the 'missing link' in the global economic triad. Third, the EU sought an alternative to the APEC process that the USA had engineered in 1993, fearing Europe's further marginalization by its exclusion from APEC membership or even observer status. ASEM was the EU's answer to this perceived American unilateralism and special relationship with Asia (Köllner, 2000, p. 7). It also provided a format through which ASEAN states could begin to re-establish strong relations with Europe based on an equal footing.

The inaugural 1996 ASEM I meeting in Bangkok brought together 25 Asian and European countries and the Commission. Twenty states were represented by their Heads of Government: four EU states chose to send their Foreign or Home Affairs Ministers, whilst China was represented by their Prime Minister rather than Chairman Jiang Zemin. The Commission had triple representation – President Santer and Vice-Presidents Brittan and Marin (Tanaka, 1999, p. 37). The objectives of the meeting were intentionally modest: its value was less to do with producing groundbreaking initiatives than establishing mutual confidence in, and the purpose of, the process. The general conclusion – from both the European and Asian participants – was that ASEM I more than achieved its goals and a more substantive expectation for future cooperation was established (Dent, 1997). This first meeting shaped the key characteristics of ASEM: these have been defined as informality, multidimensionality, partnership and a high-level focus. And, as explained by the then external trade Commissioner Sir Leon Brittan, the contrast with APEC was an important motivation:

Unlike APEC, ASEM is not confined to economic and commercial matters – although they do play an important part, as is inevitable given that the European Union and its Asian partners in ASEM together make up around half of world GDP – ASEM also includes a cultural and people-to-people dimension and a substantive political dialogue. One of its key features is its informality. (Quoted by Schmit in Fangchuan and Niemann, 2000, p. 106)

Thus, the basis of cooperation was to be primarily informal rather than institutionalized, although biennial summits and meetings for foreign, economic and finance ministers in the intervening years are convened. This approach is seen as complementary to the other formal structures for dialogue (such as ASEAN) that already existed. Theoretically at such meetings there is no official agenda (conforming with an Asian rather than Eurocentric style) with participants free to discuss whatever issues they choose (provided that there is no strong opposition to a specific topic). The 1996 Summit reflected this multidimensionality and set itself wide-ranging tasks including a new Asian–EU partnership to promote growth, as well as joint action to support global peace, stability and prosperity. Areas for practical collaboration were also outlined. These covered environmental issues, international crime and drugs, as well as less sensitive initiatives covering economic, scientific and cultural collaboration and an enhanced level of political dialogue. The two sides did not necessarily share the same expectations from ASEM I. Human rights were a European concern whereas the Asian participants preferred an exclusive focus on trade. Remarkably, and perhaps revealingly, the ASEM agenda does not envisage any meetings for Development Ministers. Reminiscent of Europe's relations with the ACP, the notion of partnership rather than dependency was the motivating factor: however, in contrast to the Lomé experience, Asia appears to have been more successful in asserting the equality of the partnership. And finally, and as outlined above, the process is focused intentionally at the level of the political elite. However, it would be hard to characterize the ASEM process as intense since personal relationships at the Heads of Government level are difficult to sustain. On the EU side, the period covering ASEM I–III (1996–2000) has seen major changes at the political elite level in the three key states of UK, France and Germany further compounding the difficulties faced by the biennial gatherings.

The degree of informality is, of course, underpinned by regular bureaucratic contact. The responsibility for coordination is with the Foreign Ministries, with two representatives for ASEM and two for the EU (the presidency and the Commission). The Senior Officials' Meeting plays a role similar to that of COREPER, bringing together foreign affairs officials from both sides to discuss the political dialogue informally. It performs an essential function in ensuring that the actual ASEM Summit can be productive. A similar role in preparing the economic agenda is played by the senior officials' meeting on trade and investment and to a lesser extent that of the meeting of finance officials. Less regular contacts are maintained in the area of customs and science and technology. ASEM has also undertaken a number of initiatives to promote business, cultural, trade and investment contacts outside government. Among these are the Asia–Europe Business Forum; the Asia–Europe Foundation; and the Asia–Europe Environmental Technology Centre.

The second ASEM meeting held in London under the British presidency was overshadowed by the 1997 Asian economic crisis that effectively stalled many of these joint proposals and posed new challenges for the EU–Asia relationship. By way of illustration, in 1998 the growth in GDP was 2.9 per cent for the EU, but shrank to – 2.5 per cent for the Asian ASEM countries. At the political level areas of potential future policy difficulties began to be informally raised. This included both human rights and labour practices, arms control and non-proliferation issues in particular. The question of Myanmar/Burma and its possible inclusion in the Asia–Europe dialogue was to prove intractable with the EU adamantly opposed to its formal participation in any form – including observer status. This issue saw a series of lower level ASEM meetings postponed during 1999. Political discussions were wide-ranging covering subjects pertinent to the EU (the Euro, enlargement), to Asia (Cambodia, the Korean peninsula) as well as international issues of common interest (Kosovo, non-proliferation, drug trafficking and organized crime) and aspects of economic and financial cooperation. The issue of human rights was again raised by the EU, albeit with only limited success. Human rights questions remained particularly sensitive for Indonesia (East Timor) and China (internal affairs) and the position of Myanmar continued to divide the EU from its ASEM partners.

Practical progress was made in cultural, educational and scientific cooperation with support for several joint Asia–Europe centres and foundations. These included the Asia–Europe Foundation in Singapore, the Asia–Europe Centre in Malaysia, and the Asia–Europe Centre for environmental technologies in Bangkok. Two potentially substantive joint plans were also launched – the 'Trade Facilitation Action Plan' and the 'Investment Promotion Action Plan'. The focus of the trade plan – only non-tariff barriers were to be examined – symbolized the modest, cautious and non-controversial nature of the ASEM agenda. Challenging and divisive economic issues (let alone political ones) were avoided. The most significant of these is the EU's application of anti-dumping regulations against particular Asian exports. Six ASEM countries are among the top 10 countries for violating the EU regulation, with China being the worst offender with 34 violations from 1990–98 (van Reisen, 1999, p. 147). One can seriously question the real motivations behind the EU actions. After all, it is the low labour costs that give China, India and other Asian countries one of the few areas of comparative advantage in the global economy. Rather than supporting these countries by providing broad access, the EU appears more concerned with defending its domestic industries in these areas that find it hard to compete by applying anti-dumping regulations. In such circumstances, the tension between the demands of a benevolent external development policy and aspects of internal EU economic policy cannot be reconciled. Another difficult issue that remained unresolved was the membership of ASEM. From the 'Asian' side India, Pakistan, Laos, Cambodia, Myanmar, Australia and even New Zealand have all expressed either formal or informal interest in participating in ASEM: from Europe the CEECs and Russia have also indicated their interest. However, a consensus on enlargement among the current Asian ASEM members proved illusive and a decision was deferred until ASEM III. Lastly, the 1998 meeting surveyed the future of the ASEM process and the next summits scheduled for October 2000 in Seoul, Korea (to be followed by a fourth summit in Denmark in 2002).

Safeguarding the momentum created at ASEM I and II was defined as the major challenge given the often intangible benefits that ASEM claims. Did the process provide comparative advantages that other linkages could not? Europe's enthusiasm for a new 'Millennium' WTO Round also remained controversial despite a recognition that development aid needed to be better incorporated within their approach to global trade liberalization (something the ACP states were to also raise within the context of renegotiating of Lomé). In 1999 the outgoing European Vice-President and Commissioner for external trade (Sir Leon Brittan) outlined several reforms designed to improve the position of ASEM and the developing world within the WTO (*Agence Europe*, no.7481, 1999). In particular, trading priorities – as defined by the Third World – had to be included on the WTO agenda. This included providing free access to all industrialized countries' markets for the world's 48 Least Developed Countries; WTO assistance to overcome the technical expertise and skilled human resource problems; and, enhanced cooperation between the World Bank, IMF, the UN and the EU to ensure policy consistency and effectiveness. However, these sentiments and the existence of both the ASEAN and ASEM fora should not be taken to mean that an automatic consensus exists among the EU on all aspects of relations with Asia. Evidence of internal fragmentation – or at least of continuing spheres of sovereignty – within Europe's approach to Asia was publicly exposed by their failure to forge a consensus among the Fifteen during 1999, in support of the Thai candidate, Deputy Prime Minister Supachai Panichpakdi, for the Directorship of the WTO. European opposition to an ASEM candidate questioned the purpose and sincerity of the dialogue. Furthermore, this failure to act with a single voice can hardly improve Asia's appreciation of the integration process or the EU's ability to be either a single or an influential international actor comparable to the USA.

The London ASEM Summit also adopted an Asia–Europe Cooperation Framework and created an Asia–Europe Vision Group with a mandate to look at long-term perspectives and directions. The 1999 ASEM Foreign Ministers' meeting received their recommendations and in the following year the Commission issued its own response, 'Perspectives and Priorities for the ASEM Process into the new decade' (COM/2000/241) designed to shape the EU's approach to ASEM III. Clearly, there was some concern that after five years the dialogue had to graduate to a more substantive level or risk the loss of momentum and purpose. As the Commission document warned 'Seoul will have the task of confirming and enhancing the importance of this partnership between our two regions, and indeed of maintaining its momentum and relevance, to counter any sentiments of 'fatigue' in the ASEM process' (Commission, 2000a, p. 2). Building on the original three pillars of activity that defined ASEM (political, economic, cultural and intellectual), a range of general priorities were identified. In the political sphere an emphasis was placed on focusing on issues of common interest and improving mutual understanding in areas where EU and Asian views differed. Implied moral hierarchies were explicitly eschewed in favour of equality of partnership: consequently, issues of aid and 'good governance' were taboo within ASEM, a choice that would have been unthinkable in the ACP context. Practical initiatives included intensifying existing high-level and informal dialogues, networking and a greater use of collaborative action in other international forums. In the economic sphere, whilst the Commission priorities were not antagonistic to development issues, the emphasis was very much on the role of business and trade. A common approach to strengthening the rules-based multilateral trading agenda of the WTO in the wake of Seattle was seen as a high-level priority. Public and private linkages as well as business dialogues between the two regions were similarly singled out. In the cultural and intellectual sphere the roles of research, civil society and in particular educational exchanges were identified as areas where ASEM could demonstrate a distinct role and comparative advantage.

The Commission also suggested five specific priorities for which concrete outcomes at Seoul could be expected. These focused on:

- *Regional and Global security.* Here ASEM's informality was seen as an effective mechanism for developing closer mutual understanding on traditional 'soft' issues (conflict prevention, peace-keeping and humanitarian assistance) as well as so-called 'new security issues' (such as international crime, terrorism and cyber warfare).

- *Trade, investment and regional macroeconomic cooperation.* The WTO was the most effective agent for realizing these goals and building a consensus through ASEM's informal process was identified as pivotal.
- *Consumers' dialogue.* This was proposed as a new area where common interests could be usefully combined, especially in food safety.
- *Educational exchanges.* Building on the work of ASEM I and II a fivefold increase in educational exchanges was proposed over a 10-year period. The sponsorship of a prestigious scholarship programme was also floated.
- *Enlargement.* Although the question of increasing the Asian side of ASEM was probably too contentious, the issue is one that will not go away. For the EU, the inclusion of Myanmar – currently an ASEAN member state – is highly problematic; conversely, the inclusion of India or Australia present radically different but equally challenging issues for the Asian states. Such an enlargement would fundamentally change the context of ASEM.

Without demeaning the importance of such issues, the question has to be asked how far the ASEM framework is necessary for their discussion and resolution. If the over-riding strength of ASEM is informality, then why not address these topics on a purely *ad hoc* bilateral basis. Is the region-to-region process either warranted or indispensable?

ASEM III was held on 20–21 October 2000 in Seoul. Again, 25 states were represented by their Prime Ministers or Presidents and Foreign Ministers: President Prodi and External Relations Commissioner Patten represented the Commission. The outcome of the meeting differed only marginally from the Commission's indicative agenda – although as was the case for ASEM II unanticipated international events dominated the political focus. In Seoul, the Korean Peninsula provided this context with the meeting issuing a 'Declaration for Peace'. ASEM partners offered to facilitate confidence-building measures, enhance regional stability with a view to the eventual reunification of North and South Korea – but embarrassingly, the EU was unable to take a common response to the question of establishing diplomatic relations with North Korea. Also within the political pillar, an important beginning, however modest, was made on the question of human rights – a topic that had been vetoed at the previous two summits. New ASEM priorities were also identified including disarmament, non-proliferation, international crime, drugs and migration. Unspectacular statements were issued on East Timor, Kosovo and the Middle East. In the economic pillar, intensification of ASEM I and II measures on trade and investment were called for; agreement was attained on support for a new WTO round; bridging the 'digital divide' was identified; and mechanisms to address the negative effects of globalization called for. And under the cultural cooperation pillar, educational exchanges became the priority. Agreement was reached on a 'Trans-Euroasia Information network', the development of ASEM tertiary exchanges and a range of other networks. No progress was made on extending membership beyond the existing principle of each side determining its own composition. Thus the EU's wish to see India included was thwarted and Asia's (specifically Malaysia) response to incorporating Australia or New Zealand was that membership would have to be through the EU half of ASEM! The only concession was that ASEM non-members were allowed to participate in common ASEM projects.

Future challenges

Clearly, ASEM has increased the profile of Asia within the EU's policy priorities. Whilst this was necessary, is it a sufficient reason for maintaining the ASEM framework as the principal mechanism for EU–Asian dialogue? To what extent has rhetoric masqueraded as progress? Among some EU member states initial commitment to ASEM was somewhat reluctant largely because of their already heavy summit obligations. The challenge for ASEM is to counter the growing general perception of 'forum fatigue' by graduating ASEM from its symbolic origins to a more substantive policy output level – without jeopardizing the informal, multidimensional and high-level advantages associated with the current dialogue (Yeo, 2000). Others have been more critical of the elitism of the process, seeing the lack of public involvement as a fundamental problem. The future legitimacy and viability of ASEM appears to depend on a greater role for civil society in the process – both in Europe and Asia (Köllner, 2000, p. 11). At both a practical and symbolic level, the establishment of a permanent secretariat could contribute to this development.

The non-contentious nature of the political dialogue also potentially threatens the future development of ASEM. Whilst a gentleman's agreement to avoid political topics that were divisive may have been the necessary price to pay in order to instigate the dialogue, ASEM runs the obvious risk of becoming effectively vacuous if 'sensitive' issues continue to remain taboo. Obviously, the problem of human rights and labour practices present major obstacles. In more general terms, the basic premise of ASEM – two regions coming together for dialogue – is arguably flawed. While the EU can justifiably be described as a region that speaks with a 'single voice' (whether vocal or timorous) in a variety of forums, the ten Asian states associated with ASEM do not function as a similarly cohesive group – or even exist collectively outside the ASEM context. There can be distinct and diverse positions within the Asian side of the process. This can lead to inconsistent expectations and, in part, explains the minimalist outcomes from the biennial summit. The evolving position of Japan is particularly important in this respect. Japan has only reluctantly been drawn into the ASEM framework. It has involved (from Japan's perspective) a sensitive if subtle downgrading of its special trilateral relationship with the EU and the USA as the Asian corner of the global economic triad (Tanaka, 1999).

ASEM has been considered a defensive response to the challenges presented by Europe's main economic rival, the USA. The promise of APEC within the region produced a European counter-weight. It was also defensive in the sense of applying a cautious approach to tariff reduction and liberalization – whatever the popular rhetoric of ASEM declarations might say. However, it was anticipated that the launch of the ASEM process would be a significant watershed and provide the missing link between Europe and Asia. The experience of the early years of ASEM suggests that these ambitions remain optimistic and little of substance had emerged from the process by the end of 2000. No significant new relationships have been established beyond the status quo or provided through the

WTO and many of the issues that frustrated the EU–ASEAN dialogue remain unresolved at ASEM. Quite how ASEM relates to the EU–ASEAN framework also requires greater clarification if duplication is to be avoided. Mirroring the general question posed in the introduction to this book – does the EU have a distinctive Third World function – perhaps the greatest challenge is what, if any, distinct role does ASEM provide? Again, the informal application of the principle of subsidiarity is useful in focusing attention (Segal, 1997). Simply, what can be done best at the ASEM level, what at the ASEAN-level and what should remain the legitimate sphere for bilateral member state policy? Despite the expression of early satisfaction, this crucial question remains fudged – perhaps by necessity. The limited institutional and policy formulations of ASEM to date make it difficult to define a substantive distinct and superior character beyond informality. The prospect of the 're-nationalization' of relations between Asia and Europe should not be discounted. Perhaps bilateral relations are in many ways 'better'.

The heterogeneity within the ASEM membership can reduce the cohesion and effectiveness of the group. On the Asian side, the tensions between Japan and the other members, the inclusion of China, as well as the parallel expectations of ASEAN membership cumulatively suggest limited scope for a common agenda among Asian ASEM states. Diversity also characterises the EU's ASEM perspectives: different views on what constitutes the Asian cornerstone of the relationship (China, Japan or ASEAN) are evident and clearly the member states will – to a degree – have diverging interests within Asia separate from any common EU multilateral position. Lastly, the imbalance within the so-called three pillars of ASEM remains a concern. As one critic has observed, there is a tendency whereby 'political dialogue and cultural and civic relations are treated merely as functional prerequisites for successful economic relations' (Schmit, 2000, p. 120). Under these circumstances, public awareness and support by civil society will remain marginal – a scenario that may well undermine the continued viability of ASEM.

More positively, the EU does seem to have discovered a deeper appreciation of the growing importance of the region and the need for an enhanced relationship. The long list of meetings agreed to at both ASEM I and ASEM II at least institutionalize an ongoing dialogue, a necessary precondition for greater cooperation. The current stage of the EU–Asia relationship could be viewed as being about building bridges that might – in years to come – lead to more fruitful outcomes. But such a scenario ignores the two decades of EU–ASEAN dialogue that has failed to deliver substantive agreements. Without a concrete economic objective, ASEM III and beyond is in danger of becoming rapidly insignificant and irrelevant within the Asia–Pacific region (McMahon, 1998, p. 247). APEC and intra-regional FTA agreements are already more advanced than ASEM. But at present there seems little prospect of a consensus emerging to raise the ASEM agenda to a more productive level, comparable say, to the transatlantic agreement between the EU and the USA (Dent, 1999, p. 6) or in matching the APEC objective of an Asia–Pacific FTA by 2020. Indeed, the commonly held greatest virtue of ASEM – its informality – makes such a development almost inconceivable. An example of where a substantive ASEM role could emerge is in a joint approach to development cooperation that incorporates Asian solutions rather than simply applies European past practice. In this way, policies that are more culturally sensitive might be possible and 'conditionality' seen as less of an inappropriate demand. Thus ASEM could provide a suitable vehicle to combine EU and Asian experiences leading to a more effective and applicable synthesis.

In conclusion, how does ASEM compare with the EU's general pattern of relations with the developing world? First, it clearly further compounds the problem of defining what constitutes the Third World. ASEM includes advanced industrial and technological societies such as Japan, Korea and Singapore as well as underdeveloped countries such Thailand, Vietnam and Indonesia. Once again, geography creates at least as many problems as it solves. Second, ASEM indicates to some degree that institutionalized relations are not always necessary – or effective – in generating dialogue. Third, it also suggests that economic parity is essential if political conditionality is to be excluded: good governance and human rights have not played a universal role in shaping the EU's dialogue partners. Fourth, the history of EU relations with ASEAN and ASEM also underline the limited role that trade preferences can play in development. Despite receiving no preferential concessions, Asian trade with the EU has grown over the past decades whilst that with Europe's privileged partners has virtually collapsed. And fifth, the EU's motives for re-establishing a dialogue with Asia illustrate Europe's wider agenda to become an effective international actor and its activism in confronting American global unilateralism. In the post-Cold War context there are no longer any *domaine reserves* that the EU is obliged to respect.

The Aid Dimension

A unique peculiarity of the EU's policy structure is the ALA (Asia–Latin America) Committee. The ALA Committee is composed of member state representatives who meet monthly to review and approve all Asian and Latin American programmes that exceed €2 million. Consequently, the ALA Committee is jointly responsible for EU aid to 34 countries across both these continents. This approach appears to defy logic by grouping together a wide range of geographically and economically diverse recipients in Asia and Latin America under a single category – for example, Brazil and Argentina with Yemen, Cuba and India. For the very worst reasons pertaining to Eurocentric administrative compartmentalization, it combines eight Central American states, ten from South America, six from South East Asia, six from South Asia and four from the Middle East, Central and East Asia! This bureaucratic invention was initiated in 1974 in response to the acknowledged gap in European relations with non-ACP developing countries. As a group, the ALA states have been dealt with on an *ad hoc* basis with financial support coming directly from the Community budget and with programmes largely confined to humanitarian and emergency aid. The Maastricht Treaty and subsequent Council Resolutions have sought to prioritize and expand ALA aid in line with other EU development activities. In particular, the 1992 Council Regulation 443/92 broadened aid objectives to include human rights, gender, democratization, good governance and environmental issues in the main policy objective of poverty eradication. During the 1990s ambitious 'third generation' agreements were signed with many Latin American countries that incorporated democratic principles as well as development cooperation procedures, although this does not include any uniform policy on structural adjustment conditionality.

If EU–Asia trading relations have been comparatively modest, then Asia has been similarly treated in the deployment of European aid. To compound matters, prior to the 1990s aid did not necessarily go to those in the greatest need: political considerations have weighed heavily in the choice of recipient countries. For example, China only began to receive aid in 1985 and similar patterns can be found for the states of Indochina (Vietnam, Cambodia, Laos and Myanmar). Typically, the very poorest Asian countries were not the main aid recipients – these were primarily the ASEAN countries, such as Thailand and Indonesia. The only exception to this was the Indian sub-continent that received aid irrespective of implied conditionality. The scale of the aid problem distorts even the most generous of programmes when examined on a per capita basis. Nonetheless, the EU contribution remains small. For example, between 1976 and 1988 aid to Indochina totalled just 151.1 million ecus, or the equivalent of 1.33 ecus per capita. Even South Asia, the most favoured of the Asian regions, received only 2.17 ecus per capita (representing 2367 million ecus) (Grilli, 1993, p. 288). With the exception of South Asia, EU aid has not been a major Asian development factor and for many states bilateral member state aid remains more important. Of course, if taken cumulatively Europe's presence is enhanced and the Commission claims that the EU does practice a comprehensive global aid programme. Conversely, critics have described the presence of EU aid as 'paper thin, not only in China and Indochina, but also in the Indian sub-continent' (*ibid.*, p. 289). The aid that does exist is almost totally for agriculture and food aid. In contrast to the ASEM initiative that was designed to rejuvenate the lethargic EU–Asia relationship, no equivalent relaunch of aid to Asia has been developed. The obligatory political conditionalities that now shape the EU's external relations in general can be seen as one of the disincentives to revising the EU's aid distribution.

Table 2.4 describes more recent Asian aid distribution for the decade 1986–1995. The value of aid has grown over the period. More significantly, these SCR figures underline the problem of

TABLE 2.4 *EU aid to Asian countries, 1986–95 (m. ecus)*

Rank order by value	Country	Value of commitments	D/C ratio* %	Rank order by D/C ratio
1	India	932	54	9
2	Bangladesh	686	67	7
3	Philippines	271	40	14
4	China	264	70	5
5	Pakistan	260	67	6
6	Indonesia	172	55	8
7	Cambodia	152	41	13
8	Vietnam	147	54	10
9	Thailand	139	116	2
10	Afghanistan	137	na	na
11	Laos	70	39	15
12	Nepal	62	45	11
13	Sri Lanka	60	91	3
14	Yemen	40	119	1
15	Bhutan	21	85	4
16	Mongolia	9	42	12

Note: * D/C disbursement/commitments ratio.

TABLE 2.5 *EU aid to Latin American countries, 1986–95 (m. ecus)*

Rank order by value	Country	Value of commitments	D/C ratio* %	Rank order by D/C ratio
1	Peru	327	57	7
2	Nicaragua	253	54	9
3	Bolivia	246	68	4
4	Guatemala	188	44	14
5	El Salvador	188	62	6
6	Brazil	137	64	5
7	Chile	135	70	3
8	Colombia	106	48	12
9	Ecuador	100	50	11
10	Cuba	90	55	8
11	Honduras	89	48	13
12	Mexico	63	73	2
13	Paraguay	46	50	10
14	Venezuela	44	18	16
15	Argentina	44	0	18
16	Panama	34	26	15
17	Uruguay	30	13	17
18	Costa Rica	29	127	1

Note: * D/C disbursement/commitments ratio.
Source for both tables: Commission (1999).

actually disbursing those limited funds that were allocated for aid. Only seven states had a disbursement rate of over two-thirds and the ratio for the largest programme (India) was only just above 50 per cent. As is discussed in Chapter 3 this pattern has become a generalized problem for the EU – irrespective of the geographical location of aid the actual delivery and expenditure of funds can be frustratingly slow and often remains incomplete. The necessity for transparent accounting and the individual conditions associated with each project make time lags almost inevitable. Table 2.5 provides similar data for Latin America. Here, only four states achieved a disbursement rate of over two-thirds and eight could manage no better than 50 per cent rates. Of the seven states to receive the greatest levels of aid, only two reached the two-thirds level.

Table 2.6 looks at the changing pattern of aid over a decade. During the first half of the 1990s EU aid to Asia increased by 82 per cent, and to Latin America by 68 per cent. However, as a percentage of the EU's overall aid, the ALA share declined over this five-year period due to the shifting aid priority towards the CEECs (to 13.6 per cent of EU total aid). This was reversed in 1995 when EU aid commitments to both Asia and Latin America reached a record level of €1.2 billion). This represented 17 per cent of the EU's overall aid budget and was close to half the level of aid provided to the ACP states. Except for 1986, Asia has always been the greater recipient of EU aid and over the 1986–95 period consumed 58 per cent of the ALA aid budget. However, on a per capita basis greater funds have gone to Latin America. In both Asia and Latin America EU support has been predominantly targeted for food aid, humanitarian projects and NGOs. The longer-term sustainability of this aid remains an area where the EU contribution could undoubtedly be improved.

A recent addition to the EU's ALA policy has been a specific focus on 'uprooted people' and refugees. The 1997 Council Regulation 443/97 created the legal base for this EU action to counter the effects of civil wars. This has generally taken two forms: in post-conflict situations where resettlement and rehabilitation initiatives act to consolidate peace processes; and where conflict continues, the financing of operations designed to increase stability. During the 1990s Asia rather than Latin America has exhibited a greater degree of conflict and need for

TABLE 2.6 *EU aid to ALA countries, 1986–95 (€m.)*

	1986	1987	1988	1989	1990	1991	1992	1993	1994	1995	1986–1995
Asia	140	257	226	426	317	383	470	504	451	696	3870
Latin America	160	156	159	210	222	286	338	401	390	486	2808
ALA Total	300	413	385	636	539	669	808	905	841	1182	6678
% change		38	–7	65	–15	24	21	12	–7	41	

Source: Commission (1999).

TABLE 2.7 *EU ALA aid for uprooted people, 1997–99 (€m.)*

	Asia			Latin America			TOTAL
	1997	1998	1999	1997	1998	1999	
Total Budget	38	38	37.95	21.35	21.35	21.24	177.89
Actual commitment	36.12	37.62	29.55	20.86	15.22	20.72	159.1
% of budget allocation	95	99	77.9	97.7	71.3	99.9	89.7

Source: Commission (2000b).

refugee assistance. However, as was the case for aid in general, while Asia attracted a larger total sum, Latin America has received higher per capita help. The raw totals are given Table 2.7. These funds financed a total of 111 individual operations – 67 in Asia and 44 in Latin America. In Asia, two-thirds of commitments went on resettlement aid whereas aid in Latin America was channelled to refugees, displaced persons, returnees and supporting reconciliation processes (Commission, 2000(b), p. 14).

Lastly, one specific, if untypical 'aid' contribution was the EU's response to the Asian financial crisis. EU member states provide around 30 per cent of funding for the IMF, 27 per cent for the World Bank and 14 per cent of the Asian Development Bank. Cumulatively, Europe is the greatest provider of financial support to Asia providing some 18 per cent of the total value at €27 billion. In comparison with the USA, in 1998 the EU's development and humanitarian aid to Asia was twice that of America and the funding for three-quarters of the then existing debt-relief schemes came from Europe (Schmit, 2000, p. 109).

Conclusion

To summarize, there are both general as well as specific criticisms that can be levelled at the EU's aid regime towards Asia and Latin America. First, an area of significant general criticism invokes the theme of the three 'Cs' outlined earlier in the book. Historically there has been a weakness in coordinating EU and member state policies towards Asia and Latin America, as well as in increasing the coherence and complementarity between different Commission DGs and policy objectives. Whilst coordination can involve complex administrative structures and tasks, clearly the greatest impediment remains an absence of political will (either through disinterest or by intent). Second, the heterogeneity of countries with Asia and Latin America – let alone between the two regions – in terms of needs, patterns of income distribution and relative poverty levels, has resulted in a suboptimal use of scarce aid resources. There are no comparative advantages of using the same administrative structure to deal with countries as economically diverse as India and China and Argentina, for example (Commission, 1999, p. 31). If the ALA grouping is maintained, at a minimum reform should differentiate between several categories of country based on income levels, poverty ratios or some other regional criteria. Third, the distribution of aid seems clearly to disadvantage Asia.

Chapter 3

Decision-making and Reforming Institutional Structures

This chapter focuses on the administration of the EU's development policy. It begins by examining the internal reforms to the EU Commission structure and responsibilities, contrasting the 1995–99 Santer administrative organization with that of the Prodi Commission after 2000. Here, the review of the management of the EU's external assistance programme as well as the reorganization of DG responsibilities is discussed. The chapter concludes with an analysis of ECHO and the degree to which humanitarian aid operates administrative autonomy free from questions of conditionality. This emphasis reflects the growing public and institutional concern that the EU's ability to deliver its development agenda has been largely frustrated by poor administrative structures. The backlog of financial commitments and the delays in implementing projects reached an unacceptable level and too often practices did not adequately respect the EU's legal obligations. Consequently, administrative structural reform became the precondition for a more effective EU development policy without which future policy initiatives on poverty reduction were bound to fail.

The structure of the Santer Commission, 1995–9

The first full post-TEU Commission lead by President Santer complicated the distribution of administrative responsibility for development issues. Whilst DGVIII remained the focus for Lomé relations, three other DGs plus the autonomous European Community Humanitarian Office (ECHO) were involved in aspects of development work. The friction with DGI (external economic relations) was particularly sensitive and much of the impetus for the Green Paper initiatives towards free trade for the ACP can be traced to this division. This fragmentation saw

DGI responsible for trade and commercial policy (with its geographical spread linking OECD countries with China, South Korea and Taiwan). DGIA was the focus for CFSP policy as well as for relations with the CEEC, Turkey, Cyprus, Malta and countries of the former Soviet Union. DGIB concentrated on the Mediterranean, Middle and Far East as well as Latin America. DGVIII remained exclusively concerned with ACP affairs with the addition of responsibility after 1995 for the newly democratic South Africa. ECHO stood apart from these structures and took responsibility for humanitarian assistance (van Reisen, 1999, p. 53). This administrative puzzle was further complicated by the competition within the College of Commissioners for seniority and policy dominance. The pre-1995 struggle between DGI Commissioner Sir Leon Brittan and his DGVIII counterpart Manuel Marin over determining the shape of future EU–South African relations has been widely documented (see Holland, 1994) and provides an illustration of a more general model of bureaucratic competition.

The administrative logic that determined these combinations emphasized region rather than policy area in designating responsibilities. It was contentious at the time of introduction and proved, ultimately, to be flawed. Geographical differentiation was seen as an increasingly archaic perspective in the face of globalization. Policies were not country or regionally specific, but general. Indeed, the very existence of the WTO underlined the similarity of treatment between countries rather than their claim to uniqueness. Consequently, the Santer reform of Commission portfolios appeared inconsistent with contemporary trends and an inappropriate framework for addressing issues of complementarity, coordination and coherence (see Chapter 4). Compounding the problem was the staff imbalance. As the 1999 Committee of Independent Experts report on Commission activities concluded, in some areas (especially ECHO) too few staff were often responsible for too large a budget. The notion of a burgeoning Brussels bureaucracy was never further from the truth. An earlier DAC Report was similarly critical of the EU's limited expertise. The number of specialist staff in key areas – such as women and development – was considered too limited. For example, in DGVIII as late as 1998 there was just one designated advisor in gender policy and one individual working exclusively on poverty reduction policy. The scope of EU activities had raced ahead of the capacity of its permanent staff to implement such policies. In order to work, the EU's programme increasingly came to rely on the use of consultants to complement its limited core staff, further complicating efficiency and lines of responsibility. As one commentator concluded, both centrally as well as in the field:

> the administration of the Commission on development aid is badly organised as well as understaffed . . . has caused incoherence in the work, and has severely restricted the skill acquisition in the Commission. It is clearly not a sound policy for ensuring a competent development administration. (Van Reisen, 1999, pp. 54–5)

One view sees the responsibility for this staffing situation lying with the member states. Undoubtedly, the Council sought to rein-in the growing authority of the Commission that occurred under President Delors. First, the principle of subsidiarity was introduced to eliminate the seemingly automatic drift of policy towards the EU-level of competence. But second, the member states together with the Parliament have imposed financial ceilings on staff recruitment that effectively prohibited expansion. And third, there was a tradition of member states demanding that their nationals be predominantly responsible for certain policy sectors. Cumulatively these factors have constrained the responsive capacity of the Commission. An alternative view argues that the problem lies within the Commission itself and that inefficiency and an absence of adaptability are the main sources of policy failure. The transfer of staff between DGs remained cumbersome and the nationality quota system created bottlenecks. Flexibility rather than size remains the key criterion.

The staffing levels of the Commission are modest by the standards of international organizations. Both staffing issues and effective coordination were the subject of review in 1998. The proposed solution was the creation of a new grouping, the 'Joint Service for the Management of Community Aid to Non-Member Countries' (usually known by its French acronym, SCR: Service Commun Relex). The SCR became operational in July 1998 with a mandate to develop greater policy coherence and utilization of staff resources and to manage all aspects (technical, operational, financial, contractual and legal) of EU aid. Somewhat paradoxically, it was also seen as a tool for introducing decentralization in the management of aid to third countries and promoting local 'ownership' of aid projects. Its geographic focus was global – not confined to just the ACP – and involved crosscutting policy responsibilities. Food aid, environment, AIDS, democracy, human rights and CFSP, for example, were part of the SCR domain. The only exception was emergency humanitarian aid that remained exclusively under the direction of ECHO.

The SCR was divided into six directorates each with the following responsibilities:

Directorate A: Central and Eastern Europe, countries covered by Phare, Tacis and Obnova programmes, CFSP, democracy and drugs projects.

Directorate B: Economic, technical and financial cooperation with Lain America, the Mediterranean, Middle East, South and South East Asia and China, forestry, environment and gender programmes.

Directorate C: EDF projects for the ACP, South Africa and Overseas Countries and Territories plus food aid, population, rehabilitation, refugees, AIDS and anti-personnel mines.

Directorate D: coordination of external relations budget and financial monitoring, financial implementation of major assistance programmes (EDF, Phare and so on), and auditing and supervisory activities.

Directorate E: Legal unit responsible for overseeing the administration and tender of all contracts.

Directorate F: horizontal tasks, such as SCR human resources, relations with other EU institutions, information as well as project evaluation.

http://www.europa.eu.int/comm/scr/

However, in keeping with fiscal constraints and the Commission's employment culture, the SCR recruited staff (some 640 in total) from the existing Directorate Generals concerned with external relations. The obvious consequence of this was to further reduce the staffing levels in these areas: roughly one third of DGVIII and DGIA were reassigned reducing staff levels to

408 and 563 respectively (van Reisen, 1999, p. 57). However, the SCR did produce initial results.

Undoubtedly, the SCR was a much-needed innovation to bring together the disparate development focus within the Commission organization. It was also a direct response to the treaty-based demand for the four Cs – complementarity, coordination, coherence and consistency (see Chapter 4). Its immediate impact was modest, however. One of the prime tasks for the SCR was to reduce the time between the definition of development projects and the actual disbursement of funds. For the year 1999 the Commission disbursed €4.9 billion out of a budget commitment of €7.9 billion, a proportion roughly similar to the previous year. This involved managing 11 640 projects and 16 448 contracts (*Agence Europe*, 28 February 2000, p. 13). Within one year of its launch, however, the new Prodi Commission revisited the problem of development coordination and the SCR was once more the subject of modification.

The 2000 administrative reforms

The appointment of the Prodi Commission in late 1999 provided an opportunity for the EU to re-examine its general administrative structures, as well as address some of the publicly acknowledged shortcomings noted in the 1999 Committee of Independent Experts investigation into Commission fraud and mismanagement. The reforms applied to the development sector were the most radical in its history and were 'a bid to cut out waste and bring more coherence to its much criticised €9 billion aid budget' (*European Voice*, 23 March 2000, p. 1). As should be clear from the previous section as well as from other chapters in this book, the EU's development policy has lacked a hierarchical structure and the policy autonomy retained by the different actors did little to promote coherence or coordination. The reorganization was helped by the choice of Poul Nielson as a Commissioner and his appointment by Prodi to the development portfolio. Whilst the Nice, Amsterdam and Maastricht treaties have given the President of the Commission enhanced powers to organize portfolios and influence the composition of the Commission, it still remains the case currently that the member states retain the right to propose 'their' Commissioner. Consequently, Prodi could only utilize the individual talents as moderated by the member states. In the past, there has been a tendency for some member states to propose the name of a Commissioner more for domestic political reasons rather than for a purely European rationale.

Commissioner Poul Nielson was proposed as a Commissioner by Denmark and has a strong record both as a committed European and in development. His parliamentary career began in 1971 and he was chairman of the Danish European Movement at the time of Denmark's accession to the EU. From 1994–9 he was the Minister for Development Cooperation in Denmark's Social Democrat Government. Thus his commitment to the EU and his experience in development policy made him an appropriate and strong choice for DGVIII. The choice of Patten as one of the two British Commissioners (replacing Sir Leon Brittan) and his appointment to External Relations was significant. The ambit of the External Relations Directorate-General was expanded considerably by Prodi and covered all countries other than the ACP, although its policy sphere did include responsibility for the SCR, human rights, democratization, multilateral organizations as well as CFSP. Consequently, many regard the External Relations DG as the lynchpin of the Commission. Clearly, Patten's experience as a former senior Conservative Cabinet Minister as well as the last British Governor of Hong Kong has made him an influential political figure with the Commission College. The appointment of Pascal Lamy, a protégé of Delors, as Commissioner for Trade was a necessary political gesture to placate France.

From an administrative perspective, the dispersal of external relations typified by the Santer Commission was reintegrated – but only to some extent. Nielson became Commissioner for Development (DGVIII) in overall charge of development policy and humanitarian aid, including ECHO. Chris Patten was appointed as Commissioner for External Relations (DGI) with control of the SCR as well as responsibility for external trade relations, Delegations in all third countries, the coordination of external policies and the CFSP. Trade Commissioner Pascal Lamy had oversight of external trade and instruments of trade policy. His Directorate-General was involved in all trade-related matters, including GSP and the trading relations incorporated in the successor to the Lomé Conventions. DGVIII continued to deal with only development issues in the ACP countries although its scope was expanded somewhat to include ECHO activities. Development relations with Asia, Latin America, the Mediterranean and elsewhere fell under External Relations, the domain of Chris Patten.

Many of those familiar with the history of Europe's development policy fear, despite good intentions, that the latest reforms can only serve further to weaken the role of DGVIII and that the policy objective of poverty reduction will be compromised. First, whilst there are expectations that appropriate geographical desks in DGVIII will be consulted when CFSP or external relations issues are involved, clearly, Patten may employ development issues to promote his other sectoral responsibilities, particularly the execution of an EU foreign policy. Second, by institutionally isolating the ACP from other developing areas within the Commission structure, the probability of dissimilar policies being pursued can only be enhanced. Third, de-linking trade and development by removing all ACP trade issues from DGVIII control may result in the ACP's particular interests being marginalized within broader concerns. Divorcing development expertise from trade expertise can hardly encourage increased coherence between the two policies. As various development lobby groups have pointed out it is unlikely that EU trade considerations will be significantly influenced by development considerations. Furthermore, the contradictions between the thematic and geographical policy structure might lead to the unintended consequence of increased dissonance in development policy. The implicit identification of development as an ACP phenomenon (separate from Asian and Latin American developing countries) may simply increase 'ghettoization' and policy fragmentation. If nothing else, surely the Commissioner for Development should at least be responsible for *all* developing countries, not just those assigned to the ACP?

Thus although development policy *per se* is to be controlled by one person (Nielson), the practice of managing the programmes will remain spread between DGs and Commissioners and it would be surprising if Patten did not come to dominate this process. Another factor that is as important as the structural changes to portfolios is the ability of the individual Commissioners to work in a cooperative and collegial manner – something that should not be automatically assumed if past practice is to be a guide. The ability of these Commissioners to forge a collaborative rather than competitive relationship between their arms of the bureaucracy will be a significant factor in determining the success of EU development policy over the 2000–05 period. All three were first-time appointments as Commissioners and no doubt all are keen to make their own respective sectors a success and enhance their reputations and future chances of reappointment and promotion. Under such circumstances, enhanced collegiality may not be the most effective strategy.

In line with the earlier DAC analysis, both Nielson and Patten have agreed that the chronic in-house staff shortages are a priority area. For example, the EU's €100 million programme for India is administered by a total of seven staff compared with an equivalent British bilateral programme worth €150 million that employs 200 staff (*European Voice*, April 2000). The May 2000 reform proposals also recommended that the SCR grow to around 800 and be given greater responsibility for designing, implementing, monitoring and assessing a wide range of – but not all – development schemes. The existing distinction between the DGs who were responsible for policy and the SCR who were responsible for the financial management of projects also often delayed delivery. One potential staffing solution under consideration is the possibility of 'externalizing' project management by creating a central specialized office for this function (mirroring the role of ECHO to some degree). This would permit the employment of additional specialized staff (funded through the operational funds earmarked for specific projects) but allow the Commission to retain overall control. In the wake of the mismanagement problems previously identified in ECHO, Commission supervision is essential. An alternative solution looks more towards devolution: the Commission's own Delegations in third countries could assume greater involvement in project management. Of course, this would involve additional staff resources that may be impossible to achieve.

The European Parliament has also been vigorously involved in the reform debates and has consistently presented a broad notion of coherence between development and all EU policy sectors – including the CAP. The 1999 restructuring of the Commission (whilst an improvement on the Santer organization) was criticized for being inadequate to the task, particularly the continued division of responsibility for foreign policy between three Commissioners. In its February 2000 plenary session, an overwhelming majority passed a Resolution calling on the Commission to publish an annual report on coherence and development policy. More radically, it called for a further reorganization of Commission portfolios to promote better co-ordination of aid policies, including a new inter-Commission working group on coherence that involved DGs responsible for agriculture, fisheries, research, trade, external relations as well as development. The Parliament also underlined (as it had done repeatedly for decades) the difficulty posed by the financial basis of development policy that further detracted from policy coherence. The principal funding mechanism for the ACP states remained the EDF – an intergovernmental mechanism based on member state contributions – and consequently outside the EU budget and parliamentary scrutiny. Whilst the Parliament is unable – on its own – to force the introduction of such changes, its constant lobbying for development issues has influenced the current reform context. The Prodi Commission are well aware of the need for Parliament's approval of future agreements with third countries as well as their authority and ability to sanction Commission failings.

In keeping with the more open approach to policy formation that began with the 1996 post-Lomé Green Paper, in March 2000 the Commission published a working document on future development policy guidelines. Within two months the Commission released their proposals for the political guidelines for future EU development policy (and, coincidentally, a report on the reform of the management of external assistance). The priority given to this review by Commissioner Nielson was indicative of the EU's acknowledgement that the status quo could not continue. If adopted and implemented the reforms could signal the most significant reformulation of development policy in the EU's history. Nielson was frank in his assessment of past EU development policy that had suffered from 'over-rigid procedures, too little flexibility on the ground and a slowness to respond compared to the best donors'. In his view, the Commission's aid system was 'too complex and fragmented' and despite being the world's largest ODA donor the EU 'grossly under-exploited' its ability to influence development (*European Voice*, 23 March 2000, p. 1).

The key elements of the new policy guidelines were familiar: to define a coherent global approach that combined trade, aid and political dialogues; to increase the impact and quality of the EU's development role internationally by seeking greater complementarity with the policies followed by the IMF, World Bank and OECD; and, at the core, a renewed commitment to fighting poverty and raising the standard of living of the poor. These policy objectives were informed by, and consistent with, those outlined at Maastricht: the alleviation of poverty and reintegrating the developing world into the global economy. However, the Commission proposal was equally sanguine about the EU's responsibility to increase its efforts to assist the poor and its ability to do so everywhere. Consequently, Commissioner Nielson floated the idea of a future EU development approach 'that focuses its attention on a limited number of areas' (*IP*, 26 April 2000). EU activities would consequently be reduced or eliminated in some areas and core tasks would be identified where the EU offers a comparative advantage and added value in relation to poverty reduction. Six such core areas were identified:

1)   trade for development;
2)   regional integration and cooperation;
3)   macroeconomic policies linked to poverty reduction;
4)   food safety and sustainable development strategies;
5)   strengthening institutional capacity; and,
6)   good governance and the management of public affairs.

Crosscutting issues (such as gender, environment and human rights) were to be incorporated within each of these core activities.

In response to the criticisms presented by the European Parliament, NGOs, civil society, several member states as well as those drawn from the EU's own experience and review of its development policy, new guidelines were proposed (Commission, 2000c). First, it was recognized that a greater degree of 'ownership' of the development process was needed that facilitated participation by civil society and the poor in third countries. Second, despite successive treaty objectives, still greater coordination was needed between the development policies promoted by EU, member state and multilateral agencies. Similarly, internal policy contradictions between development objectives and other EU policy sectors (such as trade or agriculture) still had to be reduced. And lastly, further institutional and procedural reforms were needed to simplify and speed-up the delivery of development policy output. Clearly, many of these problems were familiar and their continued presence confirmed that treaty objectives in themselves are inadequate responses. What was equally clear was that development reform would be an ongoing process and one likely to dominate the Development portfolio for the entire five-year term of the Prodi Commission.

The subsequent Development Council meeting of May 2000 examined both these and other topics and in general all member states reacted positively to endorse the Commission's new guideline proposals. Not surprisingly, the Council affirmed poverty reduction as the overarching objective of the suggested new EU policy and the emphasis on Europe's comparative advantage. It was agreed that a definitive Council position on the new policy framework would be taken under the French presidency at the November 2000 Development Council meeting. It was noted, however, that further steps were needed to increase complementarity between EU and member-state development policies. The continuing problems of EU–member state coordination were again noted and the aim of greater consultation and complementarity remained unfulfilled. A greater role for the EU in promoting macroeconomic reforms in the ACP, Latin America and Asia consistent with structural adjustment was advocated. In particular, the Council called on the Commission to focus on such policies that reduce poverty, to promote regional integration and continue to encourage the creation of free trade areas with the EU (Development Council, 2000, p. 9).

The initial reaction of development NGOs was cautious. The Liaison Committee of European Development NGOs (representing some 900 development groups) concluded that despite adopting the language of poverty reduction, the EU approach is 'essentially palliative, relies excessively on the market and does not challenge structural economic and social injustice' (*European Voice*, 27 April 2000). Others questioned whether the EU could break with its tradition of defining development priorities largely on the basis of internal EU considerations and external

policy motivations. As noted in the Introduction, colonial legacies and different phases of enlargement had largely dictated the
shape of development policy, and compromises and trade-offs
had produced the current confusion on policy and regional priorities. Despite the Commission's laudable intentions and rational approach, would the member states be willing to forgo their
individual preferences and regional interests for the greater
good? The decision of the Council (in conjunction with the Parliament) will determine if any change in policy will occur. As
the history of all EU policy sectors has shown, changing the
status quo is usually a slow and incremental process: radical
reforms – such as those suggested by Nielson – were often
diluted by competing member-state interests. To reverse this tendency it has been suggested that greater local ownership of
policy implementation and the involvement of civil society are
essential, together with measures to monitor and assess the practical effect on EU policy. Critics of the reform have also pointed
to the continuing divided responsibility for development within
the Commission. For the non-ACP parts of the developing
world it was Patten's office that shaped policy. External Relations set the budget proposals for Latin America and Asia;
consequently, some argue that the reorganization of the
Commission has only served further to marginalize the political
authority of DGVIII. Despite Nielson's appointment as overall
Commissioner for Development, in practice he is 'an emperor
without clothes' (Stocker, 2000, p. 14).

To coincide with this review of EU development policy, the
Commission also issued a critical report on reforming the management of external assistance. This review was, in part, a
response to the allegations of fraud and mismanagement made
by the 1999 Committee of Independent Experts, and in part an
obligation made by the Development Commissioner to the
European Parliament during the confirmation hearings for the
new Commission. The EU had evolved into a major actor in
development assistance. Collectively, the EU and the member
states now account for 55 per cent of all international ODA
(with the Commission alone responsible for 10 per cent) and is
the leading humanitarian aid donor. Unlike the majority of the
EU's internal policy areas, external aid is directly managed by
the Commission and accounts for 62 per cent of the budget of
all such programmes directly managed by the Commission. Its

value in 2000 was €9.6 billion (comprised of €5.3 billion from the EU budget and €4.3 billion from the EDF) (Commission, 2000c, p. 4). The creation of the SCR in 1998 was a response, but an inadequate one, to this emerging coordination problem. As already noted, bureaucratic improvements or adequate administrative resources did not match the growth in value and scope of external relations assistance. Nor was there an effective distinction between the responsibilities of the SCR and the geographic-based DGs. Consequently, it became a priority for the new Commission to overhaul what had become a dysfunctional system facing a crisis situation.

The Commission's own analysis concluded that: 'performance has deteriorated over time to the point of undermining the credibility of its (EU) external policies and the international image of the EU' (Commission, 2000c, p. 5). The report summarized the shortcomings under the following headings:

- *Staff shortages.* Whereas the volume of EU aid had increased by a factor of 2.8 between 1989 and 1999, staff levels only increased by 1.8 times, creating an estimated shortfall of 1300 management staff positions. The decision to adopt the Technical Assistance Offices subcontracting system to bridge this gap and the resultant lack of accountability was one of the major critical findings in the Committee of Independent Experts investigation.
- *Weakened control of implementation of aid.* The Committee was also scathing in its review of implementation and monitoring. The enormous increase in project approvals and legal bases for action completely undermined the Commission's ability to monitor the financial and political control of its implementation of aid.
- *Slow implementation and weak programming.* The average delay in the disbursement of committed funds had reached a staggering 4.5 years by the end of 1999 resulting in a cumulative backlog of commitments worth €20 billion. The EU's rigid annual budget cycle was largely to blame. In addition, complementary programming strategies between the Commission and the member states continued to be ineffective.
- *Fragmentation of administrative structures.* From 1984–97 the number of Directorate Generals involved in external relations trebled from two to six. Consequently, staff expertise

has been dispersed and the lines of responsibility between the DGs involved progressively blurred. (Commission, 2000c, pp. 5–6).

Whilst autonomous in its recommendations as well in the motivation for producing an external assistance report, the proposed reforms are consistent with the wider reorganization proposals developed by the Prodi Commission. The report on the reform of the management of external assistance, prepared by the SCR, outlined a series of main objectives. First, to reduce substantially the time needed to implement policies (down to 18 months from the current average of three years). Second, to improve the quality and responsiveness of project management. Third, to develop robust management procedures consistent with international standards: and fourth, to improve the impact and visibility of EU aid. To facilitate this the SCR was again reformed and enlarged. As noted above, of particular importance was the recognition – for the first time – that the EU should not attempt to perform all development tasks, but rather identify core areas. As the report acknowledged, the Commission cannot 'expect to achieve excellence in all areas of cooperation. It must concentrate its scarce staff resources first of all on a limited number of key policy areas' (Commission, 2000c, p. 8). In addition, the report favoured allowing greater cost-effective devolution of programme management in order to 'place the country in the driving seat' wherever adequate national structures permit.

Under the heading of 'an ambitious reform programme' the report advocated six linked elements that needed to be implemented coherently and as a whole as a single strategy. If implemented, these initiatives could radically alter the implementation of EU development policy over the next five years. The contents of the report can be summarized as follows (pp. 11–24).

First, a radical overhaul and unification in the programming of external assistance was called for. Echoing previous calls for coordination and coherence, it was emphasized yet again that all strands of EU policy – and those of other agencies – need to be taken into account when determining the right 'policy-mix' for each country. To facilitate this a new small, expert, interdepartmental 'Quality Support Group' – answerable directly to the external relations Commissioners collectively – was suggested and given the task of monitoring the consistency and quality of programming.

Second, a return to reunification of the project cycle – from start to completion – was identified. There are normally six stages within a project cycle (programming, identification, appraisal, financial decision, implementation and evaluation). Previously, different groups were responsible for different stages making overall supervision difficult. The new structure would see the various geographic DGs only responsible for programming decisions, and the remainder of the project cycle under the control of a new implementing body to succeed the SCR. Around 80 per cent of EU assistance programmes will be covered by this procedure. The major exception to this will be ECHO, which will retain full management of the project cycle for humanitarian actions, and programmes that demand modification because of specific and unusual factors.

Third, as noted above, the programming reforms required the creation of a new office in charge of project implementation to replace the SCR. The final form of such an office (which subsequently became known as Europeaid) remained open and the possibility of it operating external to the Commission has been mooted. A more robust administrative structure is fundamental to improving the delivery of EU development assistance. The report actually threatens that without such a staffing change the volume of EU aid programmes run by the Commission could fall to as low as one third of 1999 levels.

Fourth, greater devolution of project management to EU delegations (now represented in 128 countries) was called for, requiring the successor of the SCR to deploy staff locally rather than be exclusively Brussels-based. As Nielson commented: 'No development co-operation at arms' length will ever be effective. The Commission is now seriously trying to get geared to put its ear to the ground and listen' (*IP*, 2000b, p. 3). Clearly, delegations will see their staffing levels change favouring those operating in developing countries. As EU delegations fall under the control of Commissioner Patten, this realignment should be relatively easily achieved. Similarly, where sufficient procedures and safeguards exist, devolution may be extended to national authorities in partner countries.

Fifth, the report was aware that whilst successful administrative change involves procedural and structural reform, these in themselves are not sufficient. The promotion of a new common administrative culture throughout is essential. And lastly, to confirm the importance of this new approach and to answer those critics who called for the EU to match its rhetoric by practice, a package of urgent measures was outlined. Of greatest symbolic importance was the decision to clear the backlog of commitments some of which predate even the Santer Commission (see above).

The words of Commissioner Patten underline the importance with which this reform initiative is viewed:

> This reform will radically transform the way the Commission manages external assistance programmes. It will restore its credibility as a foreign policy actor in one major field of external EU action . . . It fulfils my commitment made at the European Parliament's confirmation hearing to expedite the reform of European external assistance management. This is a common effort of all Commissioners with responsibility in external relations fields. (*IP*, 2000b, p. 1)

Of course, the fact that these are the words of the Commissioner responsible for External Relations and not those of the Commissioner for Development point to possibly a continuing administrative, managerial and political challenge faced by the EU's policy towards the developing world. It remains to be seen whether these year 2000 reform proposals and 'the common effort of all Commissioners' will be a sufficient response, and whether the EU's external relations can ultimately exchange its traditional cacophony of voices for the clarity and direction of a single harmony.

ECHO: the European Community Humanitarian Office

The earliest attempt to differentiate between the different functions performed by the EU in external aid was the creation of ECHO in 1992. The objective was a familiar one – to establish an effective organizational structure and to make the EU more visible. ECHO was introduced at a time when the EU was undergoing one of its periodic attempts to undertake a *saut qualitif* in the level of integration. Although neither ratified nor fully implemented until November 1993, the political decision to create a European Union had already been taken at the inter-governmental level at Maastricht. The development of the CFSP, Economic and Monetary Union (EMU) and 'the hour of Europe' in the former Yugoslavia cumulatively presented the oppor-tunity for the EU to redefine itself as an international actor and to assume a central role in the post-Soviet Union power vacuum. The demands for greater and more frequent humanitarian interventions presented the fledgling EU with an obvious and practical opportunity to put these ambitions to the test. Circumstances, of course, were influential and the post-1989 geopolitical world could not be ignored. Disasters – both natural and man-made – in Bangladesh, Eastern Europe, Albania and Yugoslavia, for example, demanded a better response internationally. In many cases, the then existing Euro-pean administrative structures and emergency aid arrangements were inadequate for this new and evolving context. Conse-quently, for both internal and external reasons, the creation of ECHO is best seen as an aspect of Europe's general attempt to become an international actor and to take responsibility for improving the capacity and coordination of all international agencies to respond.

At the time of its introduction, many development specialists were critical of the administrative and policy dichotomy. EU development policy remained governed by the Commission DGs, whereas humanitarian assistance became the exclusive domain of ECHO. It was argued, with some justification, that humanitarian assistance was more effective when it formed part of, rather than was divorced from, a wider and longer-term development policy approach. Indeed, this administrative and policy separation seemed implicitly inconsistent with the Maastricht goals of complementarity, coherence and coordina-tion in development policy in general. These concerns notwith-standing, ECHO was a much-needed response to the pre-1992 fragmented implementation structure. Humanitarian aid had been administered by a number of different Commission DGs, often involving different legal bases and budget lines. In essence the EU perspective was focused more on acting as a funding agent rather than on the actual implementation process, dimin-ishing the 'visibility' of the EU as an aid participant. As ECHO itself argued, previously Europe had not directly administered humanitarian aid and had acted more as a banker than a partner. ECHO was created to change this perception: however, as experience of the 1990s has shown, monitoring and effective implementation are two distinct processes prone to a wide range of practical and administrative problems.

The administrative separation of ECHO was reflected in the original decision not to include this new portfolio within any existing DG. Thus from inception under the Delors Commission till the resignation of the Santer Commission in 1999 the Commissioner for Development (first Marin, followed by Pinheiro) was not responsible for ECHO. Between 1995 and 1999 ECHO was the sole responsibility of a single Commissioner, Emma Bonino. Only under the Prodi Commission was it decided to reincorporate ECHO under the control of the Development Commissioner. This original autonomy reflected a belief that the immediate needs of humanitarian aid were qualitatively and procedurally different from the more enduring policy perspectives demanded by development in general. The fact that after seven years' experience the decision was reversed suggests that the original dichotomy may well have been false and that the costs involved in applying a longer-term perspective are outweighed by the benefits of coordination. Of course, having a single Commissioner and dedicated staff did help to identify and distinguish initially the unique function of ECHO. This autonomy was also useful in enhancing the EU's capacity to take direct action as well as mobilize personnel and resources. Its independence was also a useful characteristic in coordinating EU-level humanitarian action and those operated bilaterally by the member states and other international agencies. The demands placed on ECHO were also unique within the typical Commission structure. Whereas other DGs had comparatively stable environments (in terms of financial commitments, policy development and project implementation), the very nature of humanitarian assistance demanded a less predictable context within which ECHO had to operate. For example, ECHO funds amounting to €764 million were spent in 1994 whereas in 1996 the level of commitment was €441 million (van Reisen, 1999, p. 52). Furthermore, the type of activity varied significantly from year to year with different emphases on refugee assistance, famine and food assistance, and disaster relief for example.

TABLE 3.1 *ECHO organizational structure, 2000*

Group	Responsibility
Commission	Commissioner Nielson (Development and Humanitarian Aid)
ECHO unit 1	ACP countries
ECHO unit 2	Central and Eastern European countries; NIS countries
ECHO unit 3	Asia, Latin America, Mediterranean and the Middle East
ECHO unit 4	General affairs; relations with EU institutions, donors and international organizations; disaster preparedness; crisis support; statistics.
ECHO unit 5	Human resources; training and NGO contractual relations
ECHO unit 6	Finances; auditing

Source: http://.europa.eu.int/comm/echo/en/present/who2_en.html

The Prodi Commission reorganization saw ECHO loose its own separate Commissioner and responsibility is now covered by the broader Development and Humanitarian Aid portfolio held by Poul Nielson. By Commission standards, ECHO currently operates with just a small administrative core in Brussels (114 people) with an additional staff of 70 experts in the field. The core structure is divided into three geographically based operational units and three management/strategy focused units (see Table 3.1). In mid-2000, field staff were operating in some 39 countries. The ACP states had the widest representation (18 countries), the CEECs/NIS 9 and the remaining 12 spread between Asia, Latin America, and the Middle East. However, the CEECs (as well as the countries of the former Yugoslavia) had the most intensive representation. There were five ECHO operations in Bosnia-Herzegovina alone (in Bihac, Banja Luka, Mostar, Sarajevo, Tuzia) two in Croatia (Knin and Zagreb) as well as the Federal Republic of Yugoslavia itself (http://europa.eu.int/comm/echo).

What then, are the exclusive tasks of ECHO and how are these distinct from the EU's other development initiatives? According to ECHO, its mandate from the EU is 'to provide emergency assistance and relief to the victims of natural disasters or armed conflict outside the European Union. The aid intended to go directly to those in distress, irrespective of race, religion or political convictions' (http://europa.eu.int/comm/echo). This covers emergency humanitarian aid, emergency food aid, the mobilization of relief and personnel, disaster prevention and pre-paredness and the necessary coordination of funding and legal bases for action. A 1996 Council regulation (EC 1257/96) described ECHO's mandate in the following terms:

- To save and preserve human lives in natural and man-made disasters during emergencies and their immediate aftermath;
- To provide the necessary assistance and relief to people affected by longer-lasting crises such as civil wars;
- To finance the delivery of aid and ensure that it benefits those for whom it is intended;
- To come to the aid of refugees and displaced persons in the country or region where they are, and help them re-settle when they return home;
- To conduct short-term rehabilitation and reconstruction operations to help victims recover a minimum of self-sufficiency, *taking account where possible of any long-term development objectives*; and,
- To prepare for disasters, in particular by setting up early warning systems and financing prevention measures in high-risk regions. (http://europa.eu.int/comm/echo) [my emphasis].

Related activities cover activities such as feasibility studies, monitoring humanitarian projects, the training of specialists and the coordination of disaster prevention measures, anti-personnel mine clearance operations, as well as the pervasive function of raising European public awareness about humani-tarian issues and the EU's leading international role. As noted above, the core legal base for these activities is Council Regu-lation 1257/96: this is supported by a further 1996 Council Reg-ulation (2258/96) and Commission Communication (COM(96) 153). In addition to setting out the framework for ECHO's activities, the first 1996 Regulation also established the Human-itarian Aid Committee (see below). The second 1996 Regula-tion addressed the need to undertake emergency aid rehabilitation and reconstruction projects in developing countries that were consistent with broader development policy operations. Similarly, the Commission Communication drew attention to the need for coordination between relief activities, rehabilitation and development between ECHO and other branches of the Commission. In addition, Article 254 in past Lomé Conventions, Article 72 in the Cotonou Partnership Agreement and a number of European Council Declarations have extended the scope and basis for EU humanitarian action.

Unlike the trade and assistance relationships governed by formal agreements such as Lomé, importantly ECHO assistance does not employ political or economic conditionality. Aid is given only on the basis of emergency need. In the words of a Development Council statement, the EU's principles are that

> humanitarian aid, the sole aim of which is to prevent or relieve human suffering, is accorded to victims without discrimination on the grounds of race, ethnic group, religion, sex, age, nationality or political affiliation and must not be guided by, or subject to, political considerations and that humanitarian aid decisions must be taken impartially and solely according to the victims' needs and interests. (Development Council, 2000, p. 14)

Over the 1990s the level of ECHO aid matched that of the member states' bilateral aid, and the EU (ECHO and member state contributions together) has become the largest humanitarian aid donor in the world. In 1991 the value of EU aid was just 195.3 million ecus; as Figure 3.1 demonstrates, EU aid has more typically been in excess of 600 million ecus. The bulk (around 85 per cent) of this assistance is channelled through the EU's donor partners rather than dispersed directly by ECHO. The partners include UN agencies and a wide range of NGOs (see Figure 3.2). Two UN agencies (predominantly the High Commission for Refugees followed by the World Food Programme), and various national Red Cross agencies are by far the most important individual partners, although a greater percentage of funds are spread among numerous NGOs. Since 1993 ECHO has operated a Framework Partnership Agreement that provides a standard contractual basis for assessing partner humanitarian organizations. As of 1999, 182 partner organizations had been vetted and approved through this process.

FIGURE 3.1 ECHO's 20 main partners in 2000

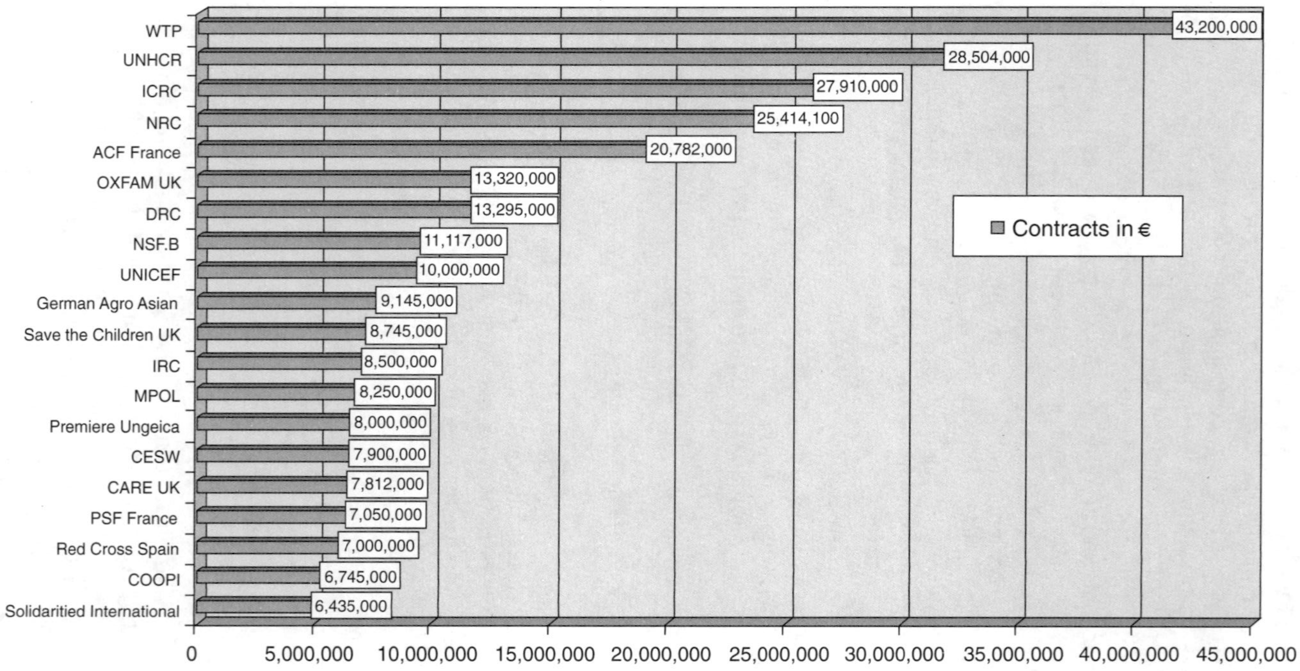

Partner	Contracts in €
WTP	43,200,000
UNHCR	28,504,000
ICRC	27,910,000
NRC	25,414,100
ACF France	20,782,000
OXFAM UK	13,320,000
DRC	13,295,000
NSF.B	11,117,000
UNICEF	10,000,000
German Agro Asian	9,145,000
Save the Children UK	8,745,000
IRC	8,500,000
MPOL	8,250,000
Premiere Ungeica	8,000,000
CESW	7,900,000
CARE UK	7,812,000
PSF France	7,050,000
Red Cross Spain	7,000,000
COOPI	6,745,000
Solidaritied International	6,435,000

Source: http://Europa.eu.int/comm/echo/en/stat/statistics3.htm

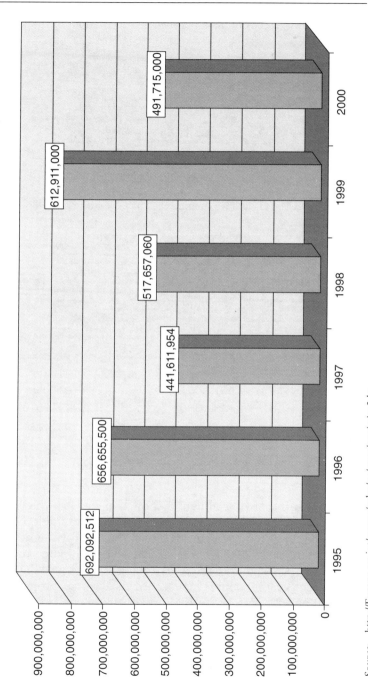

FIGURE 3.2   Financial decisions for EC humanitarian aid 1995–2000 (amounts in €)

Source: http://Europa.eu.int/comm/echo/en/stats/statistics3.htm

FIGURE 3.3   Trends in main beneficiaries of ECHO aid, 1996–98

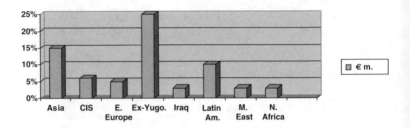

FIGURE 3.4   ECHO's main types of expenditure, 1998

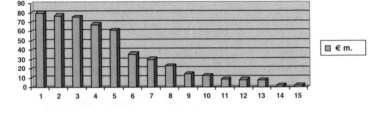

Key: 1 = Personnel   2 = Emergency rehabilitation   3 = Transport
     4 = Food products   5 = Sanitary products   6 = Others
     7 = Water sanitation   8 = First aid products   9 = Other services
     10 = Reserve   11 = Agriculture   12 = Training
     13 = Temporary shelter 14 = Visibility programme   15 = Distribution costs

Source: http//europa.eu.int/comm/echo/en/stats/chiff_en.html

The most recent official figures show that in 1998 the value of aid contracts approved by ECHO totalled 558.5 million ecus comprised of 1366 different projects. Not surprisingly, the largest share of ECHO contracts has consistently gone to the former Yugoslavia and to the ACP. Taking 1998 as an example, 32 per cent of the value of aid contracts went to projects in the ACP and 25 per cent to the former Yugoslavia (see Figure 3.3). The main types of expenditure (given in Figure 3.4) were personnel, rehabilitation, transport, food and sanitation costs, which collectively accounted for roughly 70 per cent of the budget allocation.

The creation of the Humanitarian Aid Committee (composed of the ECHO and member state representatives) in 1996 was an important innovation dedicated to improving the central coordination of aid between donors. Whenever the Commission approves an emergency aid operation valued between €2 million and €10 million, the member states must now be notified in writing within 48 hours. Where appropriate, ECHO drafts a 'global plan' for strategic action for a particular crisis or region with the objective of coordinating ECHO's strategy with those of other donors – the member states and the wider international donor community – which is then subject to Humanitarian Aid Committee review and approval. This centralized attempt to promote complementarity and coordination is also reflected in the field: routinized and systematic procedures have been introduced to facilitate the regular exchange of information between all donor agencies. Conversely, the member states have agreed to use a uniform 14-point reporting system to inform ECHO of new bilateral aid initiatives. This information is also circulated via the Internet to all concerned within 48 hours. The cumulative database on member state and ECHO aid is an invaluable tool in realizing cooperation and effective complementarity.

The EU currently provides in the region of 30 per cent of global humanitarian aid, with the member states providing a further 25 per cent. Since its inception, ECHO has been responsible for dispersing more than €4 billion. How, then, is the aid budget managed? There are three elements to ECHO's financial basis. First, funds are provided directly through the normal annual EU budget process that requires the Council and the European Parliament to approve or amend the Commission's proposal. Budget Chapter B7–21 covers humanitarian aid; under this heading five geographical or thematic areas are specified. Second, the European Development Fund can be accessed (under Article 254 of Lomé and Article 72 of the Partnership Agreement). Third, there is provision for an emergency aid reserve (introduced at the 1992 European Council meeting). This latter procedure is an essential element in the EU's ability to respond quickly to unforeseen crises and can involve significant additional funding beyond that provided in the budget. For example, the amount released from emergency aid reserve in 1999 was an additional €346 million. The accompanying Table 3.2 summarizes the allocation from the budget and EDF resources for 1998 and 1999.

TABLE 3.2   *ECHO expenditure by source of funding, 1998, 1999*

Funding basis	Ecu m. 1998	Ecu m. 1999*
EDF – Lomé IV Article 254	37.38	50.00
General EU budget line		
B7-210: aid, including emergency food aid for populations in all developing countries suffering disasters or serious crises	283.09	162.8
B7-214: Humanitarian aid for CEEC populations	135.10	98.00
B7-215: Humanitarian aid for populations of NIS and Mongolia	37.04	45.00
B7-217: Operations to help refugees, displaced persons and returnees	17.04	18.00
B7-219: Operational support and disaster preparedness	8.00	7.00
TOTAL	**517.66**	**380.85**

Note: * = provisional.
Source: http://.europa.eu.int/comm/echo/l

ECHO can either finance the full cost of an operation or enter into co-financing arrangements with other donors. Support is not subject to discriminatory conditionality and the duration is set only by the circumstances of each case. The type of activity varies considerably and as noted above can cover mine clearance schemes, medical services and supplies, food relief, construction of housing or shelters, infrastructural reconstruction, transport, logistical support and so on. Training schemes in humanitarian operations can also be funded, as are information campaigns to raise European awareness of humanitarian issues and relief. ECHO funded 19 such European awareness campaigns in 1999. Past practice has occasionally found the monitoring of projects less than perfect. However, in the wake of the 1999 inquiry into Commission malpractice, ECHO monitoring procedures have been tightened. Council Regulation 1257/96 requires the regular evaluation of aid operations to determine their efficiency, whether objectives have been met as well as to help improve future practice. ECHO has increased its expertise in programme evaluation considerably, although critics can point to both the difficulty of measuring the success of aid and to the costs involved in pre-, ongoing and post-evaluation schemes. However, the use of EU budget monies demands public accountability through such measures – although costly – and their vigorous and comprehensive application cannot be avoided.

In summary, ECHO's function and performance has been subject to considerable review since 1999 – including independent evaluations as well as the Commission's own analysis. The May 2000 Development Council meeting addressed these reports. Whilst it concluded that 'the existence of ECHO has been and remains amply justified' and provided at least as efficient and cost-effective humanitarian aid as any other international organization, there were areas where improvements were needed (Development Council, 2000, p. 13). Criticism included the choice of partners, coordination, gender dimensions of aid, assessment procedures and responsiveness. However, it was acknowledged that ECHO can only fund projects and relies on partners in the field for implementation who should share the responsibility for any perceived failures.

More constructively, a series of recommendations were proposed. These included: developing a better EU emergency response capacity, particularly for natural disasters; increasing 'visibility' of EU action; further enhancing coordination particularly through improvements to the Humanitarian Aid Committee; and, linking relief and development objectives more effectively. The previous dichotomy between a strategic long-term approach to development policy and the more immediate humanitarian emergency relief had created a grey zone where coordination and sustainability were occasionally compromised. Assistance, in fact, is better viewed as a continuum linking ECHO's emergency relief and rehabilitation functions with the phasing-in of other Commission strategies and policies. This so-called 'linking relief, rehabilitation and development' approach together with a revised ECHO mission statement was the subject of a further Commission communication in July 2000.

Conclusion

As the discussion of the administrative reforms of 1999–2000 illustrated, effective development policy requires a strengthened bureaucratic capacity. The evolution of the EU's development administration, especially under Santer, failed to match increased scope with administrative capacity. Whilst the Prodi Commission has displayed an awareness and concern for the problem, it remains to be seen if the recent administrative reforms have provided a sufficient panacea. If they have not, then the inadequacies of past development policy implementation look likely to be repeated and even compounded.

Turning to ECHO, it is reasonable overall to regard the experience as a success. The funds that the EU now devote to humanitarian aid are larger than those of the member states and ECHO has extended the EU's 'civilian' external presence globally. No international actor or agency is without defects, but under the new 1999 Commission reorganization ECHO has been responsive to adapting its processes and procedures to make EU aid more effective, complementary and coordinated. This expanding international role bolsters the *communautaire* nature of Europe's development policy and has successfully replaced bilateral action as the more important focus. This evolution is, of course, in stark contrast to the mixed intergovernmental emphasis that continues to define EU–ACP relationships and frustrates scholars who look for unmuddied characterizations of the EU's international actor status. This uneasy conglomeration of competences, decision-making styles and motivations does, however, reflect the reality of the EU's external presence for the developing world. Any change is more likely to reflect the outcome of the integration debate within the EU itself, than any new consensus on the optimal approach to development policy. The importance of understanding the multilevel governance issues within the integration process is fundamental to understanding the present and predicting the future (see the concluding chapter in this book for a discussion of these theoretical issues). Whilst EMU and CFSP have seen the tide towards a *communautaire* approach to external relations becoming the dominant (if not exclusive) focus, it lies with a future IGC to extend the EU's legal competences even further. Until such a treaty reform is undertaken, mixed competences will continue to define the fragmented elements of Europe's development policy.

Chapter 4

Complementarity and Conditionality: Evaluating Good Governance

This chapter addresses two broad conceptual issues: first, the introduction of the principle of complementarity guiding the internal organization of European policy; and second, the application of conditionality – both political and economic – in the EU's relations with the developing world. Whilst the commentary is intentionally generalized, much of the empirical evidence is drawn from the Lomé Conventions. To that extent Lomé provides a reflection of the EU's more general global approach: what is proposed in agreements with Asia or Latin America, for example, usually originates in the discussions previously held with the ACP. The application of Lomé – latterly Cotonou – is also useful as it provides the most comprehensive EU perspective dealing (as it has since 2000) with 77 ACP states in total.

Political conditionality has become one of the most disputed policy areas between the EU and the developing countries. European demands for greater accountability by recipient countries have seen the introduction of a series of related principles applied and evaluated – good governance, democracy, human rights and the rule of law in particular. Economic conditionality has a longer history and is drawn from an international rather than specifically European agenda. The definition, application and evaluation of these concepts, however, remain contentious. In addition to these externally imposed EU criteria, the Union has also set itself a performance agenda to enhance the delivery of European development policy. The notion of complementarity (and the related ones of coordination, coherence and consistency) has come to dominate EU development policy, albeit with mixed success. This chapter examines both the external imposition of political and economic conditionalities by the EU and its own internal requirements effectively to mesh EU-level and member state bilateral policies. In both these internal and external spheres the results have been mixed.

Complementarity

Writing in the early 1990s, Grilli in his seminal work on European development policy, summarized Europe's disappointing experience of constructing a common development approach in the following terms:

> Despite the progress achieved, Europeanization of development aid is still nowhere in sight . . . Multilateralization of EC aid, the most direct route to Europeanization of external assistance . . . failed to reach decisive results. Less direct forms of Europeanization of aid, from making assistance practices more homogeneous among EC members to the establishment of more common aid objectives among EC partners, have not advanced much either. After a promising start, this process seems to have slowed down to the point where progress is hardly discernible. (1993, p. 74)

With the notable exception of Lomé, Europe's presence as a development actor remained fragmented, *ad hoc* and fundamentally bilateral. If somewhat tentatively, for more than two decades the Commission had been calling for some form of coordination. By the end of the 1980s the Council did endorse this position at least with respect to the ACP states and Structural Adjustment Programmes (SAPs). The endorsement, however, continued to reflect member state sensitivities. Existing bilateral autonomy in development aid was maintained and no precise remedy was advocated beyond 'an exchange of views and information . . . to increase consistency and convergence between the approach of the Commission and the member states at all levels' (Council, 1989, p. 118).

It was at the Maastricht IGC that this deficiency was finally addressed at treaty level by incorporating the principle of complementarity as a policy objective. Only since 1993 has this principle – in theory – become a key aspect of EU policy in general, as well as in the development sphere in particular. At one level the principle is simple enough: the Treaty requires the Commission and the individual member states to work in tandem so as to produce policies that neither duplicate each other, nor more seriously, promote contradictory objectives. However, the actual translation of principle into practice has typically been less easily achieved.

In part, the origin of the problem lies with the Commission. The decade in which Jacques Delors was Commission President was characterized by a rapidly expanding role for the Commission and an implicit federal and harmonization agenda. During the Maastricht debates the Commission clearly saw the principle of complementarity to its advantage and envisioned member state development policies eventually becoming aligned with a common EU policy. In a sense, this was in keeping with the Commission's preferred view on subsidiarity – that the centre was the natural level for policy implementation not the member states. Such a perspective was, of course, bound to conflict with a number of member states and the Council's response was to reassert the importance and autonomy of bilateral development policy to some degree. As was the case with other innovative aspects of the TEU, pragmatism as much as ideology guided practice; it soon became apparent that the Commission's more ambitious agenda was politically unacceptable. Consequently, an emphasis on coordination was substituted to promote complementarity. This compromise has only been partially successful.

Defining appropriate policy spheres for the EU that are distinct from those of the member states has been particularly fraught and complex. In particular, the process can present implicit threats to the Commission's legitimate sphere of authority as well as have serious budgetary consequences. Critics maintain that the nature of European development assistance remains typically '15 + 1' with the Commission either filling in the gaps or simply duplicating the roles and initiatives operated by the member states. However, others have argued for the EU's comparative advantage and defined specific roles that add value at the EU level. These include, for example, the EU's greater economic and political neutrality; its ability to marshal greater amounts of financial assistance than any single bilateral programme; its greater choice of agencies for implementing of aid; a greater geographic spread of aid; and the longer-term security and predictability offered by assistance through programmes such as Lomé (Bossuyt *et al.*, 1999, p. 6). A core issue for member states, however, is the financial implications of this choice. Should funding be primarily directed through bilateral programmes or through EU-level initiatives? In the context of shrinking aid and development budgets there is little possibility of additional monies being allocated, just the decision of which mechanism to use to achieve policy goals.

The logic of bureaucratic self-interest – and survival – is a powerful one. Consequently, whilst there has been some progress towards implementing this principle since 1993, competing political and bureaucratic factors have often conspired to moderate its effect. As one recent analysis concluded, 'complementarity still appears to be a political slogan rather than a practical reality' (Bossuyt *et al.*, 1999, p. 1). For third country recipients, the added complexity and administrative costs associated with this multiplication of delivery agents can be considerable and result in a less than optimal use of EU and member state resources.

One example that can be used to illustrate the problems of achieving complementarity is in relation to poverty reduction – the EU's key development objective. In a study undertaken by the European Centre for Development Policy Management the application of complementarity during the first five years following the implementation of the TEU was assessed. Four major weaknesses were identified that outweighed the gains made through increased consultation and an exchange of information and learning between the Commission and the Council. First, it was found that the control of policy remained a top-down excessively centralized approach. Second, the sequencing and linkages between different poverty reduction policies were found to be lacking. In particular, Council resolutions on implementing complementarity seemed to have little influence in modifying the member state-level policy. Third, the EU actors remained largely divided in the level of commitment to the principle of complementarity and suspicious of the role it played in the wider political agenda between the Commission and the Council. Lastly, it was concluded that complementarity was largely a one-way street. The presumption was – on the part of the member states – that it was the Commission's role to ensure that EU policies became complementary to bilateral policies, not vice versa (Bossuyt *et al.*, 1999, pp. 12–13).

Looking to the future, there are a number of indications that the EU has recognized that a more effective and meaningful implementation of complementarity is needed and that improvements must be made. In part, the pressures for change have come from the awareness that sustainable development is enhanced by such collective action and the practical necessity to provide aid donors with value for money. More specifically, because both the EU and member states have considerably expanded their development priorities and interaction with civil society, often their ability to administer and implement such a wide range of programmes individually is compromised. Indeed, one of the main thrusts of the investigation into administrative malpractice (which led to the resignation of the Santer Commission in 1999) was that the Commission, in particular, had increased its areas of activity without having the necessary human resources to do so effectively. Cooperation based on complementarity may provide a remedy to this shortcoming. The possibility for enhanced capacity and capability within the Prodi Commission is remote in the post-Santer political climate. Alternatively, and more radically, recent reforms have called for the EU to replace its centralized bureaucratic approach to development in favour of decentralizing decision-making to local offices. Such a move would be in keeping with an emphasis on 'local ownership' of development initiatives – but contrary to the Commission's own bureaucratic self-interest.

Perhaps the most compelling rationale for emphasizing the importance of complementarity, however, is derived from the EU's own self-image and ambition. The words of the 1981 *London Report on Political Co-operation* that first called for Europe to become a significant international actor and to shape and not merely respond to international events has been at the heart of the EU's external relations ever since. Undoubtedly, a more effective EU presence could be established in the international community if Commission and member-state activity benefited from greater complementarity. Such arguments involve the nature of the integration debate itself. And of course, the prospect of an enhanced role for the EU is antagonistic to those states that advocate a strictly intergovernmental agenda for Europe's future. As noted in the Introduction and developed in the Conclusion to this book, such macro-theoretical ideas have a direct impact upon the shape and future of EU development policy and can under some circumstances play a greater role than issues that are specifically developmental in nature. Conversely, the Commission may also regard enhanced complementarity with suspicion if it is used to re-nationalize aspects of development policy, reduce EU budgetary allocations and constrain the EU's external role. Quite how committed the various European actors are to enhancing complementarity and their underlying motivations for doing so, remain crucial questions for determining the future impact of an EU-level development policy.

As also noted in the Introduction to this book, EU policy-making in the 1990s established a number of additional general principles designed to support and promote complementarity: these were coordination, coherence and consistency. Coordination and coherence, like complementarity, were given legal recognition in the Maastricht Treaty, whereas the principle of consistency was subsequently incorporated in the Amsterdam Treaty of 1997. Collectively the introduction of these 'four Cs' was tantamount to recognition that previous policy frameworks had been inadequate: past experience had proved that the EU often faced profound difficulties in achieving effective policy collectively. Coordination provides a practical mechanism for enhancing complementarity. It focuses on coordinating the administrative actions of the member states, the Commission and recipient countries to maximize the effectiveness and execution of EU development policy. To bolster this trend, from Maastricht onwards the Council has issued a series of resolutions promoting this perspective covering development topics as diverse as gender, the environment conflict resolution, poverty, education and food aid (van Reisen, 1999, p. 230). The principle of coherence was introduced to ensure that all areas of EU policy are compatible with EU development objectives. This requirement was further enhanced by the addition of 'consistency', which involves linking all the EU's external activities (CFSP, economic and development) in a consistent and logical manner. Cumulatively, it is hoped that by operationalizing these principles effectively, the past experiences of contradictory policies being adopted either by different arms of the Commission or by member states can be avoided. If belatedly, policy-makers have come to appreciate that often decisions taken on matters to do with Europe's internal market, for example, can have unanticipated and unintended consequences for third countries outside the Union. An obvious example of this is the CAP:

changes to price support mechanisms can influence agricultural exports which in turn may impact significantly on certain developing country producers. The implications, however, are not just limited to agriculture but spread across a wide range of policies that are increasingly been determined at the EU rather than national level. This interpretation is consistent with both the multi-level governance and path dependency theoretical models discussed in the Conclusion. Of course, in practice the level of commitment to realizing complementarity, coordination and coherence depends ultimately on political will. It remains to be seen whether the ambitious intentions agreed to in resolutions and treaties are matched in practice. Agreeing on the need for consistent and coherent policies is not the same as changing national behaviour to achieve that goal. And even where there is an intention to make such changes, bureaucratic processes can be slow to respond. Consequently, despite the legal authority of the Maastricht and Amsterdam Treaties and numerous Council resolutions, inconsistencies and even contradictions are likely to persist in EU development policy for the foreseeable future.

Conditionality: good governance, democracy, human rights and rule of law

Conditionality can be dichotomized in a variety of ways: between political and economic aspects; internal and external supervision; or between positive and negative applications, for example. Conditionality can also be prescriptively explicit or general in its description, take legal or informal forms or be peculiarly 'European' and new in nature or derived from existing global standards and definitions. Political conditionality links rewards (such as a preferential trading agreement, aid or other forms of assistance) with both the expectation and the execution of policies in a third country that promote the goals of democracy, human rights, the rule of law and good governance. Economic conditionality is concerned with linking rewards to the adoption and promotion of specific macroeconomic policies (such as structural adjustment programmes, liberalization and free trade areas). Typically, both political and economic conditionality is externally monitored (by the EU) although in theory at least it is possible for the recipient states to perform this task through internal domestic mechanisms. Positive and negative forms of conditionality simply contrast promised benefits for future desired action with the threat of punitive sanctions where specific policy guidelines are violated (and such punishment is often automatically triggered). Explicit conditionality can prescribe in great detail the mechanism, form and outcome of a policy; alternatively, conditionality may just describe general outcomes and goals leaving the methods and policies used to realize these to individual choice (mirroring to some degree the distinction in EU law between regulations and directives). Typically, it is argued that to be effective conditionality must take a legal treaty-based form to enable actions to be justicible and visible: however, in the area of political conditionality informal expectations may in practice be equally effective. Finally, both political and economic conditionalities can either draw on approaches defined by international organizations that are universally recognized or create specific policies that apply to a particular context.

What has been the underlying rationale for conditionality? Obviously there is no single rationale promoting the EU's application of conditionality. A major influence has been the changing external political environment. The post-1989 democratization process within Eastern Europe provided the catalyst and convinced the European Parliament of the necessity for future EU international agreements to contain explicit guarantees to strengthen fledgling democracies. Significantly, the 1987 Single European Act had given the Parliament the power of veto in agreements with third countries and even prior to the fall of the Berlin Wall Parliament had sought to introduce human rights clause in a number of cases (Smith, 1998, p. 260). Up until that point, Europe's external relations had generally been noted for their apolitical content (Grilli, 1993, p. 102). Second, the original ambitions of the Maastricht Treaty were highly optimistic of Europe's international role. It was envisaged that the CFSP would result in the EU becoming a significant international actor and, as such, Europe would be well placed to shape international affairs. Consequently, the Treaty provided an explicit role and responsibility for the EU to promote global democracy and development. Article J.1 specified these as central objectives of EU foreign policy as expressed through the CFSP process: Article 130u specifically linked these political conditions to EU development policy. As a result, the 1990s saw the revised Lomé as well as new agreements with Latin America and Asia all include political conditionality as an 'essential' element (and by 1995 these agreements also had suspension clauses in cases of democratic and human rights violations [Smith, 1998, p. 264]). Third, it has become accepted wisdom that sustainable development can only result where there are secure and effective institutions that promote democracy and civil society. Experience had shown that economic conditionality was, by itself, inadequate. Thus, good governance, for example, has become a developmental prerequisite, not an optional extra. Fourth, many third countries have sought democratic conditionalities as a means for promoting and embedding domestic reforms. In part, the EU can be the umbrella under which domestic governments can protect human rights, the rule of law and democratic accountability more effectively than they can independently. Other states, of course, do not take such a sanguine view and regard conditionality as essentially inconsistent with sovereignty. Lastly, European public opinion has been influential in demanding the EU resources are effectively managed and not used to support authoritarian regimes.

Good governance

The concept of 'good governance' has only found a voice in the EU's development vocabulary since the 1990s. Its introduction – together with that of human rights, the rule of law and democracy – as a form of political conditionality, has progressively complemented the trade relations basis typical of earlier EU development policy. Thanks to a politically emerging European Parliament, reference to this principle has now become mandatory in all formal agreements between the Union and third countries – developed, developing and transitional. As is often the case, whilst the formal Treaty expression of the concept can be clearly defined, operationalizing the concept has proved to be less easily achieved in practice. What, then, does the EU understand by 'good governance' and is this interpretation shared by the developing world?

First, and importantly, good governance is a broad and inclusive idea that can be expressed through a variety of measures. It includes all aspects of the management of public affairs –

economic, political and administrative – and requires that such management be 'transparent, accountable, participatory and equitable' and 'encompasses every aspect of the state's dealings with civil society, its role in establishing a climate conducive to economic and social development and its responsibility for the division of resources' (*Dialogue*, 1999, p. 34). Central to this is a belief that good governance implies the establishment of competent and effective institutions consistent with democratic principles. Evidence of corruption is inconsistent with the principle. Article 5 of Lomé IV linked the principle of good governance to the goal of sustainable development, although it did not make it an essential element of the Convention (unlike, democracy, human rights and the rule of law, which were). The difficulty in measuring levels of 'good governance' no doubt precluded this: just how 'good' was good enough? Had the principle been an essential element it would have been subject to scrutiny and differentiation and used, where necessary, to justify sanctioning any state that failed to meet the EU-defined standard of good governance. It is this role of the EU as legislator, judge and jury of the principle that presents the greatest difficulty. A cynic might also point out that the EU's own standard of good governance is imperfect given the findings of corruption that led to the resignation of the Commission in 1999, or the election in Austria of an extreme-right coalition government. Either event in a vulnerable developing country could well have seen 'good governance' abrogated.

Nonetheless, there are a number of features that can be identified as indicators of good governance (although inevitably these overlap to some degree with general democratic principles). First, there is equity in administration and resource allocation that is guided and protected through an impartial application of law. Second, good governance depends upon the state possessing the capacity to administer and manage the allocation of resources effectively. No matter how good the intention, the capacity to act remains crucial. Third, transparency in decision-making, accountability and scrutiny are fundamental. And lastly, development decision-making should be open and participatory with accessible mechanisms whereby all members of civil society can be involved and informed (*Dialogue*, 1999, p. 35). The Cotonou Partnership Agreement that succeeded Lomé IV went to considerable lengths to define the elements legally – although once again these were not given the force of an 'essential element' (see Chapter 7).

Human rights, democracy and the rule of law

In assessing human rights the EU relies on internationally accepted universal principles enshrined in the UN Charter, the Universal Declaration of Human Rights and elsewhere. Clearly, human rights are fundamental to good governance. However, the EU's self-appointed role as sole adjudicator with respect to the developing countries is not without critics. In the Lomé Convention and the Cotonou Partnership Agreement, for example, the EU has an exclusive right to judge when human rights have been breached despite repeated calls by the ACP for the equivalent of an independent EU–ACP court to perform this function.

Respect for the law and the independence of the judicial system are again fundamental principles applied by the EU. Impartiality, equality before the law and the citizen's right to redress grievances form the 'essential' elements of all other EU-developing country relationships. In contrast to good governance, any breaches in these legal requirements are more readily recognizable. Assessing 'democracy' however, can be more problematic.

Democracy's security and development have become the new mantra for relations with the Third World. The new wisdom argues that only through democratic institutions and norms can economic development effectively be pursued. The obvious question is, of course, which form of democracy does this best? The nuances of democracy are almost boundless: to avoid becoming bemused by the labyrinth of this debate, the following basic elements are considered as the essential core around which a practical assessment of democratic behaviour can be measured. Democracy is a political system based on respect for the law, implying rights (including civil rights), where the rulers are accountable to the population who can through peaceful and accepted procedures change those leaders at periodic intervals. Democracy implies control of power through checks and balances. There is no one single constitutional framework that guarantees these conditions: legitimate democracies can, and do, take many forms. When defining and evaluating democratic procedures and 'good governance', Eurocentric myopia must be avoided. The challenge for the EU remains how best to judge democratic performance. At the simplest level the following aspects of civil rights are commonly considered as essential prerequisites to political rights. 'Freedom of communication and speech and writing, freedom of assembly and of petition, freedom to form associations and engage in peaceful protest, and freedom from arbitrary arrest and lawless punishment' (Engel cited in Hanf, 1999, p. 4).

Obviously, there are some extreme situations where it is relatively easy to agree that there have been serious breaches in democratic behaviour. *Coups*, such as the one that occurred in Fiji in mid-2000, for example, are the most easily identifiable. As the case of the Fijian *coup* discussed later in this chapter shows, however, determining an appropriate response within an acceptable timeframe can prove harder to achieve. Outside such crisis situations, regular elections offer the EU a basic and practical yardstick with which to measure 'democracy' and provide a mechanism through which conditionality can be successfully applied. Free and fair elections are clearly the leitmotif of democracies and increasingly election observation has become the recognized measure for assessing the quality of this democratic practice. However, election observation or monitoring – if it is to be of value – has to be regularized, comprehensive and employ rigorous criteria. *Ad hoc* and impressionistic stamps of approval are inadequate. Consequently, a precise methodology is required to secure 'a more substantial assessment of an election's democratic quality' (Hanf, 1999, p. 6). This will focus on every aspect of the election cycle from the drafting of the electoral law through to the final allocation of seats.

Prior to the creation of the CFSP, the EU had not been formally involved in election monitoring. Since late 1993, however, the EU has become increasingly active in election observation. Indeed since the Union's first monitoring experiences (in Russia and South Africa in 1993/4) the EU has become at least an equal partner with the UN in validating the 'free and fair' nature of elections in third countries. This change was in response to Treaty obligations to support the development of democracy globally, its own implicit agenda to become a major international actor, as well as a direct consequence of third countries demanding such a role from the EU in order to provide international credibility to their electoral processes. The EU is well suited to this role. Its varied membership makes it less likely to impose a single model of democracy as its assessment criterion. Practices within the Fifteen vary considerably, but are equally valid expressions of democratic election. Of course, the conduct of elections and this kind of quantifiable assessment forms only one aspect of the wider question of good governance. Its empirical nature makes it an appealing and useful indicator but not a complete measure. In crisis situations, however, the role of election monitoring plays a vital role – as the examples of South Africa and Zimbabwe discussed later in this chapter illustrate.

Economic conditionality: liberalization, structural adjustment and debt

The hallmark of current EU economic policy towards the developing world is an unquestioning commitment to the philosophy of trade liberalization. Based on the Maastricht Treaty conviction that development is fundamentally dependent upon reintegrating the developing countries into the world economy, the EU has increasingly turned to free trade as its preferred option. Often, the arguments as much resemble fanatical fervour as they do economic rationality. Essentially, whether the EU is acting within the WTO, bilaterally with any OECD state or with the developing worlds of Asia, Africa, Eastern Europe, Latin America or elsewhere, the philosophy is dominated by economic liberalization.

The prolonged and often acrimonious negotiations between the EU and South Africa during the late 1990s best illustrate this new catechism. Prior to 1995 all of Europe's relations with the developing world involved some degree of preferential concessions on the part of the EU. The most established and formalized of these relationships was the Lomé Convention, which – as we have seen in Chapter 1 – gave the ACP countries nonreciprocal access to the EU market for a range of goods and products. In general, the Lomé approach had typified EU behaviour towards the rest of the developing world. After its transition to full democracy and the election of President Mandela in 1995, South Africa opened a dialogue with the EU with the expectation that membership of Lomé – or at least a similar arrangement – would be the basis of the new relationship. What actually transpired was that the EU effectively insisted the economic relationship be based around a free trade area (FTA). Never before had the EU sought to make this the basis of its relations with any developing country. After some minor concessions, in 1999 an agreement was signed that committed both to establishing a free trade area, albeit over an asymmetrical time period extending over 12 years for South Africa. Free trade, however, is not an absolute notion from the EU's perspective. Specifically, the EU sought (successfully) to exclude the vast majority of agricultural goods from the agreement. The internal politics relating to the CAP were of greater significance than the soundly argued economic development arguments of Pretoria. Thus trade liberalization is not an equal partnership. The South Africa example was in many regards a test for the subsequent general application of this new economic philosophy by the EU. Consequently, it was unavoidable that FTAs became the focal point for the post-Lomé IV discussions of 1996–2000 and have come to characterize the new Cotonou Partnership Agreement.

In part, a free trade agenda has been a consistent theme throughout the EU's history: the novelty was its application to such widely disparate economies. FTAs were also seen as consistent with the EU's long-standing ideological support for regional integration. In a sense the agreement with South Africa was unique in that the FTA was bilateral. The EU's objective is rather to promote regional groupings – say the Pacific Island states, East Africa and so on – with which to formalize multilateral FTAs. Such an objective is internally driven, as the motivation behind the Union itself is the belief that regional integration is a better form of both political and economic organization. Consequently, the promotion of regional integration outside the EU is something that is impossible for the Union to oppose.

Bolstering this ideological commitment is the more practical argument of trade. As the world's largest trader (representing around 38 per cent of global exports), it is in the EU's direct self-interest to support the role of the WTO in regulating the global economy. As an open multilateral trading system based on rules, market access commitments, enforcement through a dispute settlement system and a future liberalization agenda, the WTO both mirrors and facilitates the EU's wider social and economic agenda. In such a context, the EU has significantly more to gain from general trade liberalization than it has to lose from opening up its markets to the developing world. Of course, the EU can also argue that it is in the long-term self-interest of the developing countries to embrace trade liberalization. It is a matter of personal preference to determine the extent to which the EU's insistence on FTAs can be construed as altruistic. There can be no doubt, however, that the confluence of American and European views has combined to dictate the fundamental purpose of the WTO. The creation of global rules demanding equal treatment (based on 'most favoured nation': MFN) for like cases in trading relations have been effectively used by the EU to argue that aspects of the previous preferential arrangements with the developing world were no longer sustainable. Even were the EU to want to maintain non-reciprocal arrangements, WTO rules have reduced the areas where this can operate legally (WTO Article 24 prohibits such non-reciprocal regional trade agreements). The Lomé IV Convention was successful in obtaining a WTO waiver for non-compliance with the MFN principle for ACP states. Its renewal after February 2000 was a matter of debate. The options were between the EU lobbying for a further waiver (which was far from guaranteed); accept the extension of MFN to all developing countries (not just the ACP); seek to redraft the WTO rules to make allowances for the EU's particular North–South context; or embrace FTAs as a standard basis for all trade. For some, it is suspiciously convenient for the EU to employ WTO rules as an excuse for introducing free trade arrangements when FTAs are clearly its preferred economic option for the developed and developing world.

The EU's approach to international economics has become largely consistent with the mainstream policies of the Bretton Woods institutions. Indeed, making EU policy consistent with IMF and World Bank policies has become an additional aspect of coordination. Since 1996 the Commission and the World Bank have adopted a series of measures towards a joint approach to Structural Adjustment Programmes (van Reisen, 1999, p. 70). Whilst Europe's autonomy remains clear, increasing an implicit consensus between these institutions has emerged on macroeconomic development issues. Despite being a major contributor (providing over half of all Official Development Assistance – ODA – for example) the EU has not supplanted the influence of the USA in these fora. One explanation why a more distinct EU perspective in these international organizations has failed to emerge is purely institutional. The role of the EU in the IMF, World Bank and the UN is diluted because membership is through member states bilaterally: the EU as such does not have a seat and consequently Europe is unable to project its own exclusive voice. Obviously, the recent attempts to ensure coherence and coordination between national and EU-level policy has gone some way in moderating this; however, in terms of influencing the agenda of the Bretton Woods institutions Europe continues to punch well below its weight. Of course, development policy is not unique in this regard and this pattern is generally reflected wherever policy areas are shared between the EU and the member states.

The incorporation of SAPs as a form of conditionality first emerged during the negotiations for Lomé IV. Funds were earmarked and only made available for distribution where specific macroeconomic policies were undertaken by the recipient state. In fact the EU had become a reluctant convert to this economic orthodoxy and the motivation for adopting this approach came from the wider international community. From the 1970s onwards the poor performance of developing countries – especially those in Africa – were increasing explained in terms of the domestic constraints placed upon their economies. The combination of overvalued exchange rates, high tariffs and rates of taxation, together with government-controlled producer prices were regarded in part responsible for the uncompetitive nature of many developing economies. This logic, coupled with the collapse in world prices for many primary commodities, led to what was at the time an irresistible policy conclusion. Domestic structure of production incentives had to be changed and the chosen international agent for this process became Structural Adjustment Programmes.

The EU did not enthusiastically embrace SAPs and their negative consequences saw their popularity wane considerably by the end of the 1990s. Nonetheless, they became formal aspects of conditionality for a decade under Lomé IV. The EU through its member states has sought to influence the design of SAPs by the IMF to accommodate EU priorities more directly and thereby counter – to a degree – the predominance of Washington in setting the Bretton Woods agenda. The imposition of SAPs also symbolized the changed balance in the original concept of partnership that defined European–ACP relations.

Prior to Lomé IV Europe accepted the principle that developing countries had the democratic and sovereign right to determine their own aid priorities. The accelerating decline of primary product economies during the preceding decades effectively undermined the acceptance of this principle as well as emasculated their bargaining power. As Grilli notes, the EU was 'in effect trying to establish control over the policy environment governing the use of the aid resources as a condition of the disbursement of part of its economic assistance' (1993, p. 38).

One of the most catastrophic consequences of the post-1970 economic crises faced by the developing world was the accumulation of indebtedness. The combination of mismanagement, declining revenues and the effective devaluation of local currencies due to the liberalization of exchange rates demanded by structural adjustment, saw most developing countries unable to service their borrowing requirements. Africa has been the worst affected. By 2000, Africa's cumulative debt stood at US$375 billion, and equated to three-quarters of the continent's GDP and four times the value of its annual exports (*The Economist*, 2000, p. 50). Europe's approach to this issue has been both tardy and reluctant. The initial response was that debt, *per se*, was not an EU-level problem. Developing countries were typically indebted to various international organizations or had financial obligations to individual member states. The European Union accounted for less than 5 per cent of the developing countries' global indebtedness. Indeed, the general character of EU financial assistance to the ACP countries was in the form of grants not loans. Consequently it was argued as early as 1988 that the EU was not the appropriate mechanism for orchestrating debt relief. Either the G7 or the so-called Paris Club was given the initial responsibility for handling the issue. Grilli has suggested that this was especially revealing. It indicated that any debt concessions would be made unilaterally and not subject to the normal ACP–EU process of negotiation: simply, the 'form and substance of the European debt initiative could not have been farther away from the model of Lomé' (1993, p. 39).

The pattern over two decades illustrates the scale of the financial challenge. According to a leading UK lobby group, Jubilee 2000, the debt for the very poorest group of countries (the so-called 41 Highly Indebted Poor Countries: HIPC) has risen by an average of 7.4 per cent per annum each year since 1980, whilst these HIPC economies have recorded just a 1.1 per cent growth over the same period. In 1980 total HIPC debt stood at US$58 billion: by 1997 the total was US$199 billion. The plight of two countries (Madagascar and São Tomé and Príncipe) – both ACP members – was particularly severe. More than 60 per cent of their revenue went on debt servicing alone. In a response to this deteriorating situation, debt relief was reintroduced on to the EU agenda through a Danish initiative in 1995 (van Reisen, 1999, p. 122) and policy initiatives developed in the following year. However, the major initiatives by EU member states have predominantly been bilateral and outside the EU framework. In the most important contemporary example – the HIPC initiative of the late 1990s – the EU's contribution and role has been disguised by a number of member states acting bilaterally (principally the UK and Germany, with Italy and France in support – see below). As well as constituting the four most important EU member states, these four also share responsibility through the G7 group and membership of the boards of the IMF and World Bank. However, the importance of the link to the EU is clear. Thirty-five of the 41 HIPCs were members of the ACP group under Lomé IV and the EU is the world's biggest aid donor. The impact of the HIPC will principally be determined by the EU acting both multilaterally and bilaterally through its member states.

The HIPC Initiative found its way on to both the World Bank and IMF agendas by late 1996 and by 1998 the Council of Ministers issued a formal decision announcing the EU's participation in the scheme. Funds of €40 million were set aside with the monies coming from the interest accrued through the non-disbursement of the EDF, a condition that the ACP states did not regard as particularly generous (Council Decision, 1998). In contrast to this collective approach, 1999 saw both Germany and the UK lead new bilateral initiatives on debt, followed by Italy in 2000. Whether this was because of Millennium euphoria or a reflection of the transition to Social Democratic leadership in Europe at the end of the twentieth century is a matter of personal judgement. One lobby group Eurodad (European Network on Debt and Development) described the novel process as 'a competition between creditors for the title of world debt relief champion'! (http://www.oneworld.net). The Blair Government went on record as committing the UK to the UN goal of halving the number of people living in absolute poverty by 2015. The year 2000 was the British target for beginning a systematic programme of debt reduction for all 41 HIPCs, with funding coming from the proposed sale of the IMF's gold reserves. The German Government of Schröder complemented this by suggesting that SAPs be cut from six to three years (but still play a central role in debt conditionality) and that in exceptional cases aid debt could be completely cancelled. These ideas shaped the eventual 1999 'Cologne Initiative' at which the G7 agreed to provide improved debt relief to a number of HIPCs (the similar attempt in 1996 had proved disappointing). Under the new initiative some 33 countries (with a combined population of 430 million) became eligible for debt relief and estimates put the level of relief at US$70 billion, reducing the HIPC indebtedness by more than 50 per cent (*The Economist*, 26 June, 1999b, p. 23). Estimates suggest that around 15 per cent of the expenditure of HIPC countries is devoted to debt servicing and as a creditor the EU is owed roughly €1460 million (van Reisen, 1999, pp. 198; 122). The situation for Africa is even more extreme: up to 40 per cent of African public revenues go towards debt relief. In July 2000, the Commission allocated more than €1 billion to the HIPC Initiative Trust Fund, making the EU the single largest contributor (*IP*, 2000a).

Whatever the actual final figures, the point made by advocates of debt relief is that cancellation of the specific EU debt involves a comparative modest amount and is one that can be accommodated within the EU's existing budget. Debt relief does not come without conditions, of course: recipient states need to demonstrate a commitment to sound economic management (which implies continuing to comply with the IMF's Enhanced Structural Adjustment Facility [ESAF] conditions, or if introduced, its new Poverty Reduction Strategy). And around three-quarters of the HIPCs fail to do so! More vociferous critics argue that the HIPC debt-relief initiative is an inadequate gesture and that the EU and the member states should cancel all debt. The EU was institutionally divided initially: this possible option was floated by Commission DGVIII (Development), but successfully opposed by DGII (Economic and Monetary Affairs) and the European Investment Bank. Further, lobby groups such as Jubilee 2000 have proposed a list of 52 – not 41 – countries that should be included in any debt initiative. Even among those who accept that the HIPC initiative is the only practical option, there is criticism of its limited application. The conditionality attached to the HIPC debt initiative revolves around an assessment of debt sustainability. The IMF stresses macroeconomic measures (such as the role of exports in servicing debt) in its decision on which countries qualify under the HIPC programme. Criteria based on human development issues and indexes are not considered. Consequently, the immediate effect of the HIPC initiative has been extremely slow: by the year 2000, just four countries had benefited from debt relief (http://www.oneworld.net). The example of debt relief also serves to emphasize (albeit negatively) the constant challenge of complementarity for the EU. As shown above, in this key development policy area the EU is at the mercy of the member states and their respective domestic lobbies. It is almost an impossible task to expect the Commission to coordinate the British, German, French, Italian and Scandinavian proposals on HIPC policy let alone make these complementary with the EU's own position. The EU seems unable to avoid the trap of formalizing policy goals that lead to high expectations before providing the Commission with the necessary scope and authority to execute such policies. Whilst the complexities of policy-making at the EU level can provide a theoretical explanation for this, the dissonance does nothing to enhance the EU's image as an effective and single international actor. Bilateral action has proved to be resilient and remains a core aspect of the EU's multilateral development agenda.

Implementing conditionality

Despite the dominance of a bilateral approach towards debt reduction, as the preceding sections have outlined the EU has collated a range of collective political and economic conditionalities to frame its relations with the developing world. These are commonly applied and represent the multilateral perspective based upon the consensus of the Fifteen. But just how effective and consistently has political conditionality in particular been applied?

Isolating various elements within political conditionality – human rights, good governance and so on – has presented the EU with an empirical challenge: simply, how does one measure violations? Are there degrees of compliance? Are all elements of equal importance or are some less significant? Wherever possible, the EU uses a carrot rather than stick approach. The emphasis is on recognizing, encouraging and rewarding states which maintain or move towards acceptable standards of governance, preferring to withhold sanctions as very much the last resort. However, as one recent commentary noted, the EU does not provide any data to substantiate this claim so conclusions can only be impressionistic (Smith, 1998, p. 266). Given the financial constraints under which development policy operates it is probably almost impossible to 'reward' states for good behaviour as such resources are already committed elsewhere. Where a budget allocation cannot be increased the only solution is to take funds from other existing areas, something that is itself politically difficult to achieve. An example of this dilemma occurred in mid-2000 when the European Parliament sought to increase the aid provided to South Africa under the FTA agreement. As an increase in the overall development budget was not acceptable, the Council proposed re-channelling funds previously committed to the emergency food aid budget to achieve this.

Cases of sanctions are easier to identify of course (although one should be aware of distinguishing between those sanctions agreed in principle and those actually enacted – the time lag between these two events can often be considerable). Table 4.1 provides data for the 1990s where violations of democratic or human rights resulted in the suspension of trading relations or aid. Four features are immediately apparent. First, with few exceptions, the offending countries were all members of the Lomé Convention. The explicit conditionalities introduced into Lomé in part explain this pattern. Second, around half the cases occurred prior to the TEU legally coming into force (1 November 1993). This indicates that the real change in approach predated the Maastricht debates and that whilst a legal framework adds weight, the necessary prerequisite for action is a collective political will. The third feature is, the relative unimportance of the offending states to the EU economically, as well as the notable omission from the list of other less peripheral states. The fourth is the absence of cases in Asia.

Agreements with developing countries as well as the imposition of sanctions – and their removal – require unanimity in the Council. Parliament's involvement does not extend to suspension clauses and it can be technically if not politically ignored. If action is to be undertaken through the CFSP then the additional mechanisms of either joint action or common position are required. Consequently, there is ample opportunity to employ procedural

TABLE 4.1   *EU sanctions based on violations of democracy, human rights, the rule of law or good governance, 1990–98*

		Reason for EU action		
	Year	Human rights	Rule of law	Democracy
ACP states				
Sudan	1990	×		×
Haiti	1991		×	×
Kenya	1991			×
Zaire	1992			×
Togo	1992			×
Malawi	1992			
Equatorial Guinea	1992	×	×	
Nigeria	1993	×		×
Gambia	1994		×	×
Comores	1995		×	×
Niger	1996		×	×
Burundi	1996		×	×
Sierra Leone	1997		×	×
Other developing states				
Guatemala	1993		×	×
Transition economies				
Belarus	1997	×		×
Asia				
–	–			

Source: Smith (1998) p. 267; *Bulletin of the EU* (1998–2000); European *Foreign Affairs Review* (1997–2000).

arguments and allow bilateral preferences to prevent the emergence of EU action. In addition to cases of sanctions, the EU is active in other, less punitive ways – such as issuing critical démarches or joint statements in the UN and elsewhere as well as through formal political dialogues. Increasingly, the withdrawal of EU Ambassadors from third countries has been used to indicate concern. Clearly, the negative exercise of sanctions based upon political conditionality is subject to all kinds of constraints and EU action in the past has in no sense been uniformly applied. The 'importance' of the transgressing state is often influential, as is any former colonial link with a member state. China has escaped punitive action throughout the 1990s along with a number of other Asian countries where labour practices and human rights are widely known to be suspect. The nature of the economic partnership is also a factor. It can be relatively simple to impose a trade embargo on a state with which there is very little economic interaction: where European jobs are at stake the political costs are considerably higher. Often past experiences of ineffectual sanctions (such as those applied to South Africa in 1985/6 or Yugoslavia since 1991) are sufficient to deter the EU from taking punitive measures. Many critics conclude that in terms of the application of political conditionality the EU simply employs double standards. Even those who are more sympathetic to the institutional, procedural and political constraints within which the EU operates argue that a more systematic and coherent approach is possible (Smith, 1998, p. 273). The dissonance between the EU's formal presentation of its foreign policy objectives of human rights and democracy and its performance to date has principally succeeded only in widening the publicly perceived 'expectations–capabilities gap' and compromised the EU's claim to be an important international actor.

As noted already, one of the growth areas in EU external relations has been in election observation and monitoring. Within a relatively short period of time the EU has become a recognized actor in this field comparable to the UN and arguably more highly regarded than other regional organizations such as the Commonwealth. One of the EU's earliest observation roles was in 1994 for the first non-racial democratic election in South Africa (Holland, 1994). The procedure was experimental in many respects, but the experience gained helped to refine and improve the role played by the Union in subsequent elections. The lessons derived from the South African case can be summarized as follows. First, the familiar division between Commission and member state responsibilities (and funding) required better coordination: the exercise was under the auspices of the EU but had a distinctly bilateral flavour. Second, the selection of personnel involved should be coordinated centrally to ensure comparable levels of experience and expertise. The immature status of the EU's CFSP presence means that the EU *per se* does not have its own corps of observers to call upon but must rely largely on contributions from the member states. Third, the observation should be lengthy and cover the campaigning period and role of the media and not just be confined to the immediate days prior to the election. Consequently, proper observations are costly in time, money and personnel. Fourth, whilst the 'free and fair' aspects of an election must be established, European standards pertaining to the administration of the election should not be applied too inflexibly. There is a vast difference between conducting an election on the one hand with electronically verified electoral roles and an experienced electorate and on the other where the electors may have had no previous experience of casting a ballot, where literacy cannot be presumed, or even where no accurate electoral rolls exist. An overall judgement, not administrative precision, is required and the formal conclusions of the observers will have important consequences. Where the election falls below an acceptable definition of 'free and fair' the European Parliament or the Council may invoke sanctions or suspend bilateral agreements.

The best testimony to the success of the EU as an election observer is the fact that it regularly receives a large number of requests from third countries to observe or monitor elections. Indeed a special unit in DGIA was created to oversee this development in the mid-1990s. One of the most recent and potentially problematic elections involving the EU was that of Zimbabwe in June 2000. In May 2000, funds of €2.4 million (€1.83 million from the EU budget, the remainder contributed by the member states) were approved and a final Observer Team of 190 members established. The central Observation Unit and over 100 observers were deployed in the first week of June with the remainder arriving a week before the June 24–5 election (*IP/2000c*). The UN did not undertake its usual umbrella coordinating and deployment role for the various international observer missions and the EU provided the largest contingent. In addition, the EU provided funds for training around 1400 local election monitors.

The election result saw the opposition party (MDC) win 58 seats, and the governing ZANU-PF party of President Robert Mugabe retain 61 seats. In his post-election report, the head of the EU Election Observation mission, Pierre Schori – vice-president of the European Parliament and former Swedish International Development Minister – was critical of the intimidation involved during the campaign. Although it was concluded that the voting process had been void of corruption, the election fell short of being sufficiently 'free and fair'. The EU's response was to make continued aid support partially conditional on the behaviour of the new government. In this way it was hoped that EU financial assistance programmes could be used as leverage for internal reforms, including the development of a meaningful multi-party democracy. Whilst €19 million directed towards micro-projects concerned with poverty alleviation were released immediately after the election, €2 million earmarked for rural development were suspended pending 'clarification' on Zimbabwe's land reform policy. Furthermore, it was announced that a decision on an EDF grant of €33 million for HIV/AIDS programmes would depend on Zimbabwe's democratic developments over the coming months. In a diplomatically frank joint post-election statement to the European Parliament by Patten and Nielson, the Commissioner for Development stated 'it is premature to jump to conclusions on the election and its consequences. I fully share the(ir) views that EU–Zimbabwe development cooperation will depend on visible progress in the development of new policies both in the field of good governance and economic reform' (Speech, 2000). However, some commentators were underwhelmed by this threat, and a 'carrot-and-stick' approach was the very minimum action that the EU could take given the severity of intimidation reported by the EU observers.

The *coup* in the ACP State of Fiji on 19 May 2000 presented the EU with a further challenge to applying political conditionality. The Fijian case was particularly difficult for a number of reasons. First, Fiji had been chosen by the ACP states to host the signing of the new post-Lomé Convention on 8 June 2000 (some three weeks after taking hostage of Prime Minister Chaudhry and the start of the *coup*). The new 'Partnership Agreement' was already informally known as the Suva Convention. It was more than symbolically important to sign the new post-Lomé agreement on schedule: there were concerns that the application to roll-over the WTO Lomé IV waiver would not be endorsed if the Agreement was postponed. The choice and timing of a substitute ceremonial venue lay with the ACP. Second, the Fijian export economy was reliant on its sugar concession granted through a Lomé protocol: there was no doubt that the EU was capable of imposing stringent sanctions in this one area and there were certainly expectations amongst some that this should be done. Agriculture represented no less than 93 per cent of Fiji's trade with the EU throughout the 1990s. Eurostat figures for 1999 show that sugar alone accounted for 86 per cent of exports to the EU and were worth €121 million. Third, the *coup* presented a clear opportunity to evaluate the EU's character as an international actor. What response would the EU collectively agree to if – as happened – the democratically elected leader was not reinstated? The previous coup in Fiji (in the 1980s) took place prior to the creation of the CFSP. After the experience of seven years of joint actions, what would be the response now? And fourth, the *coup* exposed the sensitivities and difficulties associated with imposing European standards and democratic expectations as a form of political conditionality on societies where traditional tribal systems of political organization were still prevalent. The rejection of the legitimacy of the *coup* had to be balanced with respect for the Fijian indigenous processes.

The Fijian crisis began in early May 2000. The absence of any formal EU response during the following weeks was remarkable. Whilst the short-lived *coup d'etat* in the Solomon Islands was the subject of an immediate condemnatory press release, and the pre-election events in Zimbabwe were discussed in both the General Affairs Council and the European Parliament during May and June 2000, official statements on Fiji were not issued. The Development Council of 18 May did 'exchange views on conflict crisis situations in developing countries' but these were *in camera* and no formal reference or conclusion on Fiji was issued. Certainly informal communications were made suggesting that unless a return to democracy were forthcoming, Fiji's sugar protocol access would be suspended; the ACP states were also asked to nominate an alternative venue for the formal signing of the Agreement. Cotonou, the Benin capital, was selected and the official ceremony went ahead on 23 June 2000 (see Chapter 8). Somewhat ironically, six Pacific island states became new members of the post-Lomé agreement (Cook Islands, Nauru, Palau, the Marshall Islands and Niue and the Federated States of Micronesia) boosting the ACP Group to 77 states. Remarkably, at Cotonou the question of Fiji's suspension was not raised and a Fijian Government representative was permitted to sign the Partnership Agreement.

Conclusion

The contrast between the EU's active participation and international leadership in the Zimbabwean case and its apparent silence on Fiji presents a confusing image of the EU's development and foreign policies. Both countries were ACP states and subject to identical forms of political conditionality; both rely substantially on access to the European market for their trade; and both reflect a British colonial past. Whilst it could be suggested that the Fijian issue was better mediated through the Commonwealth or was a direct Australasian and New Zealand foreign policy issue, such reasoning merely exacerbates the perception that the EU is not an effective global actor. Even where the EU has a clear mandate it still does not, necessarily, choose to act even with the added weight of its own CFSP high representative, Javier Solana.

In conclusion, both the goals of complementarity and conditionality, if successfully executed, would enhance the EU's international character. However, as this chapter has argued, developing EU-level policies that meld with those of the member states as well as with Europe's internal policy priorities is complex, challenging and probably impossible to realize perfectly. The link between development and democratic principles of good government has become the accepted and inevitable face of North–South relations; the degree to which this conditionality is supervised and sanctioned remains variable, almost idiosyncratic. This seemingly variable application of conditionality, however, detracts from the EU's international credibility and influence. As is often the case with the EU, there is a tendency to exaggerate the expectations for new policy competences, whether this is for the CFSP, EMU or development and poverty reduction. Indeed, a cynic might accuse the EU of blatant and repetitive false advertising. Successive treaties have underlined the EU's policy on complementarity as well as introduced political and economic conditionalities – yet, there has been a worrying gap between the rhetoric and practice of what has been promised and expected. Of course, this failing is not unique to the EU: what is unique, however, is that the EU cannot rely on a long history of international action to bolster its reputation. It is judged, and can only be judged, on how it deals with the present and in the area of development policy its current performance is at best mixed, at worst disorganized and incremental.

Chapter 5

Regimes, Trade and Trading Relations

This chapter opens with a discussion of trade policy and the link to development policy within the EU. More than any other policy sector, trade has become pervasive touching almost all aspects of EU policy, both internal and external, and for some analysts trade is 'arguably the most important policy area influencing the developing countries over which the European Union has competency' (van Reisen, 1999, p. 129). Originally, Europe was able to separate development for its normal trading perspective. However, this compartmentalization has progressively broken down and trade issues have contaminated much of the development agenda of the 1990s – some would argue even to the extent of becoming the principal focus for EU relations in the twenty-first century. The subsequent sections of the chapter present the patterns of trade for the ACP, Latin America, and the other developing countries of Asia. Both these empirical and theoretical discussions are necessary. The empirical data provides a basis for analysis, whilst trade policy debate provides the necessary broader context through which to fully understand EU development policy.

EU trade policy

The history of the EU's trading relations with the developing world records the transition from particular and specialized arrangements to a contemporary approach that seeks to treat all countries as much alike as possible, ignoring to a large degree differences of geography. This change was dictated, in part, by the successive Treaty reforms of the 1990s that instigated the new policy objective of integrating the developing countries into the global economic system. But it also reflects the earlier decision to establish a common commercial policy in the original

Treaty of Rome which empowered the Commission as the most important trade negotiator, albeit one ultimately subject to member state oversight. Thus, external trade in goods became an undisputed exclusive EU competence. As Meunier and Nicolaidis state '[F]rom its very creation, the European Community had spoken in international trade negotiations with a single voice', something that distinguished the European integration process from all other forms of preferential trading arrangements (2000, p. 325).

Article 133.1 of the Consolidated Treaty reiterates the formal basis for the conduct of EU trade policy as set out in the 1957 founding Treaty of Rome:

> The common commercial policy shall be based on uniform principles, particularly in regard to changes in tariff rates, the conclusion of tariff and trade agreements, the achievement of uniformity in measures of liberalisation, export policy and measures to protect trade.

Armed with this legal authority, for more than three decades the European Community replaced the member states in trade negotiations and entered into collective trade agreements. In the context of the post-Maastricht suspicion on deepening integration and the reactivation of member state sovereignty through subsidiarity, this previously unchallenged legal authority was tested in 1994. Eight member states opposed the right of the Commission to act as the EU's sole representative for trade competences in the newly configured WTO. The Court of Justice in its reasoned decision confirmed that the EU had sole competence to conclude international agreements on trade in goods: however, they also found that the EU and member states had 'shared competences' for trade involving 'new issues' such as services, for example, until such time that there was a political consensus to transfer authority to the EU (Meunier and Nicolaidis, 2000, p. 336). The importance of the political context to both economic policy and legal frameworks was clearly apparent.

Formally, Article 133 specifies the decision-making procedures for trade policy by identifying three phases in policy-making and the respective roles played at each stage by the various institutions. First, the Council on the basis of a proposal from the Commission determines the setting of objectives for trade negotiations. The Commission's proposals may be modified by consensus by the Article 133 Committee before passing these on to COREPER and subsequently to the General Affairs Council which then frames the negotiating mandate. Typically, mandates are 'flexible' – or general – reflecting to a degree the lowest common denominator process of consensual decision-making styles. Second, where the EU has an exclusive competence, the Commission on the EU's behalf undertakes the conduct of the negotiations. At this stage the Commission can exercise significant autonomy. Third, the final outcome and decision-making authority remains in the hands of the Council, decided by QMV (Qualified Majority Voting) or unanimity depending upon the treaty basis for action (Woolcock, 2000, pp. 376–85). Other characterizations, such as that by Meunier and Nicolaidis, follow a similar three-stage process (in their case distinguishing between the initial mandate, ongoing representation and ratification). The European Parliament has no formal power under treaty provisions for trade policy, although its assent is required if a treaty or association agreement is involved or where budgetary issues or the co-decision procedure is invoked.

Despite these legally circumscribed roles, the Commission has increasingly taken on greater *de facto* importance (especially in relation to Europe's dialogue with the WTO) largely because of the need to be seen to be 'speaking with a single voice'. In practice, the EU's decision-making process for international trade is dependent on an extensive consultation process between the Commission and the Council. During trade negotiations the Article 133 Committee (which is composed of representatives from the member states and DGI) serves this essential function, although there is some evidence that the members states have begun to reassert their authority at this level (Johnson [1998] cited in Meunier and Nicolaidis, 2000, p. 332). On occasions, the Commission is forced to go beyond its formal negotiating mandate. This first happened in 1992 over the EC–USA 'Blair House Agreement' and most recently in 1999 in the FTA negotiations with South Africa. However, whatever concessions or innovations the Commission makes in discussions with a third party remain subject to EU approval – either via the Article 133 Committee or in the General Affairs Council itself. As the South

African case illustrated, the Commission cannot expect the Council to accept whatever deal it negotiates – a reality that is often as frustrating for third countries as it is for the Commission. Contrary to the imagery of 'speaking with a single voice', a more familiar reality is the problem of conflicting policy agendas between member states, as well as between different DGs, making dealing with the EU as a trade partner a complex and slow process. To further complicate matters, as noted above some member states, backed by the Court of Justice, have even begun to question this automatic transfer of sovereignty to the supranational level. The Amsterdam Treaty also went some way to reasserting the idea of a shared competence (Meunier and Nicolaidis, 2000, p. 325). Consequently, where trade issues intersect with other aspects of development policy, the EU response can be unpredictable.

By almost all measures the EU is a dominant presence in world trade. The EU accounted for almost 38 per cent of the total for global exports in 1997 (van Reisen, 1999, p. 129). Other estimates for 1996 put the value of the EU's exports to the rest of the world at 620 billion ecus with a trade surplus of 46.3 billion ecus. As Smith has noted, the EU is 'not only a major presence in the world trading system; it also trades at a profit' (1999, p. 275). Yet, the underlying nature of EU trade policy remains the subject of concerted, and heated, debate. Whilst 'Fortress Europe' was always an exaggeration and the EU has clearly become more multilateral in its approach and moved away from crude protectionism, the strength of this new commitment to trade liberalization remains in dispute. Experience has shown that there can be deep differences in trade culture and philosophies between some member states. A traditional dichotomy divided the protectionist South from the free-trading North in the Community of the original Six. With the progressive expansion of the EU this balance and geographical metaphor has fluctuated, and with it so has trade policy (pp. 277–80). Nonetheless, the tension between global liberalization for exports and internal market protection remain an undeniable part of Europe's policy equation. Van Reisen takes an extreme position in arguing that such 'tension between two economic paradigms, leading to different practices at various policy levels creates contradictory policies that are incoherent with the objectives of EU development policy' (1999, p. 130).

An additional complication has been the EU's pursuit of region-to-region groupings as an aspect of its global trade policy, particularly in those areas where EU links had been historically weak (through organizations such as MERCOSUR or ASEAN, for example). Nor is trade any longer a discrete policy sector: decisions increasingly have repercussions across – or linkages to – other policy areas, including the environment, civil society and development. Consequently, who has the competence to determine trade policy objectives will also have a considerable impact on related policy areas. This linkage is perhaps nowhere better illustrated than in the post-Lomé negotiations and in the EU's general approach to reconceptualizing the basis of its development dialogue. Traditional development strategies and priorities clashed with a changing trade context that in many ways either constrained or predetermined the range of options available. The question of linkage may also have another dimension: some go as far as to suggest that it is now difficult to differentiate trade policy in terms of internal or external spheres.

The clearest example of the internal EU policies having an adverse external linkage is in agriculture. The current CAP reflects more than three decades of intra-EU political compromises and incremental trade-offs. Only belatedly has the EU begun to address the disincentive effect that CAP subsidies and surpluses can have on food security in the developing world by lowering world prices. The probability of fundamentally reforming the CAP remains Europe's greatest challenge and although eastern expansion will necessitate changes in the CAP, it is hard to envisage how the interests of the developing world will influence that agenda. At best, some unintended side-effects might accrue: at worst, existing preferences and quotas that advantage some developing countries will be rescinded as the 'community preference' principle is extended.

In terms of trade relations, the developing world can be divided into two broad camps. One, the ACP states and other non-ACP Least Developed Countries that, at least until Lomé IV, benefited from negotiated trade preferences; and the other, all other remaining developing countries that were subject to the GSP regime. Whilst the differential aspects of these two approaches have narrowed over time, for the majority of developing countries despite defects Lomé remains the more privileged, and therefore more desirable framework. However, membership has not been an option for those outside the ACP. The main trade regime differences between GSP and Lomé can be summarized as follows. Lomé was the result of a negotiated agreement between the ACP and the EU; GSP, however, is conferred unilaterally by the EU and is regarded as a less secure and predictable arrangement. GSP preferences are also graduated and can decrease in value if a developing country or specific sector grows economically: in contrast, the advantages under Lomé ran for the life of the Convention, irrespective of performance. In general, both agricultural and industrial products have had better access to the EU market under the Lomé provisions.

GSP was first introduced in 1971 – four years before the first Lomé Convention – in response to the gaps in coverage of European trade policy with the developing world. In theory, GSP was meant to be a graduated policy that reflected different stages of development, using per capita income to discriminate comparatively between richer and poorer developing countries. However, in its original form practice departed quite significantly from theory. It was not strongly income-graduated, the approach was not applied comprehensively to the developing world and commodity coverage was not universal. The focus of GSP became trade in manufactures and industrial goods (not agriculture) and the most important exemptions from GSP were textiles and clothing (Grilli, 1993, p. 23). Some quantitative restrictions were also imposed. With minor modifications, the GSP regime was first renewed in 1981. Despite its name, it remained selective, not general, in character in both country and product coverage. Consequently, its contribution to increasing exports from the developing world was not fully maximized. The transformation in Eastern Europe in the 1990s further marginalized the role of GSP and forced further reviews.

It has now become accepted wisdom to view the EU's trade policy as consistent with the trends of globalization and liberalization with political conditions superimposed (see Chapter 4). Whilst these have undoubtedly become common themes, the EU continues to regionalize its relations externally. The principal groupings are the ACP countries (which have been dealt with separately under Lomé and the Cotonou Partnership Agreement); Asia has been categorized within the ASEM process and through ASEAN; and Latin America most recently and comprehensively through the MERCOSUR process. These historically distinct frameworks share one common contemporary trading feature: the evolution from preferential access towards free trade areas. This radical departure, it is suggested, will help to incorporate the developing countries into the global economy. Trade, after all, is of greater importance than aid for promoting economic viability in the developing world. Conversely, others see this change in trade policy as a high-risk strategy and have predicted that not all developing countries will successfully adjust to the market competition associated with FTAs. The LDCs are obviously at greatest risk. The strongest critics of this process question the EU's motivation, arguing that it is not development objectives that determine this process, but the demands of EU export potential (van Reisen, 1999, p. 162). The product exceptions in the design of FTAs (principally agriculture) underline their Eurocentric rationale. Only belatedly has the EU accepted the argument that non-reciprocity had to be retained for the LDCs – both those within the ACP group as well as those outside it (see Chapter 8). All other trading relations after the year 2000 were to be based on reciprocity. Through this policy reform the EU sought to gain guaranteed access to the emerging Asian and Latin American markets, whilst retaining the advantages of its existing markets with the ACP.

In contrast to the interdependency of EU trade policy with the industrialized world, dependency has always characterized Europe's relations with the Third World. As described elsewhere, the original trading basis for Europe's relations with the South presumed a 'pyramid of privilege' that was intended to favour specific parts of the developing world. The different EU hierarchies for preferential relations with the developing world underline the complexity of maintaining a consistent EU approach across multiple agreements and frameworks – from simply GSP agreements to Lomé's non-reciprocity. Despite this presumed ACP advantage, the developing countries share of world trade has remained modest (18.6 per cent in 1997) with Africa's performance especially weak (representing just 1.5 per cent of world exports)(van Reisen, 1999, p. 129). A key question is the extent to which the resultant 'web of agreements can be effectively managed and adapted to changing circumstances'

(Smith, 1999, p. 278). The following analysis of the trade patterns provides some evidence to answer this question.

Trade

In evaluating the EU's relations with the Third World an important criterion for measuring success is the pattern of trade. The key objective of Lomé, for example, was the promotion of trading relations and the concession of non-reciprocal preferential access for ACP products was designed to increase exports to Europe and improve the EU–ACP balance of trade. Benign intentions do not always translate into actual effect, however.

As discussed previously, between 1976 and 1985 the impact of the Lomé Convention on the balance of trade was marginal. Whilst the ACP enjoyed a trade surplus with the EC, this was also the position prior to Lomé. In terms of product, the Convention had the perverse effect of promoting ACP dependency on raw materials as an export base in exchange for importing primarily industrial goods from Europe. As Table 5.1 shows, the trade patterns have been disappointing. After a significant rise in the value of ACP exports under Lomé I and II, there has been a progressive decline. In 1976, for example, the value of ACP exports to Europe was some 10.5 billion ecus: this rose to 26.8 billion ecus by 1985 but had fallen to 18.6 billion ecus by 1994. The pattern is even more worrying in terms of the ACP share of total trade. Over the same period, as a percentage of all exports to the EU, the ACP share has fallen to half its 1976 level (from 6.7 per cent to 3.4 per cent by 1994). Conversely, ACP imports from the EU have been comparatively stable, with the balance of trade generally in favour of the ACP under all four Conventions.

In contrast, whilst the ACP position has deteriorated, Europe's trade with other developing countries outside the Lomé Convention has grown considerably. From 1976–85, the ACP states maintained their position as the developing world's leading exporter to the EU; thereafter there has been a systematic decline. By 1994 the ACP group had the lowest developing country share of EU imports (3.4 per cent), behind Latin America (4.9 per cent), the Mediterranean (5.7 per cent) and Asia (15.5 per cent). In the face of such evidence, clearly the

TABLE 5.1   *EU–developing country trade, 1976–94* (bn ecus)

EU IMPORTS FROM	1976	1980	1985	1990	1992	1994
ACP	10.5	19.4	26.8	21.9	18.0	18.6
Asia	6.7	16.0	26.0	50.9	66.4	83.9
Latin America	8.3	13.7	25.8	25.7	24.8	26.7
Mediterranean	9.6	16.4	32.3	29.8	30.3	30.8
All LDCs	70.7	114.3	128.9	143.8	145.6	165.9
All non-EC	157.7	269.9	399.7	461.5	487.6	543.2
EU EXPORTS TO						
ACP	9.6	15.7	17.4	16.6	17.0	14.9
Asia	7.5	13.1	29.4	41.0	47.1	70.7
Latin America	7.7	12.0	13.5	15.6	20.4	28.4
Mediterranean	12.3	19.8	29.8	28.5	28.6	33.1
All LDCs	550.9	83.4	121.7	134.2	153.1	193.3
All non EC	141.3	221.1	380.8	415.3	436.1	541.8
World	292.9	475.1	811.8	1076.6	1137.8	1297.9
% SHARE OF EU IMPORTS						
ACP	6.7	7.2	6.7	4.7	3.7	3.4
Asia	4.2	5.9	6.5	11.0	13.6	15.5
Latin America	5.3	5.1	6.5	5.6	5.1	4.9
Mediterranean	6.1	6.1	8.1	6.5	6.2	5.7
All LDCs	44.8	42.4	34.7	31.2	29.9	30.5
All non EC	100.0	100.0	100.0	100.0	100.0	100.0

Source: European Commission (1996) *Green Paper on relations between the European Union and the ACP countries on the eve of the 21st century: challenges and opportunities for a new partnership* (Office of the Official Publications of the European Communities, Luxembourg).

non-reciprocal trading preferences of Lomé had failed to meet the objectives of the Convention.

Part of the answer to this decline in the ACP's percentage share of EU imports can be found in the composition of trade. As Table 5.2 shows, ACP exports remained essentially primary products, with less than one quarter manufactures, machinery or chemicals. A Commission Report explained the decline as a reflection of weak global commodity prices, overvalued ACP

TABLE 5.2 *EU imports from ACP states, 1985, 1991–93 (bn ecus)*

	1985		1991		1992		1993	
	Ecus	*%*	*Ecus*	*%*	*Ecus*	*%*	*Ecus*	*%*
TOTAL IMPORTS	26.2	100	19.1	100	18.0	100	14.9	100
Foods	6.8	26	4.9	26	4.8	26	4.7	33
Raw materials	3.5	13	2.7	14	2.5	14	2.4	16
Fuel products	12.3	47	6.6	35	5.6	31	4.0	27
Chemicals	0.5	2	0.4	2	0.3	2	0.3	2
Machinery, transport	0.2	1	0.5	3	0.9	5	0.6	4
Other manufactures	2.3	9	3.3	17	3.3	19	2.2	15

Source: European Commission (1995) *Trade Relations between the European Union and the Developing Countries* (Office of the Official Publications of the European Communities, Luxembourg).

currencies and changing consumption habits in the EU. Somewhat perversely, it also argued that the poor ACP export record was 'also due to the composition of the group': 45 states belonged to the group of the least developed countries and the natural markets for the non-African states were identified as North America and Australasia, not Europe (Commission, 1995, p. 20)! Why, then, persist with the Lomé preferences? Clearly, other significant factors explaining this pattern were the structure of Lomé and the disincentives to diversify away from primary products.

This pattern is further magnified when the ACP group is disaggregated. Nigeria – who export virtually just oil and petroleum – dominated ACP trade and together with the four other African oil producers accounted for 36 per cent of ACP exports in 1993. In the same year, just 10 ACP countries (all African) were responsible for 62 per cent of all ACP exports to the EU. When compared with other non-Lomé developing countries the plight of the ACP is even more extreme: only Nigeria ranked in the top 15 exporters to the EU and no ACP state made the top 15 developing country markets for EU exports.

In such a context, the main focus of the 1995 mid-term review departed from the traditional Lomé preoccupation with preferential access to a more inclusive approach for creating a better trading environment. The arguments were as much political as they were economic and reflected the agenda of the GATT negotiations. Two new Articles introduced the idea of trade development, aimed at 'developing, diversifying and increasing ACP States' trade and improving their competitiveness' domestically and internationally (Article 15a). Mirroring the commitment of the Maastricht Treaty, Article 6a calls for the gradual integration of the ACP economies into the world economy and describes the function of trade as 'energizing the development process'.

To compound this economic position, debt had become an important immediate ACP problem. Whilst the new Lomé IV Articles 239–42 introduced the issue of debt repayment on to the Community agenda, this 'major development issue' remained largely the primary domain of member states and international organizations. Europe was wary of establishing a precedent in this area. Once again, the importance of consistency and complementarity between EU and member state policy was highlighted. Whilst the recognition of this issue was welcome, Europe's collective response at this stage was cautious and respected the role of the member states. Given the EU's limited financial involvement (just 1.2 per cent of the ACP debt-servicing costs were with the EU) it seemed inappropriate and ineffective for the EU to become the dominant forum for addressing the debt repayment. Whether this view was justified or not, ignoring the Community dimension on debt stood in stark contrast to the wider Lomé philosophy of partnership.

Financial resources

The European Development Fund (EDF) has been the principal funding mechanism for European aid since 1957. The typical pattern concerning the size of the EDF (for both Lomé and its predecessor the Yaoundé Convention) saw the ACP states generally dissatisfied: the seemingly large nominal increases in funding at best only matched the increases in real costs. As already noted in Chapter 1, whilst the EDF7 budget of 12 billion ecus was a nominal increase of around 40 per cent from the previous figure of 8.8 billion ecus, in real terms the change was marginal and significantly below ACP expectations. Similarly, difficult negotiations during the 1995 mid-term review saw EDF8 funding rise by 22 per cent to 14.6 billion ecus, an increase that again disappointed the ACP. Such outcomes reflected a hardening attitude among member states as well as the limited bureaucratic resources of the ACP secretariat to lobby for a better deal. In the context of declining multilateral and bilateral aid globally, Europe's development priorities for the 1990s had shifted to Central and Eastern Europe.

Figure 5.1 provides an overview of the financial protocol 1995–2000. The EDF was the main financing instrument of Lomé and importantly EDF funds do not come from the EU budget but are composed of member-state contributions. France and Germany provide almost half of these funds (24.3 per cent and 23.4 per cent), with the UK and Italy contributing a further quarter (12.7 per cent and 12.5 per cent respectively). Programme aid has always consumed the majority of funds. Taking 1995 as a typical year, programme aid amounted to 56 per cent, followed by risk capital (17 per cent), structural adjustment (10

152

FIGURE 5.1 Lomé IV financial protocol, 1995–2000

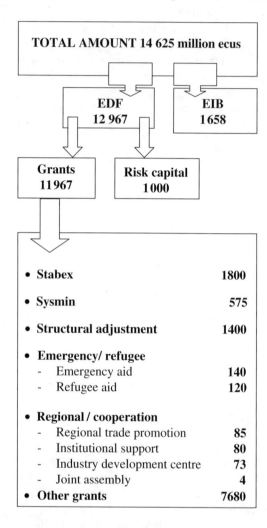

Source: European Commission (1996) *InfoFinance 1995: the European Development Fund* (Office for Official Publications of the European Communities, Luxembourg).

per cent) with STABEX and SYSMIN at 9 per cent and 6 per cent respectively. Three-quarters of all total aid to the ACP went to Africa, 18 per cent to the Caribbean and just 5 per cent to the Pacific. To place this in context, whilst Lomé funding was significant, the EU's collective aid has traditionally been exceeded by the bilateral programmes of both Germany and France. Indeed, the combined sum of the Fifteen's bilateral programmes has been around four times the Lomé figure. Taking the 1997 official development aid figures as an example, the combined total for the 15 member states was US$26.5 billion (out of a DAC total of US$47.6 billion), of which France contributed US$6.3 billion, Germany US$5.9, the UK US$3.3 and the Netherlands US$2.9 billion (http://www.diplomatie.fr).

As noted before, the time needed for the disbursement of funds has been a problematic feature of Lomé. Consequently, in order to maintain programme aid as well as STABEX and SYSMIN the duration of EDFs may overlap. Indeed, the delayed ratification of the revised Lomé IV only saw EDF8 funding become available in 1998 and even at this late stage EDF7 funds were still being allocated. If funding lapses in areas such as emergency aid or refugees, the Community budget can be utilized to bridge any short-term gap.

Other trading regimes

Outside the ACP framework Europe operates a number of different trading regimes with the developing world: GSP, Super GSP, the emerging reciprocal Free Trade Areas as well as a raft of specialized group-to-group arrangements such as between the EU and ASEAN for example. What impact have these had on trading relations? Certainly, the 1990s witnessed the progressive erosion of all forms of GSP advantages as the WTO acted to equalize treatment, making FTAs undisputedly the most privileged trading framework. Using the contrast with the ACP trading patterns as the context, comparisons of ASEM, ASEAN and Latin American trade with the EU are discussed below.

Before beginning, however, the importance of the various trading blocs requires a global context. In 1970, Europe's share of world trade was around 7 per cent; by the end of the century this had mushroomed to around one quarter. Whilst the intra-

TABLE 5.3   *Percentage EU external trade with selected third world regional groupings, 1970–94*

	% of total EU exports			% of total EU imports		
	1970	1982	1994	1970	1982	1994
Latin America*	6.7	5.2	5.3	7.9	6.5	5.0
ACP	7.6	7.2	2.8	8.9	6.0	3.4
Asian NICs**	2.1	3.0	7.6	1.5	3.2	6.2
ASEAN***	2.3	3.1	5.2	2.0	2.4	5.5
CHINA	0.1	0.1	2.3	0.1	0.1	4.5
Combined Asia/ACP/ Latin America	18.8	18.6	23.2	20.4	18.2	24.6
All Others	81.2	81.4	76.8	80.6	81.8	75.4

Notes: * = Argentina, Bolivia, Brazil, Chile, Columbia, Costa Rica, Cuba, Dominican Republic, Ecuador, El Salvador, Guatemala, Haiti, Honduras, Mexico, Nicaragua, Panama, Paraguay, Peru, Uruguay, Venezuela.
    ** = Hong Kong, Singapore, South Korea, Taiwan.
   *** = Brunei, Indonesia, Malaysia, Philippines, Singapore, Thailand.
Source: Eurostat (1998) and Smith (1999).

EU trade still accounts for the largest share of the EU's economic activity, the 1990s have seen the importance of external trade grow significantly. Most recently, the EU has actively promoted the liberalization of all forms of multilateral trade regimes in order to bolster its international trading profile and position in the world economy. However, as one study argues, this expansion and liberalizing role has been 'primarily at the expense of the less-developed countries' as EU policy (particularly the CAP) has distorted global markets and the compensation by way of Lomé and other agreements has been inadequate (Peterson and Bomberg, 1999, p. 95). Table 5.3 traces the structure of the EU's external trade from the 1970s to 1994: this period denotes the trading patterns prior to the EU's progressive shift towards free trade. Two trends are evident. First, trade with the developing world as a percentage of all EU external trade has remained fairly static; any rise has largely been thanks to the Asian NICs who can no longer reasonably be included in any contemporary categorization of development status. Second, this trend dis-

TABLE 5.4 *Comparison of EU/USA trade with MERCOSUR, 1996–98*

Exports to MERCOSUR (€bn)			
	1996	*1997*	*1998*
EU	18.5	23.3	24.4
USA	14.6	20.4	21.7
Imports from MERCOSUR (€bn)			
	1996	*1997*	*1998*
EU	14.9	17.5	18.0
USA	9.5	11.3	13.2

Source: Eurostat (1998) and http://europa.eu.int/comm/

guises other regional disparities and the fact that there have been significant winners (Asia in general) and losers (the ACP and to a lesser extent Latin America). Thus Latin America (defined in Table 5.3 to include Central America as well as South America) has been reduced in importance for both imports and exports (to around just 5 per cent) over the 24-year period, whilst as we have already seen the ACP has fallen by a larger degree to hover around just 3 per cent. Conversely, ASEAN has more than doubled its import and export trade with the EU, the Asian NICs by three- or fourfold, whilst China has the potential to emerge as the single most important partner after decades of isolation from the EU.

As noted already, the Treaty of Rome's colonial context made no mention of relations with any specific non-associated countries. Indeed, it was really only in the Maastricht Treaty that development (aid and trade) became a clear normative goal even if greater emphasis was given to symbolism over substance (Birocchi, 1999, p. 3). The subsequent Council Regulation (443/920) defined the EU's financial, economic and human development perspectives for the ALA (Asia-Latin American) countries, a policy position that will remain in effect until any regional FTAs are established. The introduction of a GSP regime in 1971 shaped trading relations with Latin America and Asia at least until the reforms of the 1994 GATT Uruguay Round. The unilateral nature of the GSP regime of course allowed the

EU, through tariffs and quotas, to limit sensitive products (such as textiles) and excluded almost all agricultural exports to Europe because of the internal demands of the subsidized CAP. The EU increasingly used other, non-tariff, measures to control EU–ALA trade. These included such things as 'voluntary export restraints' which impose a maximum figure for selected export products to Europe from specific countries. 'Rules of origin' that control products eligible for trade preferences, as well as anti-dumping legislation have further constrained the openness of ALA–EU trade. As one commentator concluded, EU trade policy towards Asia and Latin America prior to the 1994 Uruguay Round was 'in general inconsistent with the asserted pursuit of the ALA's development, being – unsurprisingly perhaps – much more concerned with the protection of European producers' (Birocchi, 1999, p. 8).

Coinciding with the emergence of the WTO, Europe has sought to redefine the nature of its economic relationship with both Asia and Latin America. As discussed previously, free trade through MERCOSUR has come to dominate the future framework with Latin America, whilst relations with Asia have shifted from an ASEAN to an ASEM focus. What has been the impact on trade of this shift – both actual and potential – in the basis of economic relations?

EU–MERCOSUR

An overview of the economic relationship between the EU and MERCOSUR was given in Chapter 2: the data presented here supplements that information and underlines the key economic trends. With respect to overall EU–MERCOSUR (including Chile) trade, the value between these two regional groupings exceeded €49 billion in 1998; and despite a 10 per cent MERCOSUR tariff on almost all goods, EU exports during the late 1990s grew steadily to over €24 billion, with Brazil the major market (ranked ninth overall for all EU exports). This, coupled with the fall-off in demand after the 1997 Asian crisis, has served to further highlight the importance of trade with Latin America in general. For MERCOSUR and Chile the EU is their main trading partner, ahead of the USA and Japan, and absorbs around one quarter of their exports. Increased FDI and greater privatization has also seen Europe's financial role in the region grow significantly during the 1990s (Bessa-Rodrigues, 1999, p. 90) although, as is the case across a wide area of the EU's external activity, the shadow of enlargement has slowed down this development.

According to data supplied by Eurostat and the Commission's own MERCOSUR external relations Web-site, trade between the EU and MERCOSUR rose considerably during the 1990s; the total value of trade flows (exports and imports) between the two blocks increased from €19 billion in 1990 to €42.5 billion by 1998, an increase of almost 125 per cent over the period. The EU suffered from a trade deficit with MERCOSUR until 1993/1994, but has enjoyed a surplus since then (in 1998 this was worth €6.4 billion). In terms of imports, the European Union constitutes MERCOSUR's main trading partner, accounting for 33 per cent of total imports in 1997; imports from the United States accounted for 27 per cent, from Japan 7 per cent, and just 5 per cent from Latin America. In terms of exports, the European Union is also MERCOSUR's main partner, accounting for 30 per cent of total exports in 1997; in comparison, exports to the United States accounted for 19 per cent, to Japan 6 per cent, and 13 per cent to the rest of Latin America. Over time, the European Union has been able to increase its market share, whereas the US share remained rather constant and that of Japan and the rest of Latin America has declined. Thus despite the existence of the North American Free Trade Agreement (NAFTA), the European Union is currently MERCOSUR's main supplier – although currency fluctuations and the presumed development of NAFTA could see this trend reversed in the medium term. Typically, the structure of the trade in goods has been asymmetrical: industrial products and capital goods are the main EU exports, whereas the principal exports for MERCOSUR are basic commodities, agricultural products and foodstuffs. Lastly, EU Foreign Direct Investment in MERCO-SUR also increased significantly during the 1990s, totalling $19.3 billion by 1997. The major investors were the United Kingdom, Spain, the Netherlands, Germany and France. The USA, however, retained its number one position as the largest contributor of FDI for MERCOSUR. The comparative wealth of Latin America when compared with the bulk of the ACP should not detract from its geopolitical and economic reality. MERCOSUR is composed of a group of economically asym-

FIGURE 5.2   Value of EU trade (exports/imports) with Asia*,1995–7
(bn ecus)

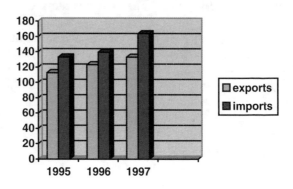

Note: * Indonesia, Malaysia, Philippines, Singapore, Thailand, Brunei, Vietnam,
Laos, China, Japan and South Korea.
Source: Eurostat (1998).

metrical developing countries, with immature democratic structures, located on the periphery of the global economy and
vulnerable to the vagaries of international economics. Despite
the internal disparities between the MERCOSUR members
themselves, let alone with those of the EU, the purpose of the
1995 Framework Agreement on Inter-regional Cooperation is
familiar – to promote regional integration and assist free trade
(see Chapter 2).

EU–ASIA

Prior to the economic crisis of the late 1990s, the EU operated
a regular trade deficit with the Asia (defined here as the eight
ASEM partners – Indonesia, Malaysia, Philippines, Singapore,
Thailand, Brunei, Vietnam, Laos – plus China, Japan and South
Korea). In 1997, for example, this group of 11 Asian economies
had a trade surplus with the EU of some €31 billion (see Figure
5.2): Asia accounted for nearly one quarter of the EU's global
imports (24.5 per cent) and close to one-fifth (18.5 per cent) of
extra-EU exports of goods. The bulk of all imports and exports
were in machinery and transportation equipment. For all of the
manufactures categories the EU operated a trade deficit with

Asia (see Table 5.5). In contrast, the trade in services has been in favour of the EU during the same period. For example, the trade in services provided the EU with a 6.4 billion ecus surplus in 1996 (with the export of services to Japan accounting for over half of the total value in this sector). Typically, the UK alone accounts for almost half of the EU's surplus. Despite the trade gap favouring Asia, for several of the member states, the Asian market is particularly important. Germany, France, the UK and Italy were the largest exporters, whilst Germany, the UK and the Netherlands were the largest importers of Asian goods in 1997 – together Germany and the UK took a massive 48.4 per cent of all Asian imports to the EU (see Table 5.6).

Another perspective on the EU–Asian relationship suggests that 'The problem for the EU with trade with East Asia is not so much its size but its rate of growth' (Grimwade and Mayes, 2000, p. 361). Whilst by 1994 the ten largest East Asian economies accounted for just 10.8 per cent of EU total imports, all bar the Philippines saw their percentage share of imports rise over the 1983–94 period (see Table 5.7). This situation was exacerbated by the imbalance in imports and exports: in 1994 exports to East Asia represented only 7.5 per cent of the EU's total exports resulting in a substantial trade imbalance. The change in the importance of China over the period is significant as is obviously the asymmetrical effect of trade with Japan. When the comparative advantage of East Asian exports of primary products and certain labour-intensive manufactures (such as clothing and footwear) are considered, clearly there may be risks associated with liberalizing trading relations through ASEM for the EU.

Normal relations with China were only established in 1975. The potential growth for trade with China (as well as the challenge posed by any trade imbalance) constitutes the most important factor in the EU's Asian trading relations. In 1980 the value of two-way trade was a mere 2.4 billion ecus: by 1998 this figure has expanded to €59.1 billion (Jia-dong, 2000, p. 3). Whilst these levels are currently only around half of that for EU–Japan trade the expanding pattern of trade with China is undeniable. It appears to be simply a matter of time until China becomes the EU's most important Asian trading partner.

A longer-term perspective that contrasts East Asia and ASEAN and other developing countries according to the

160

TABLE 5.5 *Value of trade by major product group, 1995–97 (bn ecus)*

EU	Imports			Exports			Balance		
	1995	1996	1997	1995	1996	1997	1995	1996	1997
Raw materials	8.6	9.1	9.7	9.2	9.2	10.9	0.6	0.1	1.2
Chemicals	6.3	6.6	7.7	13.6	14.2	15.5	7.3	7.6	7.8
Machinery & transport	72.3	74.3	87.1	57.5	62.5	68.3	-14.7	-11.8	-18.8
Other manufactures	46.0	49.3	59.3	32.3	37.2	38.1	-13.7	-12.1	-21.2
Total	133.2	139.3	163.8	112.6	123.1	132.8	-20.6	-16.3	-31.0

Source: Eurostat (1998).

TABLE 5.6   *Value of member state imports/exports with Asia*, 1995–97*

EU Imports from Asia			
	Bn ecus		
	1995	*1996*	*1997*
Germany	37.8	37.8	41.5
UK	28.0	30.7	37.8
Netherlands	14.6	16.9	20.9
France	14.1	14.5	17.1
Italy	10.0	9.8	11.6
Bel/Lux	7.8	7.9	9.1
Sweden	3.6	3.5	4.1
Other 7 EU states	17.3	18.2	21.6
EU 15	**133.2**	**139.3**	**163.8**
EU Exports to Asia			
	Bn ecus		
	1995	*1996*	*1997*
Germany	34.5	36.8	36.6
UK	16.2	18.3	22.5
France	17.0	16.8	19.6
Italy	14.6	17.0	16.4
Netherlands	6.3	6.1	7.0
Bel/Lux	5.3	6.1	6.3
Sweden	5.0	6.5	7.1
Other 7 EU states	13.7	15.4	17.4
EU 15	**112.6**	**123.1**	**132.8**

Note: * Indonesia, Malaysia, Philippines, Singapore, Thailand, Brunei, Vietnam, Laos, China, Japan and South Korea.
Source: *Eurostat* (1998).

percentage of two-way trade is described in Table 5.8. Whilst ASEAN only accounts for around one third of EU trade with East Asia in total, the ASEAN figure is similar to that for Latin America but more than twice as great as for the ACP group of states. In addition, trade with ASEAN has continued to grow over this period whilst that with Latin America has remained

TABLE 5.7 *EU imports, exports and trade balance with East Asia, 1983–94 (US$m.)*

Country	Imports		Exports		1994 Trade Balance
	1983	1994	1983	1994	
Thailand	1 576	7 617	1 153	6 990	−627
Malaysia	1 990	9 088	1 488	6 593	−2 495
Singapore	1 597	9 769	2 472	10 244	+475
Indonesia	1 249	7 070	2 169	4 944	−2 126
Philippines	1 007	2 319	961	2 275	−44
China	2 485	27 848	2 538	14 457	−13 391
South Korea	2 648	10 499	1 457	11 582	+1 083
Taiwan	2 845	12 790	1 402	9 988	−2 802
Hong Kong	4 027	7 655	2 819	15 211	+7 556
Japan	19 994	62 378	6 788	30 962	−31 416
East Asian Ten	39 328	157 033	23 248	113 247	−43 786
Global EU Total	621 935	1 450 699	594 172	1 500 932	

Source: Grimwade and Mayes (2000).

TABLE 5.8 *Percentage of EU external trade by regional groupings, 1975–97*

	1975		1985		1995		1997	
	Imports	Exports	Imports	Exports	Imports	Exports	Imports	Exports
ASEAN	1.9	2.5	2.7	3.0	6.3	6.4	6.9	6.3
East Asia	9.5	7.1	14.8	10.7	26.7	21.7	26.9	20.2
Latin America	6.5	8.0	8.1	4.5	5.6	5.7	5.1	6.3
ACP	7.9	8.1	7.9	5.5	3.7	3.1	3.4	2.8

Source: Eurostat (1998) and Dent (1999).

somewhat flat and – as we have already seen – the ACP has seen a dramatic collapse, especially in exports to the EU. Focusing explicitly on the ASEAN framework, trade forms the heart of the EU relationship. The composition of this trade has changed over a 20-year period. In 1980 approximately two-thirds of ASEAN exports to Europe consisted of raw materials – by 2000 around three-quarters of ASEAN's exports were in electronics, manufactures, textiles and clothing.

In summary, clearly, trade is a core element of the EU relationship with the non-ACP developing world; the contrast with the limited and declining volume of ACP–EU trade is marked. However, what is also noticeable is the overlapping frameworks used to define EU–Asian (and to a lesser extent EU–Latin American) economic relations. The EU's preference for region-to-region arrangements does not always fully correspond to the realities of regional integration in third countries. Certainly in the Asian case, the EU has been responsible for inventing new frameworks (such as ASEM) that cut across more trading economic patterns (as with ASEAN). Whilst the 'one size fits all' approach has little to recommend it, the multiplications of regimes created by the EU simply mystifies rather than clarifies the character if its international role.

Given the EU's wider global view on region-to-region free trade, the history of past relations is in many senses irrelevant for the twenty-first century. What is important from a development perspective is how different parts of the Third World can respond and compete on what will be an ever-increasing 'level playing field' without the support and advantages of preferred trading relations. Such a scenario suggests an ever widening gap between Asia and Latin America on the one hand, and the ACP on the other. The reform of Lomé notwithstanding, the Third World is rapidly becoming virtually an African phenomenon from the EU's perspective. And for both intra-EU rationales as well as external pressures, trade and the market have replaced aid and preferences as the preferred development mechanism.

Conclusion

Trade is not a technocratic policy sector – it is fundamentally political. This has never been more evident than in the 1990s debate on globalization and liberalization that penetrated the Commission as well as the member states. As one analysis expresses it, 'is the Union a force for global free trade or for protectionism?' (Peterson and Bomberg, 1999, p. 90). Whilst the jury may still be out on this question, the EU's preference for trading blocs provides evidence of both efficiency in trading relations as well as that for trade diversion by distorting the operation of a truly free global market. Within this ideological battle, the interests of the Third World have been increasingly marginalized (although the post-Seattle WTO has raised the question of inclusion of a development agenda within globalization). Similarly, the compartmentalization of trade as an 'external' issue denies the multi-level inter-related nature of the EU. An internal EU single market – even monetary union to a degree – demands (legally requires) a common external trade policy. Without this the very core of the customs union would be inoperative. Thus, the EU's external policies may be regarded as a fundamental aspect of the integration process – an argument that is developed in greater detail in the concluding chapter of this book.

Further, as has been illustrated elsewhere, trade policy – together with aid – has been a major diplomatic tool for expressing the EU's foreign policy. Of course, both trade and aid fall outside a narrow CFSP definition of foreign policy, but legal context cannot reduce the practical importance of trade as 'the EU's most potent tool of influence in foreign policy' (Peterson and Bomberg, 1999, p. 104). A consequence of this fragmented policy structure has been the proliferation of free trade arrangements with different groups of countries that reflect individual idiosyncrasies rather than the application of any general principle or common EU framework. Political choices rather than economic rationality have been the over-riding influence.

The complexity of trading relations has been compounded by the progressive application of Articles 300 and 310 that allow the EU to conclude agreements with third countries, or groups of countries. However, the shadow of the WTO means special privileges are less likely to be possible as the principle of treating like countries alike dominates. Indeed, the WTO philosophy conflicts and is in some ways incompatible with that of the EU: the WTO wants to promote uniform global free trade, whereas the EU is busy trying to create region-to-region free trade areas.

The content of free trade also differs from region to region for the EU, as special interests manoeuvre for protection creating policy contradictions that can verge on the schizophrenic. Although liberalization has clearly become the dominant philosophy of the EU, this does not mean necessarily that the approach is warmly embraced by all member states. Indeed, southern member states lead typically by France have often been characterized as instinctively opposed to liberalization because of the importance the protection of agriculture plays domestically. An example of the power of such a coalition was evident during both the MERCOSUR and South African free trade negotiations of the late 1990s where agriculture was largely excluded from the list of products for tariff removal.

The decision-making context of external trade relations is also an important component in determining the shape and outcome of the relationship. Under Article 310 association agreements require unanimity in the Council as well as the assent of the European Parliament. The interplay of the Commission (using its right of initiative in trade policy) and the Council has often proved conflictual, necessitating lowest common denominator outcomes that reflect national preferences. However, the motivation to speak with one voice has tended to result in a less strident policy being articulated. With respect to the European Parliament, here special interests can also distort the negotiated agreements significantly, although interestingly this has occasionally been to the advantage of the Third World. The Parliament was highly critical of the FTA agreement proposed for the EU and South Africa and pushed for greater concessions on the part of the EU. A similar role for the Parliament seems quite likely when it finally gets to consider the 2000 Cotonou Partnership Agreement signed with the ACP. Indeed there were signs in early 2001 that Cotonou would be the focal point for a trade dispute involving the reduced market access for ACP sugar because of the EU's new approach to treat all LDCs on an equal footing. The outline of this emerging dispute is discussed in Chapter 8 of this book.

Chapter 6

The 1996–2000 Reform Process

By the mid-1990s the old certainties pertaining to development policy were under threat and a new global agenda began to shape the EU's policy towards the Third World. This chapter examines the rationale for reform and the evolution of the debates on the post-Lomé framework that began in 1996. The chapter identifies and analyses four phases of change: the initial Green Paper options; the subsequent Commission guidelines; the negotiating mandate; and the eventual negotiating process. The discussion concludes with an assessment of the implications of the reforms for policy coordination, coherence and complementarity – the official mantra driving external relations.

The 1993 Treaty on European Union provided a general guide to the objectives of EU development policy. In general, the principles of cooperation, consistency, coherence and complementarity were – at least in theory – the criteria around which development policy was to be constructed. Article 130 states that Europe's policies should be 'complementary' to those of the member states. Both political and economic objectives are specified. EU policy has to contribute to 'consolidating democracy and the rule of law, and to that of respecting human rights and fundamental freedoms'. Economically, EU policy has to foster 'sustainable economic and social development . . . particularly (of) the most disadvantaged', facilitate the 'gradual integration of the developing countries into the world economy' and serve to eradicate poverty.

At one level the EU's policy could be seen to be consistent with these objectives. However, the realities of implementation, the problems of coherence between different EU policy sectors and actors, as well as effectiveness suggested a less complacent conclusion. If the measure of success was the alleviation of poverty, then the EU's policy record was one of failure, albeit of good intent.

Whilst the trade advantages of the Convention had been significantly eroded since 1975, it still provided these states with non-reciprocal duty-free access to Europe's single market for a wide range of specified goods (largely primary products with certain agricultural exceptions). As noted already, during the 1990s, on average the EU supplied 50 per cent of the ACP's imports and took 45 per cent of their exports. In addition there were important protocols (on sugar cane and on bananas) as well as provisions for more traditional forms of aid and assistance. Aid provided through the Lomé mechanism amounted to 52 per cent of the EU's total external aid in 1990. As noted in the introduction to this book, with the fall of communism in 1989 the ACP developing states saw EU funds switch dramatically in favour of the transitional economies of Central and Eastern Europe. Both in terms of trade and aid, the once privileged status of the Lomé states was effectively downgraded and a number of other groupings of states enjoyed better access to the European market.

By way of illustration of the changing trading patterns, in 1995 8.6 per cent of the EU's imports and 10.2 per cent of exports were with the CEECs. In contrast, in the same year the Lomé states supplied only 3.7 per cent of the EU's imports, and took just 3.1 per cent of exports. Further evidence of this decline was evident in the distribution of aid. By 1995 the Lomé states accounted for only one third of the EU's total aid – and this trend saw almost three-quarters of the EU's external aid going to non-Lomé countries by the year 2000. Critics argued that the EU was failing to implement Article 130u of Maastricht with profound implications for poverty alleviation.

In its summary review of past development policy, the Commission concluded that the Lomé principles of partnership, contractuality, predictability and security had produced an unrivalled development framework. But critically, on balance these benefits did not compensate for more serious shortcomings:

> The principle of partnership has proved difficult to carry through. Dependence on aid, short-termism and the pressure of crises have increasingly overshadowed relations. The recipient country's institutional environment and economic and social policy have often been a major constraint on the effectiveness of Community cooperation. The Union must bear

some responsibility: its procedures have also limited the effectiveness of its aid. The impact of trade preferences has been disappointing on the whole. (Commission, 1997a, p. 7)

The rationale for reform

As outlined on pages 17–18 of the Introduction, Lomé was challenged on several fronts. First, was the record of European assistance. Few, Lomé countries had seen a radical transformation in their economies: dependency continued to define the relationship with Europe. Not only had the Lomé framework failed fundamentally to improve the economic positions of the vast majority of ACP states, some critics suggested that the historic pattern of first-third-world dependency had even become more deeply embedded. This disillusionment, coupled with the domestic financial constraint on the EU budget and pressures from key member states, combined to make policy reform a priority. Consequently, the EU has insisted on economic and political conditionality to promote good governance, as well as sought to redefine the economic basis of the relationship.

The enormous changes witnessed in the international environment during the 1990s provided a second motivation for change. Prior to 1989 Europe's development policy had been exclusively focused on the 'traditional' Third World. With the collapse of communism in Central and Eastern Europe, development priorities were increasingly switched to these newly democratic transitional economies. For the EU, charity, or at least aid, increasingly appeared to begin close to home. In many ways, the integration process and the necessity of Eastern enlargement presented detrimental (if unintended) consequences for the developing world beyond Europe's borders.

Third, the parameters of the global environment changed. This presented new opportunities – and dangers – based around technology and the globalization of trading and financial systems. Crucially, the pervasive trend towards trade liberalization and the World Trade Organization orthodoxy were at odds with the traditional preferential aspects of Lomé. The WTO had begun generally to examine preferential agreements, and specifically with respect to Lomé. Although Lomé IV had been granted a WTO waiver, clearly this anomaly could not be maintained in the medium term. Whether the WTO position on Lomé simply reflected the EU's own free trade prejudices or acted as a catalyst for them is unclear. However, a free trade agenda became part of the EU's new ideology and was set to play a central role in defining the shape of the future EU–ACP dialogue.

Fourth and somewhat paradoxically, both in terms of trade and aid the once privileged status of the Lomé states was effectively downgraded and other group-to-group dialogues provided better access to the European market. As discussed in the earlier chapters, from a position at the apex of the so-called 'pyramid of privilege' in the 1970s, the ACP states saw their status progressively eroded: the CEECs, the Mediterranean associates as well as a number of bilateral agreements all provided better preferential access further marginalizing the ACP's competitive position.

Lastly, as argued elsewhere in this text, the diversity within the developing world and the obvious inconsistencies in the EU's geographical organization became unsustainable. The dissimilar treatment of similar developing countries was increasingly difficult to explain. Post-colonial ties and historical links were the obvious explanations for this tradition of differentiation. But the patchwork and incremental nature of Lomé has undoubtedly been regarded as its greatest weakness. Of course, the ACP attempted to maintain the appearance of solidarity and common interests, but even within the group a developing – least developed dichotomy began to emerge and receive recognition. While geography was not completely abandoned, in future it would have to co-exist with the criterion of development status. Both the subsequent Cotonou Partnership Agreement and the 'Everything but Arms' initiative reflected this new reality.

In response to these and other demands, in November 1996 the Commission of the EU issued its discussion Green Paper on the future of Lomé, the implications of which were to prove far-reaching for Europe and the developing world. The past motivations of altruism (based on moral arguments) and self-interest (based on a Cold War mentality) were under attack and the new intellectual rationale driving the EU's external relations now emphasized democracy, liberalized market economy and regionalism. The expectation was that the reform options would imply a reduction in the existing ACP 'privileges'. Under threat appeared to be the concept of equal partnership between the EU and the ACP countries, automatic entitlement to aid and the security of long-term treaty-based trading relations. Conversely, moving beyond the patchwork of agreements towards a comprehensive pattern of global EU development relations was possibly a better way to secure cooperation, coherence and complementarity (see Chapter 4). As we have seen, to be effective, development policies of the EU and of the member states have to complement each other; they have to be coordinated at the policy and operational levels; and they have to keep development objectives consistent (coherent) with EU trade, fisheries, agricultural and other policy sectors – a considerable task. Any new EU–ACP relationship would need to respect and operate within the parameters of these basic policy principles.

There are two levels of this problem that need to be distinguished: first, between the member states themselves; and second, within the EU. The Maastricht Treaty formally addresses the role of member states in Article 130x. It states 'The Community and the Member States shall co-ordinate their policies on development co-operation and shall consult each other on their aid programmes.' However, this Treaty obligation can only modify rather than resolve the genuine differences in objectives, priorities and mechanisms on development issues that exist among the Fifteen. For example, French development policy remains largely neo-colonial, Italy follows a more commercial approach, the UK stresses good governance whereas the Nordic states focus principally on the alleviation of poverty. Such varied perspectives make it difficult to establish even inter-member-state coordination, coherence or complementarity. So the first challenge is at the member-state, not EU, level. Member states behave in vastly different ways and there is very little shared knowledge on what each does, or the existence of institutional relations that could coordinate individual bilateral development programmes despite the aspirations of Maastricht.

The second level relates to the EU. As Article 130 stresses, complementarity is a policy goal. However, complementarity demands coordination and cooperation in order to deliver a more effective EU development policy. As argued already, for primarily historical reasons (and the incrementalism of enlargement) development policy has expanded in an unstructured and inconsistent way. But the question remains who coordinates whom within the EU framework? Can, or should, the Commission coordinate the member states? To confer new powers on the Commission is at odds with the general anti-Commission thrust of the Maastricht, Amsterdam and Nice reforms. Given such a control lacuna, it is hardly surprising that the implementation of complementarity has been slow, particularly given the conflicting agenda of restraining the role of the Commission. For policy initiatives to be workable and respect Treaty obligations, a clear coordinating function for the Commission has to be conceded.

The problem of coordination also permeates the Commission itself. As the external competences of the Union have evolved these have resulted in a diversification, not centralization, of institutional responsibility. As already discussed in Chapter 3, prior to the Prodi reorganization development policy involved seven separate actors within the Commission: DGI, DGIA, DGIB, DGII, DGVIII, DGXII and ECHO. The range of accompanying coordination problems that this led to were identified in the external review of EC aid undertaken by the OECD's Development Assistance Committee. In particular, attention was drawn to the overly complex organizational structure of Brussels compared with other donors and the problems that this posed for some recipient countries. A suggested possible reform in this area was the creation of a separate agency within the Commission whose responsibility would be to bring all these professional and technical functions together. Again, in the contemporary political climate such an enhanced role for the Commission was unacceptable.

Even if the question of accountability could be resolved, any such structural reform runs counter to one other DAC criticism: expertise and staffing levels. Around 1000 Commission officials are involved in development policy, with a further 340 in Commission delegations in developing countries. This represents a comparatively small staff when compared with those of similar-sized donors such as the USA and the World Bank. In addition to total numbers, the DAC report identified specific policy areas where expertise was most lacking – poverty alleviation, gender, population and the environment. In such a context, policy coordination is handicapped, 'coherence' becomes unpredictable and complementarity may be sacrificed. A more effective EU development policy will require improved management with increased budgetary implications.

The Green Paper and the new agenda

Although technically the Commission Green Paper was just a consultative document, the four options outlined suggested that a substantive, perhaps paradigmatic, change was anticipated. The Green Paper options were:

- *The status quo*: this saw the existing contractual system of non-reciprocal preferences maintained, if moderately reformed. However, there appeared to be a lack of political will in Europe to follow this path, and it was questionable whether the ACP itself retained the cohesion and collective interests to negotiate as a single bloc.
- *GSP*: a uniform application of the EU's Generalized Scheme of Preferences for the ACP states, thereby removing trade from any future Europe–Third World agreement. This would remove the ACP preference and the anomaly of differential treatment for different parts of the developing world.
- *Uniform reciprocity*: after an asymmetrical transitional period all ACP countries would be required to extend reciprocity to the EU in line with WTO rules. Essentially, this provided for an EU–ACP free trade area. A possible pointer to such a future direction was the Free Trade Area proposal offered to South Africa by the EU in 1996–7.
- *Differentiated reciprocity*: in this option different groups of states or individual countries were to receive different reciprocal arrangements with the EU, again based on free trade arrangements.

What was the case for the status quo? Clearly, the ACP states were in a position to lobby for a largely similar agreement provided there remained a consensus to do so. Dismantling the existing ties would be a difficult and time-consuming undertaking and the EU would probably have preferred to avoid a head-on confrontation. The existing institutions, particularly the ACP–EU Joint Assembly, had established roles and functions that were also resistant to reform. However, the ACP states remained in an essentially dependent relationship. As past revisions of the Lomé Convention had shown, generally the EU can successfully insist upon its policy proposals, leaving the ACP with a virtual *fait accompli*. The negotiation dynamics are inevitably unequal. Consequently, any ACP desire for the status quo was not a sufficient condition; member-state acquiescence was the necessary prerequisite – and increasingly that could not be presumed. At the heart of the dilemma were the concerns referred to above: a history of mixed results; the changing global development context; the inconsistencies in the EU's global arrangements; and, the increasingly dissimilar nature of the African, Caribbean and Pacific components of the group. As one commentator at the time remarked: 'Will the ACP ever mean anything more than the group of developing countries which have a privileged link with the EU? Can they exist outside this relationship vis-à-vis the UN and its many agencies?' (Lowe, 1996, p. 27).

Arguments in favour of the status quo stressed the contractual integrity of Lomé that facilitated a degree of regime certainty. The Convention also differentiated between LDCs and created specialized preferences (albeit imperfectly). Lomé also provided unique access to a range of sensitive European agricultural markets prohibited to other third countries. Conversely, the case against the status quo argued that the necessity for an annual WTO waiver undermined the certainty of preserving the existing Lomé trade preferences – one of the key characteristics of the Convention as identified by the Commission in support of the status quo. Second, this uncertainty undermined investor confidence and inhibited the much-needed flow of foreign direct investment. Third, the framework did not provide any additional impetus to the regional integration processes among ACP countries. Last, accession to the Lomé Convention prohibited any ACP state or grouping from participating in regional trading arrangements involving any other developed countries.

The post-Lomé alternatives

Turning to the implications of the other options, the application of a uniform GSP would have the advantage of harmonizing the non-reciprocal preferential trade regime bringing the EU into full conformity with WTO rules. Non-Lomé LDCs would finally receive equal treatment from the EU. Further, it would abolish the treaty impediment that prevents ACP countries from engaging in regional partnerships with other developed countries (such as NAFTA or APEC). Conversely, under such a GSP regime ACP countries would no longer be treated uniformly as preferences would reflect differential levels of development. The reduction in preferential margins for the more developed ACP agricultural exporters would be significant and the existence of the Lomé Sugar Protocol threatened. Except for the LDCs, the security of market access provided by Lomé would be affected and developing countries would forfeit any formal input into the EU's external trade regulations because the GSP is a unilateral EU instrument. Finally, the aid and trade linkage established through Lomé would be severed and its founding principle of partnership eroded.

The option of uniform reciprocity is conceived in terms of WTO compatibility and is consistent with the general thrust of integrating developing country economies into the global framework (as required in the TEU). The benefits of this would include enhancing trade credibility and foreign investor confidence by contractually guaranteeing an open import market and fixed preferences. As is the case for the GSP option, regional trading arrangements with developed countries would be permissible and non-Lomé developing countries would benefit by receiving equal treatment. More critically, any such uniform treatment fails to address the marked differences in levels of development and ability to compete in a free trade environment within the ACP. Further, the feasibility of such a comprehensive approach is dependent on all signatories agreeing to a common schedule (under GATT Article XXIV.5(c)). As the Green Paper notes, such an EU–ACP free trade area would need to take 'into account their trading patterns, their differing needs for industrial restructuring, for changes in fiscal policy which could be required to accompany the dismantling of tariffs, etc. It would be impossible for a single framework to accommodate the needs and the conditions of all ACP countries'.

The option of differentiated reciprocity offers similar benefits to those of uniform reciprocity but addresses the different levels of development and priorities found within the ACP. What was envisaged was that each region or sub-grouping of the ACP (or LDCs in general) would have a specific reciprocity schedule tailored to particular needs. This would allow for differentiation and assist regional integration processes. However, reciprocity is still the defining characteristic and as such represents a significant step along the free trade continuum. Obviously, any regionally specific scheme undermines the uniform nature of the existing Convention. For example, individual commodity protocols and agricultural preferences would have to be renegotiated leading to differentiation in treatment within the ACP. Feasibility is also a consideration. Not all ACP member states necessarily wish to belong to, or form part of, any existing regional integration process. Such states would be left with having to negotiate separate bilateral FTA agreements with the EU that are compatible with GATT/WTO criteria. Even where asymmetrical free trade defines the new relationship, some form of protection will have to be provided to the 'losers' amongst the developing world (particularly the LDCs and those African countries excluded from European assistance because of their poor records on human rights and undemocratic governments). The precise content of this asymmetry remained a matter for negotiation.

Overall, the Green Paper gave strong indications that FTAs (as defined in the June 1995 Council Conclusions) were very much part of the new development agenda; as such, the contrast with the Lomé regime was profound. If the existing policy framework was incapable of achieving the development goals of Article 130 or of enhancing coordination, coherence and complementarity, which of the Green Paper reform proposals provided a better context? The late 1990s saw a new international development agenda emerge that stresses a number of related factors: a) differentiation between richer and poorer countries; b) concentration of resources to the poorest; c) graduation of the more successful developing countries away from aid; d) promotion of the role of the private sector; and e) the integration of the LDCs into the global economy. These priorities also influenced the European debate with many arguing that a regional focus better met these concerns. The traditional aid route to development lost ground to a belief in emphasizing trade reform and private capital. As such, well-constructed regional groupings could facilitate increased intra-regional trade flows and investment patterns.

Supporters of Lomé argued that none of this was necessarily incompatible with the Convention framework. Regionalism has always had a role within the ACP and the EU has actively pursued regional integration on a global scale. The post-Lomé choice was therefore not a zero-sum one: regional differentiation within an expanded ACP framework could be construed as compatible with the new agenda priorities of the member states. Alternatively, geography was not necessarily the most suitable organizing principle. Reformulating groups of countries according to differentiated levels of development (grouping all the LDCs together, for example) could be more profitable. Again, an expanded ACP framework could arguably accommodate both forms of differentiation.

Whatever the outcome of the global versus regional format debate, two ancillary issues had to be addressed: reciprocity and free trade. As noted above, two of the Green Paper options explicitly called for the removal of the principle of non-reciprocity. Again, such a trend mirrors the wider trading agenda pursued by the EU: the progressive assimilation of the developing countries into the wider global economy; and, the promotion of the longer-term objective of global free trade. For an increasing number of countries trade, not aid, is the more important key to development. For example, in 1994 the total export earnings of developing countries exceeded their combined aid by a ratio of 8:1. Whilst the very weakest developing economies may require prolonged protection, the EU's emphasis clearly favoured 'levelling-up' trading relations on the basis of normal country-to-country reciprocity. This and Europe's free trade agenda was clearly linked to WTO obligations that seek to dismantle trade barriers (albeit in an asymmetrical fashion). Whatever post-Lomé arrangements were to be devised they had to comply with the broader WTO multilateral trade liberalization programme. What was clear from this new agenda – even before the lengthy negotiations commenced in September 1998 – was that EU–ACP relations had reached a watershed.

The Commission Guidelines and policy transition

The late 1990s saw EU–Third World relations on the verge of unprecedented change: root and branch reform, not cosmetic

incrementalism prevailed. This section examines the new negotiating mandate and policy innovations that emerged out of
the Green Paper consultation exercise and resulted in the 1997
Commission 'Guidelines'.

As noted above, the Green Paper was designed to initiate a
broad participatory and transparent policy debate; over the subsequent nine months there was intense commentary on these
proposals from the ACP, member states as well as institutions
such as the European Parliament. Unsurprisingly, the more
radical aspects were strongly opposed by the ACP as well as by
the European Parliament. For example, the Parliament adopted
the Martens Report from the Committee for Development
Cooperation in October 1997 (PE 223.237). A special EU–ACP
ministerial conference was convened in addition to the normal
EU–ACP Joint Council meetings and consultation forums were
held in each of the three main ACP regions. Each member state
was invited to make its own submissions at the Working Group
level and a variety of expert bodies and interested parties from
civil society, non-governmental organizations and the private
sector were consulted from February through till the final
preparatory *rapporteurs* conference in late September 1997.
This broad inclusive approach, whilst virtuous, sat uneasily with
the Commission's expressed desire to simplify and streamline
development cooperation.

Based on the results of this extensive if compressed consultation, in October 1997 the Commission issued its policy guidelines
for negotiating the future of the ACP–EU dialogue (which in turn
formed the basis for the negotiation mandate agreed to by the
Council in June 1998). The guidelines sought to reconcile 'flexibility and efficiency with a multi-pronged, integrated approach to
cooperation' thereby placing the EU–ACP partnership on a new
footing (Commission, 1997a, p. 3). In essence this meant constructing a new overall agreement with the ACP that permitted
differentiation and was open and flexible enough to accommodate changing circumstances. The five principal components are
outlined in Box 6.1 and discussed individually below.

Political dialogue

The renewed political dialogue with the developing world drew
its authority from the EU desire to enhance its capacity – and

BOX 6.1   Summary Commission guidelines

- **A stronger political dimension** was advanced that built on the existing conditionality, emphasized legitimacy and effective governance and was based on a shared political vision. A major aspect of this new dialogue is conflict prevention and conflict resolution.
- **The alleviation of poverty** was reaffirmed as the cornerstone of the new partnership. An integrated approach to achieve this was advocated and poverty broadly defined to encompass economic issues, regional integration, the global economy, the role of private enterprise and a social dimension.
- **Enhanced cooperation and economic partnership** recognized that the status quo had failed to deliver economic growth. This proposal touched on the sensitive issues of regional geography and trade preferences and called for "regional or subregional economic cooperation and partnership agreements linked to the overall EU–ACP partnership agreement". The Green Paper free-trade initiative was significantly modified in this Commission negotiating document: importantly, reciprocity was only gradually to be introduced for those ACP countries that want it. However, the exclusive position of the ACP was signalled to be abandoned as this new economic partnership would extend Lomé treatment of all Least Developed Countries, ACP or otherwise.
- **The reform of financial management and technical cooperation procedures** were advocated in order to give a practical effect to the new partnership. A simplification and rationalization of cooperation instruments was suggested, as well as a greater involvement in, and responsibility for development programmes by the ACP.
- **The introduction of geographical differentiation** whilst maintaining the ACP group was the fifth basic principle – and the most contentious. Unsurprisingly, the ACP states response to the Green Paper had been to assert the importance of its collective identity. Although

> **BOX 6.1**   *Continued*
>
> heeding this expression of political will, the Commission insisted on the need to have differentiated procedures and agreement within the collective ACP umbrella. (Commission, 1997a)

credibility – in external relations. Development policy formed one part of this wider agenda. As is discussed elsewhere in chapter 4, this political dialogue faced the enormous task, given the bilateral and multilateral nature of European and member state policy, of respecting complementarity, coordination and consistency. At the heart of this 'new and inherently political contract' was a recognition of common interests (Commission, 1997a, p. 9). These covered topics as diverse as regional peace and stability, conflict resolution, sustainable development, AIDS, human rights, and migration. Specifically, the EU sought from the ACP a commitment to pursue reforms in the political, economic, social and environmental spheres consistent with Europe's definition of 'good governance'. In return, the EU offered:

- a strong in-depth political dialogue;
- assistance with conflict resolution;
- support for the implementation of 'responsible' policies;
- institutional development;
- an enhanced social dimension to cooperation;
- development of the private sector;
- recognition of environmental aspects of development;
- trade development and integration into the world economy;
- expansion of cooperation into technology and 'information society';
- the principle of regionalized cooperation within an overall agreement;
- differentiation of the procedures and priorities of cooperation based on the individual countries' level of development; and,
- a simpler, more efficient and accessible Convention. (Commission, 1997a, p. 10)

As discussed in the Introduction, despite the pillarization of Maastricht, an essential aspect of the new relationship from the European perspective is to incorporate development policy within the ambit of the EU's foreign policy and to ensure that it is consistent with the objectives of the CFSP. Of particular significance here are conflict prevention and peace-building measures: the 1997 guidelines on conflict prevention in Africa are an example of how the EU might exercise this role. More recently, the Amsterdam reforms have enhanced the EU's capacity to act by providing both a policy-planning and early-warning unit dedicated to incipient crises, as well as extending cooperation with the WEU particularly over the prevention and management of crises.

The interdependent nature of development policy, external relations and foreign policy was once again clearly underlined and it was the objective of the new EU–ACP political dialogue to make cooperation more effective. The new international development agenda emphasizes the link between socioeconomic and political conditions; development now meant more than basic economic needs and incorporated political, social, cultural and human rights. A significant aspect of the new political dialogue will therefore focus on strengthening the capacities of civil society among the ACP.

There are no formal constraints on the scope of the new political dialogue and, whilst no list of topics existed, a number of key areas were to be consistently addressed. First, human rights and democratic principles constitute the core of the dialogue: indeed, these two conditions have been part of every agreement signed between the EU and third countries since 1995. From a Lomé perspective, the application of human rights was associated with a wide range of social, educational and gender policies. Democratic principles were similarly linked to development. Although no precise model was specified by the Commission, the EU insisted on the fundamental features of representative democracy being developed – the separation of powers, independence of the judiciary, regular free elections and the rights to information and freedom of expression. To be effective, both human rights and democracy were to be supported by a strict application of the rule of law.

Good governance was regarded as crucial to development and constituted a second permanent feature of the political dialogue. As discussed in Chapter 4, the concept of good governance involved the open and responsible management of resources, be they human, natural or economic in nature for the purposes of economic and social development. It also involved the prevention and eradication of corruption as a dialogue objective. A further permanent feature will be conflict-prevention and settlement, enhancing both the EU's credibility as an international actor as well as clearly linking development policy to CFSP. Under this heading a range of security issues were to be covered in the political dialogue: arms sales; banning and removing landmines; and the illegal trafficking of weapons. Other 'political' topics for regular discussion included illegal immigration, drugs and cross-border crime. Obviously, as issues arise and the political context of relations change these core topics will be modified or expanded. The breadth and openness of the political dialogue is its most important feature. Consequently, circumstances will dictate whether the dialogues will be multilateral, regional or even bilateral. Turning dialogue into effective action, however, may be a different matter.

Alleviation of poverty

As TEU Article 130u demonstrates, poverty has become a development priority for Europe. This has been bolstered by subsequent Council resolutions since 1993 covering: social and human development and gender equality; health, education and food security; and structural adjustment support, emergency aid, rehabilitation and development. This new vision of development (mirroring the policy debates in the United Nations forum) combining economic, social and environmental dimensions has been instrumental in shaping the EU's response to the objective of poverty alleviation. Thus, for example, combating gender discrimination and environmental degradation is linked to the question of poverty as well as the more traditional concerns of healthcare and educational opportunities. This new approach also emphasized the developmental importance of creating a climate conducive to fostering the private sector, growth, competitiveness and employment. However, despite these priorities and incentives established by the EU, the chosen development options are exclusively determined by each developing country, not imposed directly by the EU. Of course, a developing country that eschews the European model runs the risk of losing EU support if its chosen policies lack viability.

Within this context, the Commission guidelines set three main policy priorities: growth, competitiveness and employment; social and cultural cooperation; and regional integration. These three priorities were underpinned by three essential criteria: capacity development; gender issues; and environmental principles. Support for policies for growth competitiveness and employment focused on aspects such as the implementation of credible macroeconomic, trade and sectoral policies. To facilitate this with respect to the contribution made by the private sector, administrative and institutional reforms were advocated together with the development of better financial systems, EIB aid, enhanced labour relations as well as improved education and training. Despite the recognition that for many developing countries external debt was the greatest impediment to growth, competitiveness and employment, the EU at this stage continued to view this problem through a wider international prism rather than adopt its own specific approach.

Support for social policies and cultural cooperation as a development priority was aimed at reducing inequalities in access to healthcare, education, housing, water and other essential services. Once again, reducing gender inequality was an underlying motivation. Indeed, EU–ACP cooperation agreements in future will be required to integrate gender issues into all macroeconomic, sectoral and project assistance. Food security, demographic policies and strengthening civil society and labour relations were also considered part of the social and cultural development policy. And, importantly, the recognition of cultural identities and the promotion of intercultural dialogue were also viewed as elements related to the alleviation of poverty. Finally, regional integration was seen as a stepping-stone to the incorporation of developing economies into the global system. The EU was to provide general support and advice for such schemes covering elements as diverse as macroeconomic policy, regional infrastructure, institutional capacities as well as direct funding to offset the transition costs to regional integration.

The creation of an adequate institutional capacity to support development was perhaps one of the key areas in which the EU could play both a critical and a distinctive role. As the history of Lomé has shown, aid and policy direction have proved inadequate where developing countries have lacked the institutional infrastructure to implement policy effectively. Capacity building was therefore one of the guiding criteria for assessing the EU's involvement in cooperation agreements – and covered not just institutional capacities, but all aspects of civil society and economic sectors. In particular, the capacities of the state and the public service within the context of democratization were to be identified as priority areas for reform and support. An efficient state with appropriate and effective delivery mechanisms was regarded as a development prerequisite.

Economic partnership

As is widely acknowledged, the Lomé trade cooperation has been a failure; consequently, the Commission guidelines proposed a number of policy changes. First, they recommend that the traditional Lomé approach to trade based around a system of unilateral preferences be replaced by a more balanced and country-specific partnership. The underlying motivations were again the ubiquitous desire to incorporate the ACP into the world economy, to foster a common EU–ACP approach and to facilitate a greater role for EU businesses within the ACP economies. Again, capacity building was prioritized but this time was related to trade compliance and standards rather than institutions.

Similarly, whilst an overall EU–ACP agreement was to be maintained, strengthening regional integration by signing individual EU agreements with Africa (subdivided in West, Central, Southern and East), the Caribbean and the Pacific was seen as a long-term objective. The Commission acknowledged, however, that the EU's promotion of regional integration had to respect and accommodate the special circumstances of the least-developed countries – their lower level of development, additional constraints and limited capacities.

Such diversity persuaded the Commission that differentiated agreements were essential within the context of an overall agreement. This differentiation would recognize the need for differing degrees of reciprocity and liberalization timetables. It was proposed that from 1998–2000 the overall general framework would be negotiated with specialized regional agreements adopted from 2000–03. These could take the form of either non-reciprocal cooperation agreements for LDCs, or economic partnership agreements consistent with the WTO principle of reciprocal free trade areas for economically stronger ACP states. Where no new agreement could be negotiated, transition arrangements extending the current preferences were available for those ACP states: after 2003, however, the Commission argued that these transitional preferences would be replaced by the EU's comprehensive GSP regime. Once in place, the region-alized economic cooperation agreements would introduce the concept of reciprocity to trading relations and form the basis for eventual free trade. Whilst WTO exemptions would be required at least until 2003, an important longer-term EU objec-tive was progressively to harmonize developing country prefer-ences and make them compatible with WTO provisions without the need for waivers. As the sensitive banana, sugar and beef regimes have shown, such waivers are always open to challenge by affected third parties.

Effectiveness

The contractual nature of Lomé had been one of its greatest strengths. However, the actual application of aid has failed to match expectations. A major criticism was that the variety of instruments used had led to undue complexity, inflexibility and lack of transparency leading to difficulties of ensuring consis-tency between them. Simplification and rationalization of instruments was a priority. Further, the existing 'second tranche' procedure for monitoring the performance of programme aid needed to be extended. Whilst aid should reflect need, it must also reflect merit based on effective implementation. Similarly, conditionality would continue to be used to encourage policy reform – although the EU was increasingly sensitive to the neg-ative perceptions this entailed. Last, greater devolution of the actual management of aid was necessary. This could involve a switch from project aid to budget aid or transferring some deci-sion-making authority from Brussels to EU Delegations in ACP countries. As is generally the case in policy-making, simplifica-tion tends to promote effectiveness.

Geographical differentiation

The final recommendation of the Commission guidelines was to complement an overall agreement with geographical differentiation – even if critics argued that these two objectives were inherently contradictory. The overall framework was to cover the general objectives, principles and institutional aspects of the relationship. The geographic differentiation would reflect the regional dimension of political dialogue, economic and trade cooperation and integration. Clearly, there were regional differences in the political dialogue that needed to be recognized – as well as items of common concern already discussed. The possible regional economic partnership agreements sought to find more appropriate trading relations that respected the varying levels of regional integration amongst the ACP group. A key objective, however, was to construct an economic framework that could encourage greater regional integration. Finally, whilst respecting the ACP grouping, the extension of Lomé privileges to non-Lomé countries of comparable levels of development (particularly the LDCs) was envisaged. At least in principle, membership remained open.

The Council negotiating mandate

The Council's negotiating mandate for reforming Lomé was finally agreed in June 1998, with formal negotiations commencing three months later on 30 September. The timing was important: the UK held the presidency for the first half of 1998 and the recently elected British Labour Government had strong views on development priorities. The changes both from the Green Paper and the Commission guidelines – as well as the similarities – are outlined here. As discussed elsewhere in this book, irrespective of the institutional openness of the process and the novelty of the consultative Green Paper, the negotiations between the EU and the ACP were vastly unequal. Those changes that did appear in the negotiating mandate were more likely to come from the member states and even the European Parliament than from the ACP. For reasons of domestic politics there were simply concessions that the EU was unable to make and explanations of Europe's external development policy can still largely be found in an analysis of domestic politics.

As early as March 1998 the areas of conflict became evident: in particular, whether the existing levels of access and preferences could be maintained. Whilst the Council supported the

Commission's general trade liberalization thrust, a number of member states (the UK and the Scandinavian countries in particular) were critical of this being imposed on all ACP states and promoted alternative mechanisms for those ACP states unable or unwilling to move towards reciprocity and liberalization. The key issues were the treatment of the LDCs; the GSP as an alternative to FTAs (affecting 20 ACP countries); and the fate of the banana, beef and sugar quota protocols.

During the last week of the 1998 British presidency, the General Affairs Council chaired by Foreign Secretary Robin Cook approved the negotiating directives for a new EU–ACP agreement. At one level this decision indicated there was on the European side a consensus on the future direction and objectives of the development partnership. However, this consensus came at the cost of compromise, bargains and certain specific reservations. The greatest area for compromise and effective presidential brokering was in the commercial sector. The British presidency managed to forge an agreement that permitted the LDCs to retain their existing Lomé preferences rather than have to automatically adopt the new free trade regime. This meant that for these 39 ACP Least Developed Countries zero duty access to the European market was maintained for all current Lomé products on the existing non-reciprocal basis. This constituted a significant policy change from the most radical of the Green Paper proposals and whilst there was general consensus on this principle, the timeframe was more problematic. The EU was divided between those Northern states that wanted this provision to be phased out no later than 2005 and those, such as Spain, that argued for a much longer timeframe. The final EU position adopted set 2005 as the cut-off date for these non-reciprocal arrangements.

Policy towards those remaining ACP countries that were not LDCs highlighted the tensions within the European 'consensus' and emphasized the often key role played by the presidency. The Dutch, thinking beyond the ACP mandate, wanted the GSP approach extended to all developing countries; conversely Spain objected to any discussion of GSP arguing that this was outside the remit of the Lomé talks. Furthermore, France, Italy and Germany were concerned that the GSP option would negate the incentives for the ACP to move towards reciprocal free trade and actually undermine this core objective of the Lomé negotiations. In engineering a new consensus on GSP, the presidency had to address the concerns of these national delegations. It was finally accepted that any ACP country that was either unwilling, or unable, to join a free trade regime would retain at least the current preferences offered through the GSP system. This signalled a substantive change of position within the member states and was indicative of the persuasive power of the UK presidency. Consequently, with respect to trading relations at least, the 1998 negotiating mandate was more sympathetic to the ACP's development agenda than most readings of the earlier Green Paper had suggested.

Last, the negotiating mandate acknowledged that the banana regime, together with those for beef and sugar, had to be addressed within the WTO context. Consequently, the presidency proposed a 2004 review date: however, the events of early 1999 that saw a trade war erupt between the EU and the USA over banana preferences suggested that decisions on these preferences were no longer exclusively European in origin.

The underlying objectives of the EU were officially summarized by the Secretary General of Commission DGVIII as consolidating commercial ties and facilitating regional integration

---

BOX 6.2   Summary June 1998 Council negotiating mandate

- maintenance of the present Lomé rules until 2005;
- negotiations to take place between 2000 and 2005 on economic partnership agreements between the EU and six regional ACP-groups;
- the introduction of free trade by 2015 at the earliest between the EU and countries suitable for economic liberalization;
- a review of the banana, beef and sugar protocols in 2004 in the light of the new Lomé agreement and WTO obligations; and
- a general review in 2004 on asymmetrical timetables for FTAs and future measures to be taken for countries unwilling or unable to join FTAs.

within a comprehensive framework that encompassed trade, investment and development. These initiatives, however, would still require the consent of the WTO for any waivers involving non-reciprocity as well as its agreement that a 15-year transition period was acceptable. Although 65 ACP countries were members of the 132-member WTO at this time, the norm of consensus decision-making prevailed. Whether the joint aims of reducing poverty and integrating the ACP states into the world economy could be achieved through these combined initiatives remained debatable.

Unequal partners: the negotiating process

The lietmotif of the Lomé was always its claim of partnership. The 1999 negotiating process, however, was marked more by inequality and one-way conditionality than parity. Indeed, one commentator has described the negotiations 'as a situation of total power asymmetry, where the normative consensus of the EU leaves little room for concessions' (Elgström, 2000, p. 195). Not that such an outcome was particularly surprising or unique. Each of the successive Lomé revisions had seen essentially the European perspective predominate. Much has been written about the nature of EU negotiations – be these internal, external, economic or diplomatic in form. Generally, the literature distinguishes between negotiations that offer specific reciprocity (as in the case of FTAs where precise concessions and agreements are identified) and those that offer diffused reciprocity. In this latter case, exact immediate trade-offs are not the focus of any agreement, but rather longer-term less precisely defined reciprocity becomes the basis for the negotiations. Typically, such diffuse reciprocity makes agreement easier to achieve in negotiations. The issue was which of these two approaches would dominate the negotiation.

As outlined at the beginning of the chapter, four distinct phases of the reform process can be isolated: the 1997 consultative Green Paper; the 1998 internal EU pre-negotiations; the 1998 negotiating mandate; and the 1999 negotiations themselves. Turning to this final phase – the 1999 negotiations proper – significant differences were immediately apparent between the

EU and the ACP negotiating mandates. These differences are highlighted below.

Trade

The ACP negotiating mandate on trade was reactive and primarily forged in response to the EU's free trade agenda. The Lomé status quo, if not totally abandoned and in contrast to all previous revisions, was not the basis on which the ACP approached the reform process. Areas of consensus covered the necessity for a specific EU–ACP trade regime that was distinct from GSP or MFN options, and the need for flexibility in interpreting WTO guidelines on reciprocity and free trade areas. The significant differences between the EU and ACP mandates covered three issues. First, the ACP proposed a longer FTA transition phase (10 years as opposed to 5 suggested by the EU). Second, the ACP sought to retain as much as possible of the existing Lomé provisions and protocols – not just for the LDCs as suggested by the EU – but also for what the ACP denoted as 'highly vulnerable countries' and those with either 'small economies' or with economic levels only marginally above LDC definitions (such as Zimbabwe and Ghana). Third, and most optimistically, the ACP called for improved access for agricultural products and for a relaxation in rules of origin requirements. Once again, this issue underlined the linkage between internal EU political questions and external relations: simply, domestic agricultural lobbies will normally oppose CAP concessions that favour Lomé producers. In addition, the ACP were concerned that unilateral non-tariff barriers might in future emerge (based on social or environmental criteria).

Institutions, dialogue and political conditionality

Turning to the political aspects of the mandate, there was a broad European consensus on the main elements contained within the Green Paper – democratization, human rights and good governance. The increased importance of the political dialogue was also emphasized. However, as an analysis of the ACP positions reveals, there was no unanimity between the developing countries and the EU on the content and application of these concepts. The agenda was principally Eurocentric.

Unsurprisingly, political conditionality was contentious. For the ACP the concept of partnership and new forms of conditionality were viewed as antagonistic; conversely, a political 'dialogue' focused on good governance was central to the EU's notion of partnership and development. The ACP did not question the elements of conditionality introduced in Lomé IV. What was resisted was the EU's agenda to extend the scope of good governance as a development prerequisite, particularly given the varied interpretations of what constituted good governance. Whilst the ACP subscribed to the principle of good governance, they rejected the European position that it should be the principle on which trade is made conditional. They argued that good governance was in part a result of institutional development and sustained efforts to build national capabilities (especially legislative, judicial and executive): these levels of institutional development vary widely across the ACP and could only improve through continued and guaranteed support. Indeed, to make trade or aid conditional may perversely undermine such institution building.

However, the asymmetry that has typified successive Lomé agreements looked destined to extend to good governance. The concept was largely defined in European terms and by European standards that could be incompatible with individual ACP cultures and institutional capacities. Common assumptions and motivations guiding the good governance agenda could not be presumed. Not only were the standards of good governance Eurocentric, the EU exercised the unilateral right to suspend any form of development assistance if it concluded that good governance had been breached. The exclusion of any joint mechanism for measuring good governance or any joint procedures for suspension produced vociferous ACP opposition. Article 366 of the revised Lomé IV provided for suspension where one of the 'essential elements' of the Convention was breached – and good governance is only regarded as such an essential feature by the EU. The suspension clause was implemented when the Council (on a Commission or member-state initiative) decided by QMV to open consultations with an offending ACP state. The state concerned then had a maximum of 30 days to address the EU's objection. Failing this, the EU could evoke either partial suspension of the Lomé provisions (acting by QMV) or their full suspension where the member states were unanimous.

A similar pattern can be detected in the nature of the political dialogue proposed. Despite shared concerns (conflict prevention, post-conflict reconstruction and sustainable development), the EU's priorities were given a high profile (such as human rights, democracy, drugs and crime, gender equality). In contrast, the ACP agenda was marginalized: the ACP were concerned about how EU activities impacted negatively in the developing world (such as arms sales, activities of European transnationals and even nuclear testing). Migration further underlined the two perspectives. The EU saw this exclusively in terms of poverty, human rights, conflict and illegal immigration. The ACP, conversely, wanted to expand the agenda to cover the treatment of ACP immigrants in relation to Schengen and the free movement of individuals – something the EU was initially loath to do.

Institutionalizing the political dialogue was also important. Whilst there was common agreement on a flexible approach and a reinforced dialogue, the EU faced – as it does with virtually all third countries – an expectations–capabilities gap. The ACP value and seek frequent high-level contacts. The question is whether the EU can accommodate these demands in its already overcrowded international calendar. The EU also sought to expand the scope of contacts to non-state actors, or civil society. For some ACP members this posed problems pertaining to civil-state relations. Finally, the ACP and the EU had differing positions regarding future accession to the ACP group. The ACP wished to incorporate newly independent territories as well as Cuba, thereby breaking the 'colonial' perception of membership whilst the EU was reluctant to commit to this open agenda.

Other issues of dispute concerned debt relief. For the ACP this was a development priority and they have called upon the EU to cancel all debts accrued under Lomé I–IV as well as promote the issue of debt relief in other international fora. In response, the German presidency in early 1999 proposed the total annulment of debt for the most heavily indebted ACP states. Traditionally the EU had viewed this problem as one best dealt with at the level of the member states. The vast majority of Third World debt is to individual European governments and financial institutions whilst direct debt to the EU is comparatively modest. However, the German presidency initiative could see the EU become the more effective vehicle for addressing this global issue. A related ACP request concerned currency stability, and in particular the emerging global role of the euro and the impact on ACP currencies that are pegged to it.

Instruments and management

Differentiation between ACP states (that rewards successful and appropriate cooperation practices) was a key European objective. Equal treatment irrespective of past performance was no longer viable. Whilst *need* was to remain a core determinant for resource allocations (assessed according to population size, income levels, LCD status and specific vulnerabilities), this would be supplemented by estimates of *performance*. In particular, the EU would critically review the effectiveness of local financial reforms. Conversely, the ACP opposed the limitation of aid based on any performance criteria and called for the EU to meet the international standard of 0.7 per cent of GDP devoted to Overseas Development Assistance (as well as honouring its own Treaty-based objective of reducing poverty). According to 1997 DAC figures, only three EU member states met this target – Denmark (0.97 per cent), The Netherlands (0.81 per cent) and Sweden (0.76 per cent). Whilst France and Germany contributed by far the highest European ODA totals (US$6.3 and US$5.9 billion) this only represented 0.45 per cent and 0.28 per cent respectively.

To improve delivery, a simplification of development instruments, particularly STABEX, had been foreshadowed, a greater role for civil society advocated and greater flexibility in programming suggested. Again, across these areas there were significant differences of emphasis between the EU and ACP interpretations. There was agreement, however, that the new agreement should be a predictable, stable and simplified policy instrument. Consequently a long-term global agreement has been proposed (with mid-term review clauses) with financial protocols based on five-year cycles.

Whilst significant differences existed that were the subject of intense negotiations through 1999, it would be misleading to characterize the process as exclusively conflictual. There was wide agreement on the general aspects of the accord. This consensus included the eradication of poverty and the gradual integration of the ACP into the world economy; the incorporation of the private sector within development strategies; the promotion of regional integration; linkages between sustainable development and the environment; and the role of civil society in promoting peace and stability.

Conclusion

The outcome of the global versus regional format debate will inevitably have to reflect the wider trading agenda being actively pursued by the EU – the progressive assimilation of the developing countries into the wider global economy, and the promotion of the longer-term objective of global free trade. Europe's free trade agenda is clearly linked to WTO obligations that seek to dismantle trade barriers (albeit in an asymmetrical fashion). Whatever post-Lomé arrangements were devised they would have to comply with the broader WTO multilateral trade liberalization programme.

Critics have pointed to the inconsistencies within the EU's new development strategy. The emphasis of geographic and economic differentiation seemed essentially incompatible with the notion of an overall framework that respects and defends the ACP as a singular group. The obvious rationale was political. It was a necessary compromise to placate the ACP vested interests and offered at least the appearance of an agreement that recognizes the integrity of the ACP grouping. However, economically that integrity has rapidly diminished. Not only was the ACP being divided by free trade reciprocity, for the LDC the exclusiveness of Lomé was also threatened. Foreshadowing a possible future policy change, debate began to emerge around treating all LDCs, both ACP and non-ACP, in an identical fashion (see Chapter 8). Whilst such a uniform treatment is laudable, it does question the necessity of maintaining the ACP grouping. What function does it really serve? As debated earlier, persisting with this recognition of colonial ties hardly seems an appropriate principle for reform or for guiding first-third-world relations in the twenty-first century. Clearly, to abandon the overall Lomé framework would have caused serious political and institutional protest – from the ACP, some member states and European institutions. To persist with the façade of a collective agreement was perhaps the only possible choice in the transition from uniform non-reciprocity to the new regionalized free trade regimes favoured by Brussels.

Conversely, the Commission and others argue that there is nothing inherently contradictory between having an overall framework and specialized regional or country-specific provisions. That the ACP itself valued the coherence of the grouping is perhaps proof enough for its existence. The institutions, procedures as well as Lomé's own *acquis* are important foundations: to have scrapped them outright would have suggested that the previous twenty-five years of development experience had been worthless. Although imperfect, the Lomé experience can and does contribute to a better development policy paradigm.

Chapter 7

The Cotonou Partnership Agreement

It was expected that the successor to Lomé IV would be signed in Suva on 8 June 2000. The *coup* in Fiji forced a last-minute cancellation (see Chapter 4): consequently, the ceremony was rescheduled for later that month in the Benin capital of Cotonou. As discussed in the previous chapter, the new Partnership Agreement was the result of a lengthy negotiation process, the agenda of which transformed appreciably over the 1996–2000 period. Perhaps surprisingly, much of the general experience and *acquis* of the previous twenty-five years of Lomé were retained (for example, the contractual nature and benefits of long-term agreements). But past policy failures were also seen as the motivation for reform. In particular, the institutional and policy-making contexts of each ACP country were seen as serious and fundamental impediments to effective development. The past practice of uniform preferential trade access and direct aid had generally failed to transform ACP economies. As argued elsewhere in this text, the ACP's share of the EU market had declined markedly over the lifespan of Lomé (to just 2.8 per cent by 1999) and remained dependent on a narrow range of primary products depressingly reminiscent of a colonial economic structure. The economic remedy proposed by the EU was extreme – differentiation based around a commitment to free trade. These radical proposals were successfully moderated through concessions and safeguards – although the basic principle of ACP free trade areas was established, marking a paradigmatic departure from the spirit of Lomé.

This chapter examines the detail of the new Partnership Agreement, highlighting the key differences from Lomé and comparing it with the agreements under discussion with other regions of the developing world. Cotonou – if successful – may well prove to be the blueprint for the global application of EU development policy. First, however, the global changes that preceded the Cotonou reforms are summarized in order to set a necessary historical context.

Africa, at least, was always seen as associated with an integrated Europe. As far back as 1950, the Schuman Declaration argued that only integration could provide the additional resources necessary for African development. Whilst these necessary resources have yet to be delivered, integration and development have now been inexorably linked for the past half-century. The earliest period of European integration coincided with decolonization – reflected in the Yaoundé Conventions and the earlier OCT agreement and the establishment of the EDF under the founding Treaty of Rome in 1957. The enlargement of the Community in the 1970s coincided with the transition from decolonization to what was labelled (mistakenly) the new international economic order. The rationale behind Lomé I embraced both these changes and, as argued in Chapter 1, its provisions at the time were widely viewed as the most progressive in the world based, at least in theory, on partnership and solidarity (David, 2000, p. 12). The joint institutions STABEX and SYSMIN, non-reciprocity and the protocols on sugar, beef and bananas were all considered exemplary innovations of their time. With hindsight, this period proved to be one of benevolent but misplaced economic policy towards the ACP.

Within the context of the Cold War and emerging non-alignment movements, the earlier Lomé Conventions were largely precluded from any overt political conditionality. This fundamentally changed after 1989. The renegotiation of Lomé IV coincided with the watershed of German reunification and the collapse of communism in the East. Political dialogue – or perhaps more accurately political conditionality – was no longer taboo but became an essential element of a new approach to development issues. Thus Lomé IV contained policy that was expressly political and focused on human rights. The signs of a changing economic philosophy also began to emerge with the adaptation of the structural adjustment programmes of the Bretton Woods institutions becoming part of EU development policy for the first time. Similarly, Lomé IV tentatively promoted the role of the private sector in development as well as that of regional cooperation. All these shifts in development economic policy were consistent with the global trends of the 1990s that saw the market replace the State as the principle economic mechanism throughout Eastern and Central Europe.

The final historical change that preceded Cotonou saw the Lomé IV mid-term review and the Green Paper process emerge at a time when development policy was confronted by new challenges in the form of globalization and liberalization. Clearly, globalization presents opportunities but also significant risks to developing countries. Tellingly, consensus had begun to emerge on all sides that the past Lomé trading regime had failed to arrest let alone reverse the economic decline of the ACP: some went as far as to argue that it was in fact instrumental in accelerating the decline. This, together with the new WTO-based consensus and the economic development of the CEEC conspired to overturn the economic philosophy that had underpinned Lomé for the previous quarter-century. Trade liberalization, accompanied by democratic institution-building, was the new international context that the successor to Lomé was obliged to recognize, acknowledge and ultimately embrace. Consequently, the Partnership Agreement emphasizes the political aspects of development and not just the economic. The importance of institutional capacity, the support of civil society and the role of the non-state sector in promoting development underpin this new philosophy and are set to define the new context for EU development policy until at least the end of the Cotonou agreement in 2020.

It is not a factor unique to the EU that the public political response to agreements typically emphasizes common ground and downplays areas of contention or failure. Nonetheless, it must be acknowledged that constructing a new agreement that was acceptable to the ACP states and to the EU was, in itself, a significant achievement. Poul Nielson (European Commissioner for Development and Humanitarian Aid) went as far as to claim that the agreement was 'a major historical and political event'. Cotonou constituted 'a new era of a relationship based on a profound reform of the spirit, the objectives and the practice of our cooperation' (Nielson, 2000, p. 2). For the Commission, it provided an important example of a successful and open process of policy debate and helped to redress the negative aspects of globalization on the developing world that had surfaced at the 1999 Seattle WTO meeting. For their part, the

ACP states recognized that a mutually acceptable agreement had been finally achieved – albeit one that was asymmetrical and involved concessions to reconcile significant differences in areas such as the political dimension, the new commercial framework and implementation of financial cooperation.

As the EU knows from its own experience of Maastricht and Nice, intergovernmental decisions are actually only the penultimate step in the treaty-making process. Ratification by the parties involved is necessary before an agreement is concluded and this can be a lengthy as well as uncertain procedure. Lomé IV had initially expired at the end of February 2000, and was extended through to the conclusion of the negotiations in June. The ACP–EU Joint Committee of Ambassadors adopted the majority of the new Cotonou provisions as transitional measures as of 1 August 2000. The notable omission from this procedure was the financial protocol that can only be applied once full ratification is complete. This will require all EU member states and the European Parliament to approve the Partnership Agreement, as well as ratification by at least two-thirds of the ACP (51 countries). It would be optimistic to predict ratification could be completed within 18 months – by the end of 2001. Further, it remains to be seen whether the European Parliament will be as willing as the ACP to accept the compromises on free trade and progressive abolition of trade preferences.

Objectives, principles and institutional structure

The broad objectives of the Partnership Agreement are defined in Article 1 as:

> to promote and expedite the economic, cultural and social development of the ACP States, with a view to contributing to peace and security and to promoting a stable and democratic political environment.

> The partnership shall be centred on the objective of reducing and eventually eradicating poverty consistent with the objectives of sustainable development and the gradual integration of the ACP countries into the world economy. (Partnership Agreement, 2000, Art. 1)

European support and encouragement to assist in developing regional integration processes are expressly mentioned as mechanisms that can assist in realizing these primary EU–ACP objectives. In addition, Article 2 outlines four 'fundamental principles' that will govern relations between the EU and the ACP:

- The equality of the partners and local ownership of the development strategies was stressed. As the text states 'The ACP States shall determine the development strategies for their economies and societies in all sovereignty'.
- To foster the widest possible involvement and participation in political and economic affairs, the partnership is open to 'all sections of society, including the private sector, and civil society' as well as central government.
- 'Dialogue and the fulfilment of mutual obligations' is pivotal to enacting the intent of the partnership.
- 'Differentiation' in the arrangements for ACP countries and for regions (reflecting different levels of development) has become a fundamental principle, distinguishing between those more able to compete in the global economy and the least-developed countries, which will retain special protection.

This last principle is the most significant departure from the former uniform Lomé approach. The ramifications of this change are revolutionary: it paves the way for a multi-speed approach to future development that will inevitably differentiate between different regions of the ACP group. The inclusion of civil society was also given direct effect through several measures: the right to consultation and incorporation within the EU–ACP political dialogue process; involvement in projects; organizational capacity-building support; and financial assistance. The recognition of these non-governmental actors was conditional on their democratic and transparent organization 'according to national characteristics' (Partnership Agreement, 2000, Article 6.1).

The general Lomé institutional structure was retained in the Cotonou Agreement. The three existing joint EU–ACP institutions – the Council of Ministers, the Committee of Ambassadors and the Joint Parliamentary Assembly – remain operational. At its largest, the Council may involve all 92 governments plus members of the Commission. The presidency of the Council and the Chairman of the Committee of Ambassadors alternates between the EU and ACP member states. Council decisions are taken 'by common agreement' (Article 15.3). The Joint Assembly is composed of equal numbers of EU and ACP representatives (MEPs in Europe's case and either members of national parliaments or their designates for the ACP). It is required to meet twice a year, alternately in the EU and in an ACP state. Whilst it may adopt resolutions and make recommendations, it is formally a 'consultative body' (Article 17). One significant reform, however, was in the dispute settlement mechanism. Where the EU and ACP are in dispute, binding arbitration, normally using the procedures of the Permanent Court of Arbitration for International Organizations, governs.

Political dialogue and conditionality

Obviously, the negotiations surrounding the political dimension of the agreement were among the most sensitive. Not surprisingly then, the most that was possible was to agree on broad general principles and a limited number of specific issues, leaving how these might be implemented and evaluated to future practice and circumstances. For example, Article 8 stipulates that the EU and ACP 'shall regularly engage in a comprehensive, balanced and deep political dialogue'. The purpose of the dialogue was similarly anodyne: to exchange information, foster mutual understanding and develop 'agreed priorities and shared agendas'. Areas of 'mutual concern or of general significance' that the dialogue specifically mentions are 'the arms trade, excessive military expenditure, drugs and organised crime, or ethnic, religious or racial discrimination' as well as 'respect for human rights, democratic principles, the rule of law and good governance' (Article 8.4). Interestingly, political dialogue was not confined to the formal institutional framework of the Agreement but could also take place informally and at regional or sub-regional levels as deemed appropriate.

The Agreement does identify what it calls 'essential elements and fundamental element'. The distinction was important and the topic of some tension in the negotiations (Gomes, 2000, p. 11). Duplicating Lomé IV, three 'essential elements' are identified: respect for human rights, democratic principles and the rule of law. These are expected to govern the behaviour of the EU and ACP both domestically and internationally. Article 9 of the Agreement describes these in the following terms. First, human rights are defined as 'universal, indivisible and inter-related': all fundamental freedoms and human rights, 'be they civil and political, or economic, social and cultural' must be protected and promoted under the Agreement. Second, universally recognized democratic principles must underpin the legitimacy and legality of State authority (reflected in its constitutional, legislative and regulatory system, and the existence of participatory mechanisms): on the basis of these universally recognized principles, each country develops its democratic culture. And third, the Agreement stipulates that the structure and authority of government 'shall be founded on the rule of law, which shall entail in particular effective and accessible means of legal redress, an independent legal system guaranteeing equality before the law and an executive that is fully subject to the law.' In broad terms, these conditions do not depart significantly from the provisions established in Lomé IV.

Breaches of any of these essential elements may ultimately lead to a country facing suspension from the Agreement. Any party to the Agreement can bring such a breach to the Council of Ministers which, within 15 days, must then engage in 'consultation' with the offending country on how best to remedy the situation. Where consultation proves unsuccessful or is refused, or in cases where immediate action is necessitated, 'appropriate measures' in accordance with international law and proportional to the violation, may then be taken. Full suspension from the Agreement is seen as a measure of only last resort (Article 96).

In contrast, the text dealing with good governance and corruption are largely new and have not been simply duplicated from Lomé. ACP opposition to 'good governance' becoming an 'essential element' of the Agreement was sufficient to see this given the somewhat different status – that of a 'fundamental element'. Reaching agreement on common and workable definitions of good governance and of corruption proved difficult, although the text attempts to define the concept in the following terms:

... good governance is the transparent and accountable management of human, natural, economic and financial resources
for the purposes of equitable and sustainable development. It
entails clear decision-making procedures at the level of
public authorities, transparent and accountable institutions,
the primacy of law in the management and distribution of
resources and capacity building for elaborating and implementing measures aiming in particular at preventing and
combating corruption. (Article 9.3)

Achieving this broad joint definition was in itself considered a
notable success (Gomes, 2000, p. 12). Provisions for the regular
assessment of good governance are built into the Agreement,
taking into account 'each country's economic, social, cultural
and historical context'. A similar procedure to that for breaches
of 'essential elements' also exists for cases of financial
corruption with suspension again an option of last resort. This
procedure has not been extended to cover breaches of 'good
governance', however.

The risk is, however, that unless these broad principles – both
essential and fundamental – are respected and promoted, the
quality and purpose of the political dialogue will be marginalized and regarded as little more than cosmetic conditionality to
be applied in a selective manner. An area that could become the
test for this process is the greater involvement of civil society
and the business community in development envisaged under
the Partnership Agreement. From the EU perspective, the
involvement of such non-governmental actors is essential to the
consolidation of democracy, which is itself now widely regarded
as a precondition to economic development. Thus the promotion of democracy and democratic norms – bolstered through
political dialogue – has become the core element in the EU's
development policy towards the Third World. However, a
consensual definition of what constitutes 'good governance'
remains elusive, contrasting the minimalist view of the efficient
management of public affairs with an inclusive one that involves
pluralistic process, norms and a rejection of corruption. Some
commentators have argued that the democratic agenda of
Cotonou is unrealizable – and when coupled with poverty alleviation – sets unrealistic and unobtainable goals. A framework

for partnership may be able to contribute to these objectives, but it is an unreasonable expectation of Cotonou that it alone can achieve these outcomes. To avoid future disappointments and presumed policy failure, Cotonou needs to establish appropriate expectations commensurate with its capacity to deliver.

The new agreement does present the ACP and the EU with a broader basis on which to engage in political dialogue, however. In principle at least, any issue of mutual interest can be discussed. Explicit references to new topics – peace-building and conflict-prevention (Article 11) and migration issues (Article 13) – were introduced into the text providing an explicit legal basis for the development of EU–ACP joint policy in these areas. A focus will be on targeting the root-causes of violent conflict, mediation, negotiation and reconciliation processes, as well as specific issues such as military spending, child soldiers and anti-personnel mines. Critics have remarked on the oddity and uniqueness of incorporating such geopolitical concerns into a commercial and financial agreement. Largely on the insistence of the ACP, migration was dealt with in some detail in the Agreement. The 'fair treatment' of legally resident ACP nationals, the extension of rights comparable to those for EU citizens as well as action to combat employment discrimination, racism and xenophobia are all stipulated. Conversely, the EU insisted on 'a prevention policy' on illegal immigration. First, the EU hopes to normalize migratory flows by improving the social and economic conditions throughout the ACP. Second, and more pointedly, the Agreement requires the ACP states to 'accept the return of any of its nationals' found illegally resident in the EU 'without further formalities'. The recipient state is obliged to provide the appropriate identity documentation and administrative facilities necessary for repatriation, whilst ensuring 'that the dignity of individuals are respected in any procedure initiated to return illegal immigrants to their countries of origin' (Article 13.5). Initially, the EU had wanted this policy to extend to non-nationals who used ACP states to enter the EU illegally, but this was unanimously rejected by the ACP (although only shelved for future bilateral discussions) (Gomes, 2000, p. 11). Whilst the provisions of the migration policy also apply in reverse to EU nationals in ACP states, the clear motivation behind these provisions has come from a Europe concerned about increased illegal migration from the developing world.

These topics – peace, conflict and migration – are, in part, a logical consequence of the incorporation of development goals as one element within the EU's CFSP at Maastricht. Institutionally and in terms of Treaty competences, Maastricht linked development policy across decision-making pillars and gave greater legitimacy to Political Dialogue as an essential EU activity with third countries. It was no longer feasible to quarantine development policy as purely economic in content: its incorporation within CFSP made it undeniably political too. The political aspects of Cotonou reflect this intra-EU rationale as well as underline the validity and importance of conceptualizing integration from a neo-functional perspective.

Financing and the EDF

The ACP states' disappointment with the level of new EDF funding provided at Cotonou was a familiar outcome and reflected the sentiments of all the previous Lomé renegotiations. Their argument was that the priority given to poverty eradication seemed inconsistent with this financial commitment. The final level of resources for the 9th EDF was set at €15.2 billion over the five-year period 2000–05 (€13.5 billion in the EDF and €1.7 billion from EIB's own resources). This level of support was only marginally higher than the 8th EDF figure (with no increase in real terms). However, additional funds from the unspent balances from earlier EDF allocations have been carried forward, making the total of new and old funds available some €25 billion. Clearly, the greater financial impediment may be the actual disbursement of the funds effectively and efficiently during the lifetime of the 9th EDF rather than any inadequacy in the amount budgeted. The EDF's record has repeatedly shown that disbursement faces serious obstacles often due to the insufficient institutional capacity in many ACP states as well as within the Commission. At the time of the signing of the Cotonou Agreement €9.9 billion remained uncommitted from previous EDFs (see Table 7.1). Critics have noted that no targets or timetable for levels of disbursement have been set and predict that continued low levels of disbursement will also come to characterize Cotonou and undermine the main policy objective of poverty eradication (Laryea, 2000, p. 16).

TABLE 7.1   *Partnership agreement financial resources, 2000–07
(€bn)*

	Euros
• 9th European Development Fund (EDF), including: Long-term envelope (10.0 bn) Regional envelope (1.3 bn) Investment facility (2.2 bn)	13.5
• Remaining balance from previous EDF	9.9
• European Investment Bank (EIB) individual resources	1.7
	25.1

Source: *The Courier* (2000).

As is the case for the Agreement in general, financial co-operation has to be consistent with the development objectives of the ACP states. This involves respecting their 'geographical, social and cultural characteristics' as well as emphasizing the 'importance of predictability and security' (Article 56). ACP ownership and responsibility for development programme priorities and objectives was stressed (for both state and non-state actors): however, the decision on funding any projects or programmes remains solely with the EU. Article 60 defines the scope of financing to include measures to reduce debt and balance-of-payments problems; macroeconomic and structural reforms; stabilization of export earnings; institutional development and capacity-building; technical cooperation; and humanitarian and emergency assistance.

Cotonou expects that greater efficiency can be achieved by rationalizing the financial mechanisms available under the agreement. One of the implementation problems under Lomé had been the complexity and diversity of instruments that operated independently, reducing overall coherence. The EDF now only provides for two financial instruments: one that covers non-reimbursable aid such as long-term subsidies for development support; and one providing risk capital and loans as a private-sector investment facility. Thus, rather than receiving a multitude of financial allocations, ACP states will now receive a single indicative total sum for all operations covering a five-year period. In addition, the new rolling programming system will consider the performance of ACP economies in assessing financial support, and no longer make decisions that are purely based on need. The criteria for assessment will be the result of EU–ACP negotiations, recognizing the different individual political, economic and social characteristics of each state. In this way it is hoped that resources will be less prone to becoming frozen in the indicative programme budgets of countries unable to utilize them effectively. This should result in greater flexibility in the nature of indicative programming. The need for further delegation of authority to EU Delegations in ACP countries has also been recognized in the new financial arrangements.

Cotonou also specifies three significant macroeconomic policies: debt-relief; structural adjustment; and export earnings stabilization. The introduction of financial measures aimed at debt-relief is a significant break with past practice and was indicative of successful global pressure as well as of a change in member-state positions on the issue during the late 1990s (especially in Germany and the UK). Resources covered by the Agreement can now be used for debt-relief initiatives that have international approval: an undertaking has been given by the EU to examine whether additional resources can also be mobilized to reduce the debt burden. Whilst welcoming this EU initiative on debt-relief, the ACP has argued for greater EU involvement in advocating a fully funded international Highly Indebted Poor Countries programme as well as the cancellation of unsustainable debt-levels incurred by the ACP (Laryea, 2000, p. 16). Structural adjustment support – particularly that which addresses regional integration issues – is also extended in the Agreement. Joint ACP–EU assessment of such macroeconomic support is envisaged to 'ensure that adjustment is economically viable and socially and politically bearable' (Article 67). To determine whether structural adjustment programmes can receive funding, the EU has accepted the principle that provided the criteria of the principal multilateral donors (such as the IMF and World Bank) are met, then EU financial support is 'automatic'. In this way it is hoped that disbursement of funds can be accelerated and fewer Commission staff resources committed to structural adjustment programme assessments. Finally, the spirit of both STABEX and SYSMIN are incorporated in the Agreement. Long-term support is provided 'in order to mitigate the adverse effects of any instability in export earnings, including in the agricultural and mining sectors' (Article 68). In general, support can be triggered where a 10 per cent loss in average earnings occurs, although entitlement for support is limited to four successive years.

Innovations

Commissioner Nielson regarded the new agreement as a significant departure from the Lomé method in three ways: the nature of the partnership; the objectives to be focused on; and the ways and means of achieving these (2000, p. 2). The actual innovations, however, were not quite as novel as suggested by the Commission's rhetoric – only the last of these could rightfully claim to be a clear break from past practice. First, the concept of partnership was as much the defining characteristic of Lomé as it is of Cotonou. What was new, however, was the further application of good governance as a 'fundamental element' of the relationship and the responsibility and accountability of ACP in this respect. Second, the focus on poverty eradication in the Cotonou agreement combined with sustainable development and the gradual integration of the ACP economies within the global economy has successfully defined a more precise EU development role. However, such a focus is far from revolutionary. Poverty reduction has been part of the EU's formal treaty obligation since Maastricht, and informally for much longer. Whether this role is realistic or achievable remains a moot point, of course. And whilst laudable, poverty reduction is hardly an exclusive role for EU, but had become a common function of the international world by the end of the twentieth century. The subsidiarity question – what does the EU do best, and what the state – remained untested. And third, and the area where the Partnership Agreement can justifiably claim innovation, Cotonou seeks to better influence the context within which development occurs, emphasizing trade development and investment. As shown previously, the EU's remedy for this has been to depart from Lomé's trade preferences approach to embrace free trade as the better mechanism for economic growth. Transition periods notwithstanding, this constitutes a radical departure from the past uniform basis of economic relations between the EU and the ACP developed over twenty-five years.

Importantly, in contrast to Lomé's uniformity, the Partnership Agreement differentiates between the levels of development of ACP states. The Least Developed Countries remain principally governed by the traditional Lomé approach, whilst the more economically able ACP states have the new conditions for liberalized economic partnerships applied to them. Practically all LDC exports will benefit from non-reciprocal free access to the EU market by 2005 (the sugar and beef protocols being the only major exceptions to this). The EU's new approach to the LDCs reflects a wider international assessment of the particular economic situation of these states. The EU's role is, however, crucial as 39 of the world's LDCs are signatories of the Cotonou Agreement (see the following section for further discussion).

The radical reform of trading relations, therefore, applies specifically to the non-LDC ACP states. The EU regards this new approach as comprehensive and designed to enhance ACP competitiveness. A series of deadlines for the progressive abolition of trade barriers and the introduction of WTO compatible free trade have been promulgated in Article 37 of the Agreement. September 2002 has been set as the date by when negotiations on economic partnership agreements must commence with a view to their introduction no later than 1 January 2008. During this interim period the current Lomé IV trade regime will be maintained although some commodity protocols will undergo review. However, agreements on trade liberalization seem far from inevitable with all of the ACP states. Consequently, provision has been made for an assessment in 2004 to determine which of the non-LDC ACP are not in a position to move towards free trade. For these states, alternative arrangements will be examined that can provide them with 'a new framework for trade which is equivalent to their existing situation and in conformity with WTO rules'.

Even for those non-LDC states regarded as suitable, a further review in 2006 will assess whether a longer transition beyond 2008 is necessary. For those countries able to meet the original deadline a transitional period has to be agreed upon before all elements of the negotiated trade agreement are fully implemented. The wording of the Agreement is cautionary on this point noting the need to take account of the socioeconomic impact and variable capacity of ACP countries to adapt and adjust to liberalization. Consequently, negotiations will 'be as flexible as possible in establishing the duration of a sufficient transitional period . . . and the degree of asymmetry in terms of timetable for tariff dismantlement' (Article 37). No timeframe for the transition is specified, but other agreements suggest that up to twelve years is quite possible. In addition, Article 37 raises the issue of WTO compatibility in several places and calls on the EU and ACP to 'closely cooperate and collaborate in the WTO with a view to defending the arrangements reached'. Elsewhere the Agreement calls for identification of common ACP–EU interests and a more effective lobbying of the WTO agenda to promote a development perspective. Clearly conflict at the international level is widely anticipated. Given these intra-ACP–EU issues and the external challenges, the agreement signed in Cotonou in the year 2000 may only fully impact in 2020 at the earliest. Given the well-known impoverished predictive abilities of economics, it will be remarkable if these various deadlines are uniformly honoured. Despite the Agreement's insistence that the new trade agreements will come into force on 1 January 2008, clearly there is ample opportunity for delay – either justified or intentional.

The precondition for these partnerships is the development of regional groupings within the ACP grouping: the template is for group-to-group economic relationships, not for a series of bilateral and *ad hoc* agreements between the EU and 77 individual ACP actors. The challenges – for the ACP – are great. First, effective regional integration is a significant economic and political issue between ACP states and will require detailed and painstaking interstate negotiations over several years with no guarantee of success. Second, many of the anticipated regional groupings combine relatively developed ACP economies with those classified as LDCs. Regional integration that combines these two groups will be especially difficult to achieve. And third, and simultaneously, these ACP states will also have to liberalize their economies in line with international standards and may face significant political and social opposition. Under such circumstances 2008 could prove to be an unobtainable deadline for most of the eligible ACP states.

Trade liberalization is to go hand-in-hand with a wider range of cooperation across associated areas. For example, the Partnership Agreement covers competition policy, intellectual property rights, information and communication technologies, standardization, consumer protection, the environment and labour standards. Of symbolic and practical importance is the agreement to cooperate on matters of mutual concern in other international fora, such as the WTO. On balance, Cotonou certainly presents a more complete set of arrangements on which to construct the EU–ACP partnership than its predecessor. The overall aim, however, remains ambitious and long-term in nature – 'sustainable development' that leads to the 'gradual integration of the ACP States into the world economy . . . implemented in full conformity' with WTO provisions (Article 34).

The renewed emphasis on poverty reduction – with the longer-term aim of its eradication – promises that future EU policy may be more able to take account of the complexity and multidimensional nature of poverty. The past one-dimensional approach centred on preferential trade has been superseded by three priority areas of cooperation: economic development; social and human development; and regional integration and cooperation. In each of these areas, three crosscutting themes are to become the focus of the EU's policy towards poverty – gender equality; sustainable management of resources; and, institutional development and capacity-building. These are undeniably laudable aims and follow the best practice of modern development theory. But given the history of institutional incapacity and persisting limitations placed upon the staffing levels and expertise of the Commission, are these objectives realistic? Indeed, are these objectives that are best realized by the EU at all? Would the delegation of organization, authority and funding to the UN agencies be a better poverty-reduction strategy? Of course, such an abdication of the EU's global role would run counter to the more pervasive ambition for Europe to be a credible international actor.

Despite the 20-year duration of the Cotonou Agreement, this innovation was less of a departure from past Lomé practice than might be presumed. Five-year agreements and renegotiation processes typified Lomé (even Lomé IV had a mid-term review clause that was in effect a partial renegotiation). However, within Cotonou there is provision for five-yearly revisions and each financial protocol runs for a similarly limited period. Whilst major renegotiations may be avoided, the five-yearly review cycle will undoubtedly be more than just *pro forma* in scope.

Lastly, Cotonou contains a separate chapter on humanitarian and emergency assistance – reflecting partly the merging of ECHO with the Development DG under the control of Commissioner Nielson. The Agreement emphasizes the necessity for 'rapid, flexible and effective' aid for natural disasters as well as for the effects of man-made conflicts (Article 72). The main aims cover the safeguarding of human lives; funding of logistical delivery of direct aid as required; rehabilitation and reconstruction; support for displaced persons and refugees; and assistance for disaster-prevention mechanisms. Assistance can be requested alternatively by an ACP state, the Commission, international organizations or non-governmental actors.

Towards differentiation under the ACP umbrella

One of the principal objectives of the ACP states was to protect the integrity of the APC as a group. Maintaining recognition by the EU of the group collectively, rather than regionally or bilaterally, was paramount. As outlined in the previous chapter the ACP had to overcome attempts by the Commission to abandon this unique grouping in favour of specialized regional agreements. The final outcome was an uneasy compromise. The ACP umbrella has been retained, but the provisions for distinct and autonomous regional economic partnerships signals an end to Europe's uniform approach to the developing world of Africa, the Caribbean and the Pacific. Further, special provisions are also in place for landlocked and island states. Critics have suggested that this compromise is tantamount to a Trojan horse and will eventually succeed in dividing the ACP internally. Conversely, others have argued that any commonality expressed by the group was only superficial at best, and the dismemberment of the group long overdue.

The undeniable message from Cotonou is that the EU preference is to promote ACP regional integration and deal primarily on a region-to-region basis. Such a development of course corresponds to the EU's own original philosophy and is consistent with a view of integration as a global process. However, the EU also regards regional integration as the most effective route through which the ACP states can re-enter the international economy. In the words of Article 35.2 of the

Partnership Agreement, 'regional integration is a key instrument for the integration of the ACP countries into the world economy'. Practical support is given to this through Articles 29 and 30. These cover the promotion of single unified regional markets, cross-border issues as well as direct assistance for the institutionalization of regional integration. Furthermore, regional integration, if it does promote growth, is also seen as a means for realizing Europe's major development policy objective: the reduction of poverty. It may also help to bridge the gap between the LDCs and other developing countries within a particular region. All of these potential advantages are, of course, premised on the political requirement that any form of regional integration is based on and will contribute to democracy and good governance. The corresponding economic requirement – sound economic management – including the removal of intra-regional tariffs (and a subsequent loss of revenue) may prove problematic, and require a revision in the Cotonou free trade timetable.

The Pacific Islands

Clearly, not all ACP regions face the same problems or have similar resources: some are better placed than others. This may be illustrated by examining the Pacific Islands. The Pacific is a region clearly affected by the transition from Lomé to Cotonou. Under Lomé the Pacific was by far the smallest regional grouping with just 8 out of Lomé IV's 70 members (with just 6 million people): this has now enlarged to 14 out of the Cotonou total membership of 77 states and is comparable to the Caribbean's representation (with 15 states). Within the context of the ACP, the Pacific was also the least economically integrated region as only a minority of the Pacific's independent Forum Island Countries (FIC) were also Lomé signatories. However, now all 14 FICs are Cotonou signatories and the prospects for the development of a Pacific regional economic partnership agreement with the EU by 2008 look more promising.

Historically, the 14 Pacific ACP states have significant European colonial links – with the UK, Spain and Germany – and the region even more so through French Polynesia (although this has always remained outside the ACP group). The Pacific states also share many similar development constraints: subsistence economies, market isolation, limited export diversity or capacity, lack of expertise and vulnerability to natural disaster. In contrast to the eight Pacific Island states that were members of Lomé, none of the six new signatories to Cotonou have any significant trading relations with the EU. Indeed, cumulatively, these six only add 226 500 to the population for the Pacific ACP states (MacRae, 2000, p. 24). The future impact of these microstates may well be greater than their small size would normally suggest. First, the expansion of Pacific representation is important in offsetting the predominance of African countries within the ACP. Second, collectively, the island states of the Caribbean and the Pacific now form a sizeable minority and will be better placed to introduce topics of specific concern to island nations – such as global warming, economic viability and depopulation – on to the ACP agenda. Third – and of greater general importance – the FIC structure presents an obvious mechanism through which the EU can negotiate an economic partnership agreement. The Pacific offers the simplest test case for EU–ACP free trade and could conclude the first regional agreement, the success of which will determine the future of other agreements in Africa and the Caribbean. Conversely, access to the fishing and other resources enjoyed by the Pacific states under their Exclusive Economic Zone (which totals 20 million square km) may prove to be a major hurdle to an agreement. Critics of the regional free trade principle have always warned of the inequality of free trade between Europe and the developing world: for states with little to export to Europe, conceding fishing rights may be an unreasonable price to pay for enhanced links with the EU.

The least developed states

Sitting alongside this emphasis on regional integration are the special differentiated provisions for LDCs, landlocked or island states in the Partnership Agreement. The following discussion focuses on the largest of these three groups – the LDCs – but similar arguments and considerations can be applied to both the landlocked and island states. Cotonou realistically recognized the dichotomy that had always existed within the ACP but went largely unrecognized in Lomé: that between the very least developed states and the other developing countries. As discussed previously, most other international actors had long recognized this division. Cotonou uses the LDC category as the organizing principle for its economic reforms: development status under the Partnership Agreement now determines the appropriate trade regime.

Table 7.2 presents data for the 39 LDCs that are members of the Agreement and for the other 38 ACP members. As is the case for LDCs in general, these countries are predominantly drawn from Africa: for the ACP, only six LDCs (one in the Caribbean and five in the Pacific) are not African. It should be noted, however, that the definition of LDC in the Cotonou Agreement does not perfectly match that used by other agencies or follow the HDI exactly. The 2000 HDI surveyed 174 countries: significant ACP omissions were Somalia and Liberia in Africa, and 9 of the 14 Pacific Island states.

The predominance of LDCs in Africa – representing half of all African states – presents a serious challenge to the objective of integrating these countries into the global economy. Whilst the actual form and shape of regional integration that emerges is legitimately the exclusive concern of the states involved, all the possible configurations must inevitably include a number of LDCs. Indeed, Article 29 of the Partnership Agreement gives one of the objectives of regional economic integration as 'fostering participation of LDC ACP States in the establishment of regional markets and sharing the benefits'. Southern Africa – in the form of the Southern African Development Community – is generally regarded as the most viable and advanced form of regional cooperation on the continent. But even here half of the memberships are LDCs. Of course, South Africa already has the only ACP free trade agreement with the EU and this may be a useful template for extending the regime more generally to SADC. Elsewhere in Africa – East, West and Central – the prospects for engineering regional integration leading to economic partnership agreements with Brussels seem less immediately likely. In comparison, the Caribbean and the Pacific Islands (as already discussed) appear to be more probable candidates, despite the particular problems associated with regionalism and island states. Twenty-six ACP members are defined as island states under Cotonou. The question of market size may also be a distorting factor. The fifteen Caribbean ACP states have a population of 22.8 million and the fourteen Pacific Island ACP

216

TABLE 7.2   *ACP countries' Human Development Index*

(i) LDCs (39) defined under Cotonou			
Country	*Population:* *(m.)*	*HDI*	*HDI* *ranking*
Sierra Leone	4.6	0 252	174
Niger	10.1	0 293	173
Burkina Faso	11.3	0 303	172
Ethiopia	59.6	0 309	171
Burundi	6.5	0 321	170
Guinea-Bissau	1.2	0 331	169
Mozambique	18.9	0 341	168
Chad	7.3	0 367	167
Central African Republic	3.5	0 371	166
Mali	10.7	0 380	165
Rwanda	6.6	0 382	164
Malawi	10.3	0 385	163
Guinea	7.3	0 394	162
Gambia	1.2	0 396	161
Angola	12.1	0 405	160
Eritrea	3.6	0 408	159
Uganda	20.6	0 409	158
Benin	5.8	0 411	157
Tanzania	32.1	0 415	156
Zambia	8.8	0 420	153
Democratic Republic of Congo	50.0	0 430	152
Haiti ~	8.0	0 440	150
Djibouti	0.6	0 447	149
Mauritania	2.5	0 451	147
Togo	4.4	0 471	145
Sudan	28.3	0 477	143
Madagascar	15.1	0 483	141
Comoro Islands	0.7	0 510	137
São Tomé & Príncipe	0.1	0 547	132
Equatorial Guinea	0.4	0 555	131
Lesotho	2.1	0 569	127
Solomon Islands ~	0.4	0 614	121
Vanuatu ~	0.2	0 623	118
Cape Verde	0.4	0 688	105
Samoa ~	0.2	0 771	95

TABLE 7.2   *Continued*

Tuvalu ~	0.1	na	na
Kiribati ~	0.1	na	na
Somalia	8.1	na	na
Liberia	2.6	na	na

(ii) Other ACP African countries (15)

Country	Population: (m.)	HDI	HDI ranking
Senegal	9.0	0 416	155
Ivory Coast	14.3	0 420	154
Nigeria	106.4	0 439	151
Congo	2.8	0 507	139
Kenya	29.0	0 508	138
Cameroon	14.3	0 528	134
Zimbabwe	11.4	0 555	130
Ghana	19.2	0 556	129
Gabon	1.2	0 592	123
Botswana	1.6	0 593	122
Namibia	1.7	0 632	115
Swaziland	1.0	0 655	112
South Africa	39.4	0 697	103
Mauritius	1.1	0 761	71
Seychelles	0.1	0 786	53

(iii) ACP Caribbean countries (15) *

Country	Population: (m.)	HDI	HDI ranking
Haiti*	8.0	0 440	150
Guyana	0.8	0 709	96
St Lucia	0.2	0 728	88
Dominican Republic	8.2	0 729	87
Jamaica	2.5	0 735	83
St Vincent & the Grenadines	0.1	0 738	79
Suriname	0.4	0 766	67
Belize	0.2	0 777	58
Grenada	0.1	0 785	54
Dominica	0.1	0 793	51
Trinidad & Tobago	1.3	0 793	50

TABLE 7.2   *Continued*

St Kitts & St Nevis	+	0 798	47
Antigua & Barbuda	0.1	0 833	37
Bahamas	0.3	0 844	33
Barbados	0.3	0 858	30

(iv) ACP Pacific Island countries (14)*

Country	Population: (m.)	HDI	HDI ranking
Papua New Guinea	4.7	0 542	133
Solomon Islands*	0.4	0 614	121
Vanuatu*	0.2	0 623	118
Fiji	0.8	0 769	66
Samoa*	0.2	0 771	95
Cook Islands	+	na	na
Kiribati*	+	na	na
Marshall Islands	+	na	na
Micronesia	+	na	na
Nauru	+	na	na
Niue	+	na	na
Palau	+	na	na
Tonga	+	na	na
Tuvalu*	+	na	na

Key: na = HDI data not available for these countries.
    * = includes LDC countries given in Table 8.2 (i).
    + = population is less than 0.1 million.
    ~ = non-African LDC.
Sources: *Human Development Report 1999*
http://www.undp.org/hdro/HDI.html; *The Courier* (2000).

states just 6.7 million: Africa alone totals 610 million across its 48 ACP states.

The Agreement is not completely silent on these issues and does not require LDCs to adopt trade liberalization regimes. It recognizes that LDCs need to be accorded 'special treatment in order to enable them to overcome the serious economic and social difficulties hindering their development' (Article 85). Specifically, the provisions for the new economic and trade regime propose that by 2005 at the latest 'essentially all products' from the LDCs will have duty-free access 'building on the level of existing trade provisions of the Fourth ACP–EC Convention' (Article 37). But the broader policy issue remains problematic. How will future free trade agreements between any regional grouping and the EU accommodate these protectionist needs of LDCs? Detailed rules of origin and tariff controls needed by the LDCs would appear to conflict with any notion of trade liberalization and demand high compliance costs. Thus for the core ACP countries and the vast majority of impoverished citizens – those in Africa – effective regional economic partnership agreements would seem a distant prospect at best.

Conclusion

In summation, the Cotonou Agreement reflects as balanced and as equitable an outcome as could reasonably be expected from a protracted negotiation process that has involved considerable compromise and accommodation. Certainly, the direst predictions that an extreme free trade reading of the original Green Paper suggested were moderated significantly. Conversely, other than for the LDCs, the continuation of the Lomé framework has been largely abandoned and the principle of trade liberalization has effectively replaced that of non-reciprocal privileged access. Whilst the shock of this change has been somewhat cushioned by lengthy negotiation and transition periods that retain some aspects of the Lomé *acquis*, there has been a paradigmatic shift in the focus and direction of EU–ACP relations. However, these reforms are ultimately dependent on a wider global agenda and on improved institutional capacity that can enhance policy implementation. Without better, quicker and more coordinated implementation (on the part of the ACP, but also the EU) the primary objective of the Partnership Agreement – poverty reduction – will remain impossible to attain. The challenges that confront the effective implementation of Cotonou and how this agreement meshes with the most recent EU development initiative – the 'Everything but Arms' proposal of February 2001 – is discussed in the following chapter.

Chapter 8

Future Challenges: Implementing Cotonou and 'Everything but Arms'

The focus of this penultimate chapter is on the future challenges faced by EU development policy. First, the issues surrounding the implementation of Cotonou are considered; and second, the most recent policy initiative – the 'Everything but Arms' regulation – is outlined and analysed as an element of a more coherent global EU development approach.

Implementing Cotonou

Supporters of the Partnership Agreement argue strongly that, within the context of increasing and irreversible globalization, only it can possibly provide an effective framework for development. Globalization has the capacity permanently to marginalize certain ACP regions: the intention and spirit of Cotonou is to ensure that the ACP are included rather than excluded from globalization and to influence the direction of this process to secure more equitable development. The EU has expressed its political commitment to defend the principles of the Cotonou Agreement in all international fora, particularly at the WTO. Yet despite this highest level of political will, the Partnership Agreement faces a number of important challenges.

Perhaps the most fundamental challenge to be faced during the 20-year duration of the Partnership Agreement is a psychological one. Cotonou undoubtedly presents an opportunity for EU–ACP relations to prosper and may offer potentially innovative solutions to historic dilemmas. But to what extent will the new philosophy and ambitions be embraced, and to what extent will the Lomé mentality persist? It is one thing to agree to the principle of trade liberalization – quite another to implement the necessary domestic reforms to make that a reality in the ACP states. Just as it has proved unrealistic to expect all the candidate countries of the next EU enlargement to join simultaneously, it is equally unrealistic to presume that all of the 38 non-LDC signatory states will be in a position to sign regional free trade agreements by 2008. Indeed, the 2004 and 2006 review dates provide the legitimate mechanism whereby such a scenario becomes possible.

The negotiations that led to the South African FTA were instructive in shaping the trade aspects of the Cotonou Agreement. The success of the 'first wave' of ACP–EU regional economic partnership agreements will be equally instructive and influential in persuading less enthusiastic or economically less well-suited ACP states of the merits of experimenting with free trade. Thus the detailed provisions, timing and selection of appropriate states as the test case is crucial. Perhaps the Pacific Island states could provide a comparatively favourable example: whether this would persuade the African ACP states of the suitability of free trade or rather underline its inapplicability to African economic conditions remains to be seen. Of course, external factors may supersede these discussions. A new WTO Round that incorporates a sympathetic development agenda could make the Cotonou Agreement largely irrelevant. Conversely, a reversal of the recent international consensus on development could see a less sympathetic approach taken and the ACP shy away from a more intrusive, rule-based and liberalized trading regime.

A further challenge is the LDCs. Insisting on the LDCs adopting the same timetable towards economic partnership as the other better-developed ACP states (as proposed in the original Commission Green Paper) would have been catastrophic – and was successfully resisted. However, by providing essentially the status quo for these 39 LDCs, the EU has created a paradox. If, as is widely accepted, Lomé's non-reciprocal arrangements have helped to exacerbate the economic decline of the ACP, how can their continuation be advantageous? How, if at all, can the LDCs reach an economic position whereby economic liberalization becomes a possibility? Does Cotonou unintentionally condemn them to third-class status in perpetuity? Clearly, the nature and global scale of these problems go far beyond the scope of the Partnership Agreement. Nonetheless, to be effective the Cotonou Agreement will have to recognize and operate within the international economy if the mistakes of Lomé are not to be repeated.

In addition to the economic challenges, the Partnership Agreement has set an ambitious agenda relating to civil society. Lomé adopted an essentially government-to-government approach: to transform and decentralize this to involve non-state actors – some of whom may be in conflict with their government – is something the Commission has recognized may be hard to implement (Petit, 2000, p. 18). Not all ACP countries have a well-defined civil society that is capable of participating in development initiatives; in others the government may be reluctant to empower potential opposition groups. However, the development of legitimate and representative groups within civil society and their effective participation in the formulation of development policies remains a core element in the Cotonou approach. Indeed, Cotonou defines the involvement of non-state actors as a 'fundamental principle' and their involvement is required across a wide range of policy sectors covered in the Agreement (Desesquelles, 2000, p. 8). Successful development is now predicated on having effective democratic processes and pluralistic participation in order to provide the necessary institutional foundations for economic policy. Civil society is therefore an explicit and essential element of development and one where continued EU support (financial, political and even moral) will be required. Whilst this is non-controversial, it remains to be seen whether the Partnership Agreement can introduce mechanisms that will be adequate to achieve these objectives.

A somewhat more pragmatic challenge is effective implementation. The record shows that both Lomé and the EU's other aid programmes have often been characterized by tardy implementation, inefficiency and weak accountability. To address these problems, the Prodi Commission has introduced institutional-level reform by reorganizing External Relations, and the Cotonou Agreement has simplified the use of financial instruments in order to address these deficiencies. These reforms ought to increase the efficiency of the EU's programmes, but they seem unlikely to be a sufficient panacea. The EU's institutional capacity is already overloaded and it seems destined to stagnate given the increased intergovernmental impetus embodied in the Nice Treaty. A stronger and larger Commission with expanding policy competences now appears incompatible with the direction of the integration process of the early twenty-first century. Without such additional institutional capacity, the procedures envisaged at Cotonou may become impossible to implement. Similarly, better implementation demands increased capacity on the part of the ACP recipients, particularly in relation to decentralized cooperation involving a partnership between state and non-state actors (Desesquelles, 2000, 9). Without adequate institution-building (for government and for civil society), the implementation capacity for many ACP countries will be unchanged, in effect neutralizing any new policy opportunities presented by the Agreement.

As has now become widely recognized, development requires strong democratic institutional support. A majority of ACP states can demonstrate robust and deep-rooted democratic systems; but for some this process remains fragile and in its infancy. And for a number internal or external conflicts have effectively undermined democratic culture and processes – in Ethiopia, Eritrea, the Democratic Republic of Congo, Sierra Leone or Fiji for example. In such circumstances the role of political dialogue, particular conflict-prevention strategies, becomes fundamental to the success of the Partnership Agreement.

A more general challenge is whether the unique EU–ACP relationship can be maintained, or whether Cotonou signals the break-up of this 'imagined' group. The coherence of the group was first challenged in the 1996 Green Paper. Despite predictions of an imminent death, the ACP maintained solidarity throughout the post-Lomé reform process and fought off criticism of the contradictions and incompatibility within the ACP concept. Until the ACP wishes to disestablish the group there is little that the EU effectively can do. The political symbolism of the ACP label far outweighs any geographic or economic arguments. At least superficially, Cotonou has guaranteed the status quo for two decades. But as suggested already, beneath this formal unity the new economic partnership arrangements may create institutionalized tensions that result in the ACP imploding and fragmenting into discrete – and competing – regional groupings. Whereas past diversity was not an impediment to cohesion, future economic competition (disguised as 'positive differentiation') may prove to be a greater challenge. The ACP

faces considerable internal strain as it seeks to balance the interests of LDCs with those of comparatively wealthy states such
as Nigeria or South Africa. Again, Cotonou unintentionally
may have encouraged and formalized such a dichotomy by
agreeing to treat the LDCs and the other ACP states quite
differently economically.

Of course, there are countervailing political arguments in
support of maintaining the solidarity of the ACP. As a group
currently of 77 states it presents a more credible presence as a
negotiating partner that could be absent were the individual
states to interact bilaterally or regionally with the EU. And yet
the ACP does sit uncomfortably with the EU's preference for
regional dialogues internationally. Furthermore, the level of
intra-ACP trade is minimal and to the extent that it does exist
it primarily reflects regional cooperation that could exist outside
the ACP framework. The longevity of the ACP may depend on
the promotion of the group's identity beyond the EU into other
international arenas. Acting collectively at the WTO or the UN
would enhance its utility and answer critics who see the ACP's
sole *raison d'être* being its special relationship with Europe. Successive ACP Heads of Government summits have recognized
this necessity without to date finding a more effective expression in practice (Karl, 2000, p. 22). Somewhat paradoxically,
the Cotonou Agreement may provide this added impetus,
however, as the EU has committed itself to promoting the ACP's
representation in international organizations.

Lastly, the final challenge to be overcome is both familiar and
conceptual in content. What should be the EU's development
role with regard to that, of the member states and other international organizations and donors? Cotonou – like its predecessor – constitutes a unique agreement that can be considered
as unparalleled for its time. It links politics, trade and aid in an
as yet untested way and Cotonou at least contains the seeds of
a distinct EU development role. The parallel with the EU's own
CFSP is instructive. Just as Europe's foreign policy is diminished
(at least in the eyes of third countries) by the continuation of
national foreign policies (even where these are 'consistent' with
CFSP), so the EU's common development policy, as expressed
through the Cotonou Agreement, is diminished by the existence
of the bilateral development programmes operated by individual EU member states. Until development policy becomes an

exclusive EU competence, questions will always be raised as to the legitimacy of its role and effectiveness of its function. The 20-year duration of Cotonou has precluded the immediate abandonment of an EU development policy: however, the future re-nationalization of this policy sector should not be totally discounted. After all, financial support for the Partnership Agreement falls outside the scope of the EU's own budgetary resources and the continuation of the national funding basis of the EDF makes the programme highly dependent on intergovernmental accord. Conversely, an exclusive EU competence for development can be seen as self-defeating. The complexity and scale of development, particularly in relation to poverty, requires multiple actors and agencies. The EU, member states, other OECD countries, the UN, WTO and others all have roles to play. Where these are overlapping, the institution that can offer 'added value' or comparative advantage should take the lead. Such an approach remains consistent both with a broader understanding of subsidiarity and with a logical approach to development in a globalized context.

'Everything but Arms'

Both the complexity and the dynamic pace of change that has come to characterize the EU's development policy at the start of the twenty-first century was reflected in the so-called 'Everything but Arms' (EBA) proposal adopted as a Council Regulation (416/2001) on 28 February 2001. This Commission proposal to the Council was consistent with the new thrust of the Partnership Agreement and yet simultaneously suggested a fundamental break with the EU's past approach to development policy. Cotonou had introduced the principle of differentiation according to development status and offered special treatment for ACP states classified as Least Developed Countries. The Agreement even foreshadowed the general application of this new principle. However, whilst consistent to the Cotonou philosophy, 'Everything but Arms' has breeched the long-established policy of offering the ACP preferential advantages over all other developing countries. To extend non-reciprocity to non-ACP LDCs suggested – if not endorsed – a view that the ACP as a group was no longer the dominant organizing prin-

TABLE 8.1   *List of Least Developed Countries*

The ACP LDCs are:	The non-ACP LDCs are:
Sudan, Mauritania, Mali, Burkina Faso, Niger, Chad, Cape Verde, Gambia, Guinea-Bissau, Guinea, Sierra Leone, Liberia, Togo, Benin, Central African Republic, Equatorial Guinea, São Tomé and Príncipe, Democratic Republic of Congo, Rwanda, Burundi, Angola, Ethiopia, Eritrea, Djibouti, Somalia, Uganda, Tanzania, Mozambique, Madagascar, Comoros, Zambia, Malawi, Lesotho, Haiti, Solomon Islands, Tuvalu, Kiribati, Vanuatu and Samoa	Yemen, Afghanistan, Bangladesh, Maldives, Nepal, Bhutan, Myanmar, Laos and Cambodia

Note: There are 48 LDCs on the UN list: 39 of these are ACP countries. All GSP preferences for Myanmar have been suspended, and this also applies to EBA preferences.

Source: http://www.europa.eu.int/comm/trade/miti/devel/eba4_sum.htm

ciple for EU–Third World relations. The ACP had been split between the 38 non-LDCs and 39 LDCs who were now to be dealt with under an exclusive new 48-country LDC framework. Those critics who saw the Lomé renegotiation process as the forerunner to the fragmentation of the ACP group appeared vindicated.

According to a Commission press release, 'Everything but Arms' constituted a 'groundbreaking plan to provide full access for the world's poorest countries into European Union markets' and would grant duty-free access to the world's 48 poorest countries (see Table 8.1). The proposal covered all goods except the arms trade: hence the slogan, 'Everything but Arms'. European Trade Commissioner Pascal Lamy was forthright in his advocacy for the new proposal:

There has been plenty of talk about how market access for poor countries is critical if we are to tackle their growing

marginalisation in the globalising economy. Everyone seems ready to make the commitment at the political level. But talk is cheap. We now need to move beyond opt-out clauses. It's time to put access to our markets where our mouth is. That means opening up across the board, and for all the poorest countries. So we want to move to liberalise everything but the arms trade.
(http://www.europa.eu.int/comm/trade/miti/devel/eba1.htm)

The decision to proceed with the 'Everything but Arms' was in part a response to the failed 1999 Seattle WTO meeting and the perception that developing countries faced potential exclusion from the benefits of global trade liberalization. The EU's initiative was consistent with a wish to see a future WTO Round of multilateral trade negotiations successfully launched through which the interests and concerns of the developing countries can be addressed.

Given its implications, the proposal was opposed from two directions. First, a number of existing ACP beneficiaries feared their interests were being compromised by this more inclusive programme; and second, initially some of the more protectionist-minded EU member states raised critical voices. In order to placate the ACP, concessions were made on transitional arrangements for significant products: rice, sugar and bananas (see below for details). The potential impact on ACP bananas was, however, still regarded as problematic by several Caribbean states. And of course, these concessions inevitably promoted continued LDC reliance on largely unprocessed raw products with little added-value accruing. Member state concerns over the potential for fraud and the difficulties in monitoring rules-of-origin were addressed in the eventual Regulation. Specific measures were established to safeguard the EU from a flood of fraudulent imports under the proposal. A somewhat different criticism was also raised by some LDCs; rather than excluding the duty-free export of third world arms to Europe, it was argued that greater benefits would result from a cessation of European arms sales to the developing world!

With opposition largely overcome, on 26 February 2001 the General Affairs Council adopted the Commission proposal on 'Everything but Arms' as an amendment to the EU's Generalized Scheme of Preferences. As of 5 March 2001 goods from the world's 48 LDCs receive tariff-free access to the EU market for all products other than arms and ammunition. This initiative makes the EU the world's first major trading power to commit itself to opening its market fully to the world's most impoverished countries. Duty and quota restrictions were eliminated immediately on all products except for the sensitive ACP issues of sugar, rice and bananas where full liberalization is to be phased in over a lengthy transition period. 'Everything but Arms' complements the LDC content of the Cotonou Agreement and triggers a process that will ensure free access for 'essentially all' products from all LDCs by 2005 at the latest.

What is the likely effect of the 'Everything but Arms' initiative? Does the rhetoric match the economic content? According to Commission figures, the EU had become the major global destination for LDC exports. In 1998, LDCs exported goods worth €15.5 billion: of this total the EU took 56 per cent (worth €8.7 billion) whilst the USA imported 36 per cent (worth €5.6 billion) and Japan 6 per cent. However, this previous regime excluded about 10 per cent of the 10 500 tariff lines in the EU's tariff schedule, and affected 1 per cent of total trade flows. The Commission proposal and the adopted Regulation addressed these gaps by granting duty-free and unrestricted quota access to for a further 919 lines covering all products (except arms and ammunition) from all LDCs. The new list leaves out just 25 tariff lines all of which are related to the arms trade. For the first time all agricultural products are covered including: beef and other meat; dairy products; fresh and processed fruit and vegetables; maize and other cereals; starch; oils; processed sugar products; cocoa products; pasta; and alcoholic beverages. As to bananas, rice and sugar which, as stated, were not liberalized immediately, the Commissioner for Trade Mr Lamy commented:

> We have been through this line by line, product by product, and have concluded that we should now take this important further step. Of course, some of the products are relatively sensitive, but there is no point in offering trade concessions on products which LDCs cannot export. We have to make a real difference. We of course recognise that duty free access

alone is not enough to enable the poorest countries to benefit from liberalised trade. We need to help them build their capacity to supply goods of export quality, and we reaffirm the Commission's commitment to continued technical and financial assistance to this end. (http://www.europa.eu.int/comm./trade/miti/devel/eba1.htm)

For these three products the implementation of unrestricted access will take effect in progressive stages. The ACP banana protocols had also been the subject of concerted WTO action and the new provisions had to be consistent with this process. Consequently, duties on bananas will be reduced by 20 per cent annually starting on 1 January 2002 and fully eliminated at the latest on 1 January 2006. Duties on rice will be reduced by 20 per cent on 1 September 2006, by 50 per cent on 1 September 2007 and by 80 per cent on 1 September 2008 and eliminated at the latest by 1 September 2009. Duties on sugar will be reduced by 20 per cent on 1 July 2006, by 50 per cent on 1 July 2007 and by 80 per cent on 1 July 2008 and eliminated at the latest by 1 July 2009.

To compensate for the delay on fully liberalized market access, the EU has agreed to transitional procedures for all 48 LDCs that invoke duty-free quotas for sugar and rice. The quota levels are based on the best figures for LDC exports during the 1990s, plus an additional 15 per cent. These quotas will increase by 15 per cent each year during the transitional period. For LDC raw sugar, a duty-free quota has been set at 74 185 tons for 2001/2002 growing to 197 355 tons by 2008/2009. Imports of sugar under the ACP–EC Sugar Protocol are additional to this quota (to uphold the integrity of this protocol). Similarly, LDC rice has duty-free status within the limits of a tariff quota of 2517 tons in 2001/2002 increasing to 6696 tons by 2008/2009 (See Table 8.2).

The challenges posed by coherence, complementarity and coordination are clearly at play in this new approach. The suggested compromise tries to balance improved trading opportunities for LDCs with giving sufficient time and protection to EU member-state producers to adapt to changes required in the Common Agricultural Policy (particularly for the three most sensitive products). It also has to take into account the constraints imposed by agreements with other developing

TABLE 8.2 *Tariff quotas for rice and raw sugar from LDCs*

Products	2001–2002 'EU import tons'	2002–2003 'EU import tons'	2003–2004 'EU import tons'	2004–2005 'EU import tons'	2005–2006 'EU import tons'	2006–2007 'EU import tons'	2007–2008 'EU import tons'	2008–2009 'EU import tons'
Rice (1)	2517	2895	3329	3829	4403	5063	5823	6696
Sugar (2)	74185	85313	98110	112827	129751	149213	171595	197335

(1) marketing years September 2001 to September 2009
(2) marketing years July 2001 to July 2009

Source: http://www.europa.eu.int/comm/trade/miti/devel/eba4_sum.htm

countries (the ACP as well as other traditional suppliers of primary products to the EU) and, of course, be consistent with WTO thinking.

This seeming European largesse also has to be balanced against other provisions of the Regulation that seek to stabilize the effect of this liberalization and in extreme circumstances protect EU producers and the EU's financial interests. Article 2.7 gives the Commission the authority to 'carefully monitor the imports of rice, bananas and sugar' and if necessary move to 'temporary suspension of the preferences'. Typically, the EU has designated itself judge and jury in any such cases. More generally, Article 4 provides for measures to combat fraud. Under this heading is included the failure to provide sufficient administrative cooperation to verify the precise country of origin of LDC goods, and 'massive increases' in the normal levels of LDC production and export capacity to the EU. And finally, Article 5 provides for the suspension of preferences by the Commission for a range of particularly sensitive products 'if the import of these products cause serious disturbance to Community markets and their regulatory mechanisms'. A 25 per cent annual increase is sufficient to trigger this procedure. Thus, through these mechanisms the EU will carefully monitor imports of rice, sugar and bananas and apply safeguard measures where necessary.

It is hard not to suspect the EU of a self-serving compromise in relation to these omnibus provisions. The argument offered by the Commission that the motivation for these safeguards is that trading benefits should only accrue to the countries for which they are intended (the LDCs) lacks a certain conviction. The scrupulous application of anti-fraud measures has at least as much to do with placating the interests of those member states whose domestic production will be most effected by the new concessions. However, it is reassuring that an assessment of the extent to which the LDCs are really benefiting from EBA, and whether the EU's provisions on rules of origin, anti-fraud and safeguards are adequate, has been authorized. The Commission has been asked to report to the Council in 2005 on the impact of trade within the EU and for LDCs, as well as on African, Caribbean and Pacific countries and to suggest appropriate proposals where necessary.

Conclusion

Both Cotonou and the EBA are potentially groundbreaking agreements: the EBA goes beyond any other current WTO initiative and Cotonou adopts a fresh approach to development. Whilst the European initiative has been widely welcomed, clearly developing countries would benefit further if these policies were replicated by America and Japan. Of course, neither agreement addresses the non-tariff barriers that often restrict developing country exports from entering the EU market and the supply-side limitations common in many developing countries that again constrain their trade potential.

Without undermining the benign intent of the EBA, there is growing concern among some developing countries that the EBA may prove to conflict with the broader development strategies of Cotonou. In an ideal world the reform process that lead to the Cotonou Agreement would have developed in parallel with the EBA discussions – ensuring to some degree coherence, coordination and complementarity. However, the existence of two separate agreements with overlapping but not identical membership presents the ACP with a potential dilemma. The Least Developed ACP countries are party to both agreements and have a choice of frameworks: the non-LDC ACP states, however, are excluded from the benefits of the EBA and some are concerned that the market access guaranteed by Cotonou will in practice be undermined by the more generous EBA provisions provided for non-ACP LDCs.

More significantly, the free access offered to the ACP LDCs seems to nullify the necessity to enter into regional free trade agreements with the EU as outlined in the Cotonou Agreement. All potential ACP regional FTAs include LDCs. Why should any ACP LDC exchange non-reciprocal unlimited access to the EU market for a regional free trade agreement that will give the EU free access to its markets and remove its ability to raise tariff revenue at its borders? Thus, unintentionally perhaps, the EBA has at least the potential to undermine the Cotonou Agreement objective of creating regional free trade agreements. Once again, the viability of the ACP as a coherent group can be questioned. And perhaps more worryingly, the complexity of orchestrating a global approach to development policy at the EU-level that respects consistency, coherence as well as complementarity seems beyond the capacity of current policy-making frame-works. Adverse unintended consequences that characterized the Lomé experience continue to present a current danger to development policy in the twenty-first century.

Chapter 9

Conclusion: Development and Integration

The preceding chapters have provided an overview of the complex mosaic of frameworks that define the EU's relations with the developing world. The emphasis of the book reflects that of the EU itself: both historically and contemporarily the most intense dialogue has been with the ACP countries, with Asian and Latin American relations given considerably less attention. However, the debate surrounding the reform of the Lomé Convention and the changing development paradigm promoted by the EU has come to colour all sectors of European development policy. In that respect, policy towards the ACP shapes and determines the nature of the EU's Third World relations globally.

In this concluding chapter the conceptual link between EU development policy and the process of European integration is explored. Whilst atheoretical examinations of EU politics can still be found, increasingly the importance of integration theory has come to be recognized as the essential starting point for discussions of any EU activity. To understand the motivations and rationale behind European policies – as well as the chosen policy mechanisms – requires a theoretical framework. Often explanations are not to be found in the more immediate issues related to a specific policy sector, but in the wider debates concerning the kind of integration process envisaged. Understandably, most examinations of Europe's relations with the Third World have located themselves theoretically within the discourse of development studies. However, the perspective of this book has been upon the European process of establishing policies that are developmental in nature; consequently the issues pertaining to the wider integration debates are of central relevance. Simply, which of the competing approaches to integration can best explain EU development policy? In this concluding chapter, theoretical explanations that provide the greatest insight into the question of who determines the development policy agenda are considered.

Development and integration theory

A number of other texts emphasize the priority given to integration theory. For example, in *Developments in the European Union* the importance of establishing the right theoretical lenses for viewing aspects of integration is stressed. As the authors remind us, it is vital to contextualize empirical information (whether policies or decisions) within theoretical and conceptual approaches, so as to both understand the 'facts' better and to assess and develop the nature of integration theory (Cram, Dinan and Nugent, 1999, p. 17). In a similar vein, *Decision-Making in the European Union* distinguishes between three levels of theorizing (super-systemic, systemic and sub-system) and argues – rightly – that it is important to differentiate between these levels when considering the appropriate choice of theoretical framework. Simply, the level of analysis required will determine the usefulness as well as applicability of each theoretical approach. As the authors argue, 'a theory which seeks to explain or predict "big decisions", such as the launch of EMU, should not be judged by how well it explains or predicts a decision to change the way pig carcasses are measured' (Peterson and Bomberg, 1999, p. 9). Applying this logic to the focus of this book, the usefulness of grand integration theories (such as neo-functionalism or intergovernmentalism) in explaining the broad outline of EU–Third World relations should not be confused with different lower-level approaches that might better explain a specific humanitarian action or trade concessions.

The general EU literature of the 1990s has been characterized by a renewed interest in these broader integration issues: in this discussion the theories associated primarily with the work of Moravcsik, Marks, Bulmer and Peterson form the conceptual foundations for this analysis of development policy. The interesting question for this analysis is how far can these general integration theories be used to interpret the EU's policy towards the developing world? There is a danger of creating just the appearance of coherence: the application of a general approach can, through its very generality, create a false impression of cohesion and coherence where in fact the policy is fragmented and a response to different catalysts.

Liberal intergovernmentalism

At its most basic level, liberal intergovernmentalism places the state as the key actor in determining EU outcomes. Although its most influential proponent Moravcsik (1991, 1993, 1995; Moravcsik and Kalypso, 1999) specifically circumscribes the applicability of liberal intergovernmentalism to what he calls history or polity-making events, its logic and explanation has been extended by others in an attempt to form a more general grand theory of integration. However, as Sartori (1976) long ago warned, concepts do not automatically 'travel' well and the cost of increased stretching is often an unsatisfactory fit between theory and practice. Whilst acknowledging this potential constraint, many of the general assumptions of intergovernmentalism have direct applicability to theorizing the EU's development policy. Thus for intergovernmentalists, integration is fundamentally realized through interstate bargaining by rational economically self-interested governments influenced by their domestic settings and is not the outcome of any independent dynamic process or non-state actors. Crudely put, what you see is what you get: states exercise power and therefore all decisions made by the EU must reflect, to some degree, a *Realpolitik* perspective. Typically, outcomes are based on the lowest common denominator. As in international relations not all states are deemed equal, with France, the UK and Germany often the dominant actors; however the importance of all member states exceeds that of the supranational institutions which, for intergovernmentalists, are peripheral and provide an inadequate account of the EU's grand decisions.

A key aspect implicit in this examination of the EU's policy towards the developing world is who is driving the policy agenda? Liberal Intergovernmentalism provides one set of conceptual lenses for intellectualizing this question. The answers it provides are distinct, provocative and possibly mutually exclusive with other integration theories. Whether intuitively appealing, or fundamentally flawed, the importance of intergovernmentalism is that it clearly establishes an extreme explanatory pole against which other theories can be located, compared and contrasted. Thus, an intergovernmentalist perspective towards development policy argues that the policy-making process is determined by the member states. This book cites many examples that correspond to such an approach. Clearly, historically the introduction of a development focus (of Yaoundé and of Lomé) was driven by national government concerns (primarily French and British respectively). This was complemented by the emergence of a Latin American policy after the accession of Spain and Portugal. Member states were also the primary source for the increased concern for good governance and other aspects of conditionality. And although Prodi instigated the reform of the Commission, his selection as President of the Commission was a direct response to member-state pressures demanding restructuring and more effective policy implementation.

The negotiation of Cotonou provides some of the richest evidence of intergovernmentalism in EU policy-making. First, it should not be forgotten that for any agreement to proceed there had to be consensus on all points on the EU side. Whilst trade-offs and concessions are the typical mechanism for developing EU policy, this does not undermine the fundamental point that any single state can veto a consensus from emerging. The negative role of member states was evident in the constraints imposed upon the negotiating mandate given to the Commission. Agricultural concessions were largely prohibited due to expected member-state opposition. The issue of immigration and repatriation was again the result of explicit member-state involvement. More positively, the involvement of the UK and Germany was the determining factor in changing the EU position on both debt relief and on the treatment of LDCs. The change in government in the UK was instrumental in finally bringing debt relief within the ACP framework – a policy that previous EU governments had avoided. Similarly, the decision not to extend reciprocal free trade principles to the LDCs was strongly advocated by the UK, Germany and the Netherlands underlining both the legal and moral authority of member states in determining EU development policy.

The application of liberal intergovernmentalism to development policy reminds us of the primacy of the member states. The Fifteen determine the broad parameters for the large decisions that set the context for micro-policy choices. Their political will – or at least their collective acquiescence – is required.

However, there are also clearly disadvantages in using only such an elite-focused approach to policy-making. The EU institutions are marginalized in such an analysis: in the context of development policy, the omission of the Commission as a significant policy initiator is conceptually unrealistic and misleading.

Neo-functionalism

This theoretical approach has been applied to the integration process since the 1950s and its classical application is best represented by the work of Haas. Generally, neo-functionalism is identified with the opposite theoretical pole to intergovernmentalism. However, the contrast should not be seen as fundamentally antagonistic, but rather that different aspects and actors involved in the integration process are simply given a different emphasis and explanatory power. Peterson and Bomberg go as far as to state that the two approaches 'are complementary more than they are competitive' (1999, p. 15). As theory, intergovernmentalism focuses on process whereas neo-functionalism highlights context. Neo-functionalism does not deny that states are important actors; but it does argue that other supranational actors (such as the Commission, Parliament and the Court) may often be of greater importance in explaining integration. In essence, neo-functionalism tends to identify a wider range of actors and a greater complexity of relationships when characterizing integration. What it shares with intergovernmentalism is an aspiration to offer a comprehensive super-systemic level explanation of the process.

The idea of 'spillover' is neo-functionalism's most celebrated – and controversial – theoretical contribution. For Haas, spillover manifested at least three elements: functional, political and geographic. The logic is straightforward. Neo-functionalism argues that policy sectors and decisions are not isolated or autonomous. Rather they are located within a network, or policy community, and that decisions have repercussions beyond their immediate policy area. Actions that promote deeper integration in one policy area will have implications, consequences and effects upon a number of related policy areas. For example, a decision to create a European single market has influenced more than internal trade barriers. Neo-functionalists would argue that it has necessitated a common response to questions as diverse as citizenship, immigration, trade sanctions and tax harmonization.

Within the development policy context, a neo-functional-based analysis would see connections between the EU's reform of the Lomé Convention and its approach to a Common Foreign and Security Policy, enlargement and external trade relations in general. Most obviously, as we have seen, the TEU provided the legal possibility for spillover from CFSP to development policy. The EBA debates on free-market access for all LDCs arguably also display neo-functional characteristics. Having conceded that LDCs should receive special treatment in Cotonou, this policy concession crucially informed the EBA debate. Without any concessions for the ACP LDCs, support for the EBA may not have emerged. In the past, considerable debate has focused on whether this spillover effect is inevitable or 'automatic'. Whilst most now agree with Keohane and Hoffmann (1990) that any such spillover is usually preceded by an 'intergovernmental bargain', only crude intergovernmentalists deny that this dynamic is evident in the integration process. The idea of spillover merely acknowledges the inter-related nature of policy development within the EU – which can have both positive and negative outcomes.

Multi-level governance

Some of the most interesting conceptual developments of the last decade are consistent with and build upon a basic neo-functional foundation. Perhaps the most influential is the 'multi-level governance' perspective first elaborated by Marks, Hooghe and Blank. They reject a uni-dimensional theoretical framework in favour of a more complex model that identifies a range of actors across different policy levels characterized by 'mutual dependence, complementary functions and overlapping competences' (1996, p. 378). Significantly, this approach both incorporates and moderates the intergovernmentalist preoccupation with the central role of the state. The crucial modification is that multi-level governance considers that states (represented through the Council of Ministers) share decision-making authority with the supranational institutions; consequently, states – whilst they remain important actors – cannot guarantee desired outcomes and are themselves constrained by domestic interests and influences. In the context of Europe's external development relations, the recognition of other actors (such as the ACP states and the EU–ACP institutions as well as the Commission) suggests that this policy sector may possibly exhibit an even more extreme form of multi-level governance than that found for internal EU policies (Holland, 2000, p. 675).

Numerous examples of multi-level governance can be found in this book. Among them the most obvious relate to the reform of the Commission and to the Cotonou negotiations. As noted above, the member states were important in promoting the reform of Commission procedures – but they were not the only actors. The critical report that led to the resignation of the Santer Commission, pressure from the European Parliament as well as the agenda of the new Prodi Commission were at least of equal importance. A combination of national and supranational factors was at work. The Cotonou negotiations provide an even broader example. Clearly, the Commission was instrumental in setting the parameters for the debate. Although none of the Green Paper options was endorsed with qualification, the focus of the reform debate was in practice set by the Commission and by its resultant guidelines. Had the Commission not signalled a preference for regional FTAs, it is hard to see how this concept would have emerged at the Council level. Of course, as discussed above, the Council can and did modify the Commission proposals – most notably with respect to separate treatment of LDCs – but overall the framework of the Cotonou Agreement can be traced back to the Commission's earliest 1996 proposals. The advantage of multi-level governance is that it allows the analysis to accommodate the roles of non-state actors and institutions and as such adds a much-needed layer of conceptual sophistication to the basic intergovernmental theory.

The conceptual roots of multi-level governance can be traced to the earlier work of Bulmer (1983) that was influential in repositioning 'domestic politics' as a key variable in explanations of European decision-making. Clearly, too, the approach is sympathetic to the neo-functionalists' emphasis on supranational institutions, particularly the role of the Commission. At its most incisive, multi-level governance theorizes the enhanced authority of the supranational institutions at the expense of the state and national sovereignty. However, it goes beyond these earlier frameworks to stress the complexity and interacting nature of different policy levels – local, regional, national, transnational and international – that collectively shape integration. This complexity, of course, presents its own methodological challenges, but it is nonetheless a welcome correction to the oversimplification presented in many intergovernmentalist analyses.

Policy networks and new institutionalism

Another approach that is compatible with multi-level governance is the influence of public policy literature on integration theory, particularly the idea of policy networks (Peterson, 1995; Richardson, 1996). Simply, this approach argues that general public policy theories derived from national studies can be applied equally successfully to the EU policy process: in that respect they suggest that *sui generis* theories of integration are unnecessary. For example, agenda management and implementation processes have been used to enrich analyses of EU behaviour. The major contribution of the public policy literature has been at the micro decision-making level and these approaches are less able to operate at the level of grand theory. However, the recognition of interlocking policy networks at EU, state and sub-state levels is consistent with a multi-level governance perspective and helps further to challenge an exclusive reliance on intergovernmental explanations. In relation to development policy, the problems associated with policy implementation or with assessing good governance may best be dealt with through such network policy theories.

Finally, another contemporary development that is consistent with neo-functionalism is 'new institutionalism' (see Bulmer, 1994: Pierson, 1996). Here, the emphasis is on the role of the supranational institutions in shaping the EU agenda, policies and decisions. This approach confronts the intergovernmentalist view that institutions are merely objective agents and not actors with their own motivations and interests. The Parliament, Commission and Court effect and are affected by the integration process. Values, norms, the very 'politics' of interaction are used to explain outcomes. A dynamic rather than static view of institutions is assumed that clearly requires an institutional learning capacity. Not only do institutions matter, they evolve, adapt and respond within their contemporary and historical contexts. Of course, this dynamic characteristic reflects the

242 The European Union and the Third World

reality of changing political elites (at least within the Commission and Parliament) that can alter the definition of institutional self-interest at any given moment. Consequently, new institutionalism argues that outcomes are rarely optimal: policy gaps and unintended consequences are evident especially where decisions are made within the context of short-term institutional horizons. The potential conflict between the EBA and Cotonou free trade areas discussed in Chapter 8 seems a clear example of this dynamic that can be explained by new institutionalism. Historical precedent and timing are identified as crucial limitations: future options are constrained by past decisions and the logic of 'path dependency' is influential. Applying these insights to the EU's development policies again enriches our understanding. For example, it reminds us of the power of the status quo. Innovations must operate within the context of existing policy parameters and these will inevitably preclude some outcomes and favour others. Similarly, Parliament's desire to participate in the reform debates on Lomé may reflect both a concern with development policy *per se*, but it may also reflect the wider issues of defining policy competences between competing institutional actors in general. A legal or purely formal understanding of the policy process ignores these vital contexts; but inevitably, incorporating new institutionalism within integration theory further adds to the complexity and messy nature of this process.

In summary, the theoretical point being made here is a simple one: that integration theories that are typically used to explain the internal processes of European integration – and even polity-making decisions -can be used with equal validity and relevance for Europe's external relations. Thus integration theory is the appropriate conceptual framework for thinking about the EU's relations with the developing world. The decisions, non-decisions, policies and programmes both reflect and are informed by this wider integration context. However, as this discussion has outlined, the purpose of theorizing about European integration is not to find a single macro-theory. Rather it is to discriminate between alternative theories depending upon the level of analysis chosen and the nature of the actual empirical case. At different times within this book alternative theories are engaged – intergovernmentalism, neo-functionalism, multi-level governance and so on – in order to shed the greatest light upon specific aspects of EU development policy. Such an inclusive theoretical position – if somewhat frustrating for those seeking simple answers – is the only valid approach.

Conclusion

There are a number of broad conclusions that can be drawn from this survey of EU relations with the developing world. First, development policy is an undervalued and under-researched aspect of EU activity. In the academic literature it gains only spasmodic attention: as discussed above, in contrast to the analysis of most other EU policy sectors, it is rarely addressed from the conceptual premise of integration theory. In part, this discontinuity is explained by the ambiguous nature and origin of development policy. The national funding base of the EDF is symbolic of this unfamiliar blend of national and supranational competences. Whilst a distinct EU role exists, it is often conditional on national bilateral support and its function in the wider integration process clouded.

Second, and perhaps above all else, EU development policy towards the Third World is subject to the shadow of complementarity. Ensuring that the different elements of EU-level development policy are consistent and do not produce unintended consequences or conflict of interests is a substantial organizational task. The most recent Prodi Commission reforms have gone some way to addressing this at the bureaucratic level. However, as was argued in the analysis of the EBA and the implementation of Cotonou in Chapter 8, ensuring consistency across different development policy spheres remains problematic. In isolation, the FTAs under Cotonou, the provisions for ACP non-reciprocity as well as the extension of this to all LDCs under the EBA can all be regarded as rational and appropriate policy responses. But cumulatively, these individual EU initiatives contain inherent conflicts and probable contradictions. This tendency is further exacerbated when one then tries to align EU-level policies with the 15 bilateral policies of the member states. Consequently, it should not be surprising to find examples where EU policy fails the complementarity test: what is more surprising is the frequency with which complementarity is achieved.

Third, development policy forms an important aspect of the EU's international role and should be conceptualized within the broader intention to establish a single foreign policy international 'presence'. Indeed, the continuing constraints of the civilian nature of EU action make development policy initiatives an attractive mechanism for extending 'presence'. The danger, however, is once again in failing to match expectations with capabilities. As argued elsewhere in this book, it seems foolish for the EU to establish development policy goals – such as poverty eradication – that are effectively unachievable. Less grandiose, but more attainable objectives are needed to enhance the reality of the EU's presence in a global context.

Lastly, the Introduction to this book questioned whether development policy was a core function of the EU or might constitute an area for 'enhanced cooperation' under the Nice Treaty. The analysis here, especially in light of the theoretical discussion given above, argues very strongly that development policy remain a core EU activity. Popular support for the integration process requires more than monetary union or a common market. A wide and comprehensive range of policies is needed in order to generate public awareness and belief in the purpose of integration. Without external policies such as relations with the Third World, the 'idea' of Europe is diminished. The challenge for the EU is to harness its various external policy sectors to this end – to enhance the integration process. From an integration perspective it would be mistaken for the EU to surrender development policy to the national level. Both Cotonou and the EBA are ambitious attempts to redesign the EU's role. However, the greatest challenge remains defining development policy as an exclusive EU competence and in making that policy a future success.

Bibliography

Agence Europe (2000), 28 February.

Allen, D. and M. Smith (1999) 'External Policy Developments', *Journal of Common Market Studies: Annual Review*, vol. 37.

Arts, K. and J. Byron (1997) 'The Mid-term Review of the Lomé IV Convention: heralding the future?', *Third World Quarterly*, 18, no. 1.

Asante, S. (1996) 'The European Union – Africa (ACP) Lomé' Convention, *Africa Insight*, vol. 26, no. 4.

Bessa-Rodrigues, P. (1999) 'European Union-MERCOSURL: in search of a "new" Relationship?', *European Foreign Affairs Review*, vol. 4.

Birocchi, F. (1999) 'The European Union's Development Policies towards Asian and Latin American Countries', DSA European Development Policy Study Group Discussion Paper no. 10.

Bonvin, J. (1997) 'Globalisation and linkages: challenges for development policy', *Development: the Journal of the Society for International Development*, vol. 40, no. 2.

Bossuyt, J., J. Carlsson, G. Laporte and B. Oden (1999) *Improving the Complementarity of European Union Development Cooperation – from the bottom up*, ECDPM Discussion Paper no. 4, Maastricht.

Bossuyt, J., A. Koulaimah-Gabriel, G. Laporte and H.-B. Solignac Lecomte (1999) 'Comparing the ACP and EU Negotiating Mandates', *The Courier*, no. 173 (Brussels: European Commission), pp. 72–4.

Bulmer, S. (1983) 'Domestic Politics and EC Policy-Making', *Journal of Common Market Studies*, vol. 21.

Bulmer, S. (1994) 'The Governance of the European Union: a new institutional approach', *Journal of Public Policy*, vol. 13.

Bulletin of the European Communities (1998–2000) (Brussels: European Commission).

Caputo, E. (1996) 'The Case of the European Union', *Evaluating Programme Aid, IDS Bulletin*, vol. 27, no. 4.

Chirathivat, S. (2000) 'Asia-Europe Investment Relations and the ASEM Process', in *Asia–Europe in a Global Economy: Economics, Economic Systems and Economic Cooperation*, conference proceedings, Korean EC Studies Association. Seoul, Korea, 1–2 September.

Commission of the European Communities (1969) 'The External Trade of the European Community 1958–1967', *Current Notes on the European Community*, no. 5 (London: European Commission).

——(1972) 'The Enlarged Community and the Developing Commonwealth Countries: some notes on association', *European Communities Press and Information: Background Note*, 27 March (London: European Commission).

——(1973) 'Memorandum of the Commission to the Council on the future relations between the Community, the present AASM States, and the countries in Africa, the Caribbean, the Indian and Pacific Oceans referred to in Protocol 22 to the act of accession', *EC Bulletin*, Supplement 1/73 (Brussels: European Communities).

——(1986) *Ten Years of Lomé: a record of EEC–ACP Partnership 1976–1985* (Brussels: European Information Development).

——(1994) *Towards a New Asia Strategy: Communication from the Commission to the Council*, COM(94) 314 (Brussels: European Community).

——(1995) *Trade Relations Between the European Union and the Developing Countries* (Luxembourg: Office of the Official Publications of the European Communities).

——(1996) *Green Paper on Relations Between the European Union and the ACP Countries on the Eve of the 21st Century. Challenges and Opportunities for a New Partnership*, COM(96) 570, 20 November (Brussels: European Community), 89pp.

——(1997a) *Communication to the Council and the European Parliament: Guidelines for the Negotiation of New Cooperation agreements with the African, Caribbean and Pacific (ACP) Countries*, COM(97) 537 final, 29 October (Brussels: European Community).

——(1997b) *The Future of North-South Relations: Towards Sustainable Economic and Social Development*, 'Cahiers' of the Forward Studies Unit (Luxembourg: European Community).

——(1999) *Evaluation of EU Development Aid to ALA States – Phase III – Synthesis Report*, Joint RELEX SERVICE for the management of Community aid to non-member countries (SCR), 15 March.

——(2000a) 'Perspectives and Priorities for the ASEM Process (Asia Europe Meeting) into the New Decade', Working Document, COM(2000) 241.Final, 18 April.

——(2000b) *Report from the Commission on the Implementation of Council Regulation (EC) No. 443/97 of 3 March 1997 on Operations to Aid Uprooted People in Asian and Latin American Developing Countries: Consolidated Report for 1997–1999*, COM (2000) 367, 16 June (Brussels).

——(2000c) *Communication to the Commission on the Reform of the Management of External Assistance*, 16 May (Brussels).

Cosgrove-Twitchett, C. (1978) *Europe and Africa: from Association to Partnership* (Farnborough: Saxon House).

Council Decision (1998) Council Decision of 6 July 1998 concerning exceptional assistance for the heavily indebted ACP countries, *Official Journal L 198, 15/07/1998*, pp. 40–1.

Council of the EC (1989) 'Resolution of 16 May 1989 on Coordination in Support of Structural Adjustment in ACP States', *Bulletin of the European Communities*, no. 5.

Cram, L., Dinan, D. and N. Nugent (eds) (1999) *Developments in the European Union* (London: Macmillan).

Crawford, G. (1996) 'Wither Lomé? The Mid-term Review and the Decline of Partnership', *The Journal of Modern African Studies*, vol. 34.

Cruz Vilaca, J. da and J. Heredia (1998) 'The European Union and the Transformation of the Andean Pact into the Andean Community: from the Trujillo Protocol to the Sucre Act', *European Foreign Affairs Review*, vol. 3.

Dauster, J. (1998) 'MERCOSUR and the European Union: Prospects for an Inter-Regional Association', *European Foreign Affairs Review*, vol. 4.

David, D. (2000) '40 Years of Europe–ACP relationship', *ACP–EU Partnership Agreement signed in Cotonou on 23 June 2000*, supplement to *The Courier* (Brussels: European Commission).

Dent, C. (1997) 'The ASEM: Managing the New Framework of the EU's Economic Relations with East Asia', *Pacific Affairs*, vol. 70, no. 4.

—(1999) 'The Weak Link in the Triad? The Future Prospects of the European Union's Economic Relationship with East Asia' paper presented at the Sixth Biennial ECSA International Conference, Pittsburgh, 2–5 June.

Desesquelles, G. (2000) 'The Non-governmental Actors', *The Courier*, issue 181 (Brussels: European Commission).

Development Assistance Committee (1996) *European Community: Review* (Paris: OECD).

Development Council of the European Union (2000) *2263rd Council Meeting – Development – Brussels, 18th May*, PRES/00/156.

Dialogue for Democratic Development: policy options for a renewed ACP-EU partnership (1999) (Stockholm: IDEA).

Elgström, O. (2000) 'Lomé and Post-Lomé: Asymmetric Negotiations and the Impact of Norms', *European Foreign Affairs Review*, vol. 5, no. 2.

European Foreign Affairs Review (1998–2000) vols. 3–5.

European Voice (2000) 'Nielson Unveils Blueprint for Development Policy Overhaul', vol. 6, 23–9 March.

—(2000) 'Planned EU Aid Shake-up Under Fire', vol. 6, 27 April–3 May.

Eurostat (1998) Statistics in Focus: External Trade – 12 (Brussels: Commission of the EC), pp. 1–10.

Fangchuan, H. and U. Niemann (eds) (2000) *Asia and Europe – Towards a Better Mutual Understanding*, Second ASEF Summer School, 22 August–5 September 1999, Beijing: Asia-Europe Foundation/Singapore: Peking University.

Focke Report (1980) *From Lomé I to Lomé II; Texts of the Report of the Resolution Adopted on 26 September 1980 by the ACP–EEC Consultative Assembly* (Luxembourg: European Parliament).

Gomes, S. (2000) 'The Political Dimension of the New ACP–EU Partnership', *The Courier*, issue 181 (Brussels: European Commission).

Grilli, E. (1993) *The European Community and the Developing Countries* (Cambridge: Cambridge University Press).

Grimwade, N. and D. Mayes (2000) 'Trends in EU–East Asian Trade and Their Implications for Europe's ASEM Programme' *Journal of Economic Integration*, vol. 15, no. 3, pp. 363–6.

Grisanti, L (2000) 'Europe and Latin America: the Challenge of Strategic Partnership', *European Foreign Affairs Review*, vol. 5, no. 1.

Haas, E. (1958) *The Uniting of Europe* (Stanford: Stanford University Press).

Hanf, T. (ed.) (1999) *Watching Democracy at Work: Writing State of Democracy Assessments and Organising Election Observation. A Practical Guide* (Freiburg im Breisgau: Arnold Bergstraesser Institut).

Heidensohn, K. (1995) *Europe and World Trade* (London: Pinter).

Holland, M. (1994) 'Plus ça Change ... ? The European Union Joint Action and South Africa', *Centre for European Policy Studies*, no. 57 (Brussels: CEPS).

Holland, M. (2000) 'Resisting Reform or Risking Revival? Renegotiating the Lomé Convention', in M. Green-Cowles and M. Smith (eds), *State of the European Union V* (Oxford: Oxford University Press).

IP (2000a) *Press Release: Commission Sets Out Political Guidelines for the Future of EC Development Policy*, IP/00/410, 26 April.

—(2000b) *Press Release: Common Service for External Relations – Commission Shakes Up Management of External Assistance*, IP/00/480, 16 May.

—(2000c) *Press Release: EU Deploys 160 Strong Election Observation Team in Zimbabwe*, IP/00/553, 30 May.

—(2000d) *Press Release: Debt Relief: Commission Warns Against Dilution of Enhanced HIPC Initiative*, IP/00/779, 13 July 2000.

Jia-dong, T. (2000) 'The Openess of International Economic Integration and Trade between EU and China', Fifth ECSA-World Conference, conference paper (Working Group 4) (Brussels: Commission of the European Communities).

Johnson, M. (1998) *European Community Trade Policy and the Article 113 Committee* (London: RIIA).

Karl, K. (2000) 'From Georgetown to Cotonou: the ACP Group Faces Up to New Challenges' *ACP–EU Partnership Agreement signed in Cotonou on 23 June 2000*, supplement to *The Courier* (Brussels: European Commission).

Keohane, R. and S. Hoffmann (1990) 'Conclusions: Community Politics and Institutional Change', in W. Wallace (ed.), *The Dynamics of European Integration* (London: Pinter/RIIA).

Köllner, P. (2000) 'Whither ASEM? Lessons from APEC and the Future of Transregional Cooperation between Asia and Europe', in *Asia-Europe in a Global Economy: Economics, Economic Systems and Economic Cooperation*, conference proceedings, Seoul, Korea, 1–2 September.

Laryea, G. (2000) 'Effective Poverty Eradication', *The Courier*, issue 181 (Brussels: European Commission).

Lee, Chong-Wha (2000) 'Trade Issues in the ASEM Process', in *Asia–Europe in a Global Economy: Economics, Economic Systems and Economic Cooperation*, conference proceedings, Seoul, Korea, 1–2 September.

Leftwich, A. (1993) 'Governance, Democracy and Development in the Third World', *Third World Quarterly*, vol. 14, no. 3.

Lister, M. (1997a) 'Europe's Lomé Policy in Perspective', *European Development Policy Discussion Papers*, no. 2.

Lister, M. (1997b) *The European Union and the South: Relations with Developing Countries* (London: Routledge/UACES).

Lowe, D. (1996) 'The Development Policy of the European Union and the Mid-term Review of the Lomé Partnership', *Journal of Common Market Studies: Annual Review*, vol. 34.

McMahon, J. (1998) 'ASEAN and the Asia-Europe Meeting: Strengthening the European Union's Relations with South-East Asia?', *European Foreign Affairs Review*, vol. 3, no. 2.

MacRae, D. (2000) 'An Opportunity for the new Pacific ACP members', *ACP–EU Partnership Agreement signed in Cotonou on 23 June 2000*, supplement to *The Courier* (Brussels: European Commission).

Marks G., Hooghe, L. and K. Blank (1996) 'European Integration from the 1980s: State-Centric v. Multi-level Governance', *Journal of Common Market Studies*, vol. 34.

Meunier, S. and K. Nicolaidis (2000) 'EU Trade Policy: the Exclusive versus Shared Competence Debate', in M. Green-Cowles and M. Smith (eds), *The State of the European Union V* (Oxford: Oxford University Press).

Monnet, J. (1978) *Memoirs* (New York: Doubleday and Co.).

Moore, M. (1995) 'Promoting Good Government by Supporting Institutional Development', *Towards Democratic Governance, IDS Bulletin*, vol. 26, no. 2.

Moravcsik, A. (1991) 'Negotiating the Single European Act: National Interests and Conventional Statecraft in the European Community', *International Organisations*, vol. 45.

—(1993) 'Preferences and Power in the European Community: a Liberal Intergovernmentalist Approach', *Journal of Common Market Studies*, vol. 31.

—(1995) 'Liberal Intergovernmentalism and Integration: a Rejoinder', *Journal of Common Market Studies*, vol. 33.

—and N. Kalypso (1999) 'Explaining the Treaty of Amsterdam: Interests, Influence and Institutions', *Journal of Common Market Studies*, vol. 37.

Moreau, F. (2000) 'The Cotonou Agreement – new orientations', *ACP–EU Partnership Agreement signed in Cotonou on 23 June 2000*, supplement to *The Courier* (Brussels: European Commission).

Nielson, P. (2000) 'The new agreement will benefit the poorest', *ACP–EU Partnership Agreement signed in Cotonou on 23 June 2000*, supplement to *The Courier* (Brussels: European Commission).

Nunnenkamp, P. (1995) 'What Donors Mean by Good Governance: Heroic Ends, Limited Means and Traditional Dilemmas of Development Cooperation', *Towards Democratic Governance, IDS Bulletin*, vol. 26, no. 2.

OECD Development Assistance Committee (1996) *Development Cooperation: Efforts and Policies of the Members of the Development Assistance Committee, 1996 Report* (Paris: OECD).

Oman, C. (1997) 'The Policy Challenges of Globalisation and Regionalisation', *Development: the Journal of the Society for International Development*, vol. 40, no. 2.

O'Neill, R. and R.J. Vincent (eds) (1990) *The West and the Third World* (New York: St Martin's Press).

Olsen, G. (1996) 'Do Ethics Matter in International Aid Relations? A Discussion of Ethics as a Determinant of European Aid to Sub-Saharan Africa in the Post-Cold War Era', *Journal of Developing Societies*, vol. 12, no. 2.

Olsen, G. (1997) 'Western Europe's Relations with Africa Since the End of the Cold War', *The Journal of Modern African Studies*, vol. 35.

Partnership Agreement (2000) *ACP–EU Partnership Agreement signed in Cotonou on 23 June 2000*, supplement to *The Courier* (Brussels: European Commission).

Pederson, J.D. (1993) 'The EC and the Developing Countries: Still Partners?', in O. Norgaard, T. Pederson and N. Peterson (eds), *The European Community in World Politics* (London: Pinter).

Peterson, J. (1995) 'Decision-Making in the European Union: Towards a Framework for Analysis', *Journal of European Public Policy*, vol. 2.

— and E. Bomberg (1999) *Decision-Making in the European Union* (London: Macmillan).

Petit, B. (2000) 'The Cotonou Agreement is the only one of its kind in the World', *ACP–EU Partnership Agreement signed in Cotonou on 23 June 2000*, supplement to *The Courier* (Brussels: European Commission).

Pierson, P. (1996) 'The Path to European Integration: a Historical Institutionalist Perspective', *Comparative Political Studies*, vol. 29.

Ravenhill, J. (1985) *Collective Clientelism: the Lomé Conventions and North–South Relations* (New York: Columbia University Press).

Richardson, J.J. (1996) *Policy-Making in the European Union* (London: Routledge).

Sartori, G. (1976) *Parties and Party Systems* (Cambridge: Cambridge University Press).

Schmit, L. (2000) 'The ASEM Process: New Rules for Engagement in a Global Environment', in Fangchuan and Niemann (eds), *Asia and Europe – Towards a Better Mutual Understanding*, Second ASEF Summer School, 22 August–5 September 1999, Beijing: Asia-Europe Foundation/Singapore: Peking University.

Schmuck, O. (1990) 'The Lomé Convention: a Model for Partnership', in G. Edwards and E. Regelsberger (eds), *Europe's Global Links* (New York: St Martin's Press).

Segal, G. (1997) 'Thinking Strategically About ASEM: the Subsidiarity Question', *Pacific Review*, vol. 10, no. 11.

Smith, K. (1998) 'The Use of Political Conditionality in the EU's Relations with Third Countries: How Effective?', *European Foreign Affairs Review*, vol. 3.

Smith M. (1999) 'The European Union', in B. Hocking, and S. McGuire (eds), *Trade Politics* (London: Routledge).

Speech (2000) *Speaking points of Chris Patten, European Commissioner responsible for External Relations, and Poul Nielson, European Commissioner responsible for Development and Humanitarian Aid on Zimbabwe elections*, SPEECH/00/255, European Parliament, 4 July.

Stevens, C. (1983) 'The European Community and Africa, the Caribbean and the Pacific', in J. Lodge (ed.), *Institutions and Policies of the European Community* (London: Pinter).

—(1995) The EC and the Third World, in M. Ugur (ed.), *Policy Issues in the European Union*. (Dartford: Greenwich University Press).

Stocker, S. (2000) 'Time to match EU Rhetoric about the Fight Against Poverty with deeds', *European Voice*, vol. 6, 11–17 May.

Tananka, T. (1999) 'Asia–Europe Relations: the Birth and Development of ASEM' *Keio Journal of Politics*, no. 10, Keio University, Japan.

The Courier (1990) 'EEC–ACP Cooperation: the Historical Perspective', no. 120 (Brussels: European Commission).

—(2000) *ACP-EU Partnership Agreement Signed in Cotonou on 23 June 2000*, Special Issue (Brussels: European Commission).

The Economist (1999a) 'Reviving the European Connection', 26 June.

—(1999b) 'Helping the Third World: How to Make Aid Work', 26 June.

—(2000), 'The poor who are always with us', 1 July.

Van Reisen, M. (1999) *EU 'Global Player': the North-South Policy of the European Union* (Utrecht: Eurostep International Books).

Vernier, G. (1996) 'Lomé IV Mid-term Review: Main Innovations', *The Courier*, no. 155 (Brussels: European Commission).

White, H. (1996) 'Evaluating Programme Aid: Introduction & Synthesis', *Evaluating Programme Aid, IDS Bulletin*, vol. 27, no. 4.

Woolcock, S. (2000) 'European Trade policy: global pressures and domestic constraints', in H. Wallace and W. Wallace (eds), Policy-Making in the European Union, 4th edn (Oxford: Oxford University Press).

World Bank (1997) *World Development Report 1997* (New York: Oxford University Press).

Yeo, Lay Hwee (2000) 'ASEM: Looking Back, Looking Forward', *Contemporary Southeast Asia*, vol. 22, no. 1.

WWW sources cited

WWW pages cited in this text were valid and active at the time of writing; however, the nature of www pages means that such pages are periodically updated or removed. For this reason only keyword destinations are listed below for future reference:

http://Europa.eu.int/comm
http://Europa.eu.int/comm/development
http://Europa.eu.int/comm/trade
http://Europa.eu.int/comm/echo
http://Europa.eu.int/comm/external
http://www.diplomatie.fr
http://www.jubilee2000.net
http://www.one-world.org/euforic
http://UNDP.org

Index